Towards Human Rights in Residential Care for Older Persons

People are leading significantly longer lives than previous generations did, and the proportion of older people in the population is growing. Residential care for older people will become increasingly necessary as our society ages and, we will require more of it. At this moment in time, the rights of older people receive attention at international and regional levels, with the United Nations, the Organization of American States and the African Union exploring the possibility of establishing new conventions for the rights of older persons.

This book explores the rights of older people and their quality of care once they are living in a care home, and considers how we can commence the journey towards a human rights framework to ensure decent and dignified care for older people. The book takes a comparative approach to present and future challenges facing the care home sector for older people in Africa (Kenya), the Arab world (Egypt), Australia, China, England, Israel, Japan and the USA. An international panel of experts have contributed chapters, identifying how their particular society cares for its older and oldest people, the extent to which demographic and economic change has placed their system under pressure and the role that residential elder care homes play in their culture. The book also explores the extent to which constitutional or other rights form a foundation to the regulatory and legislative structures to residential elder care and it examines the important concept of dignity.

As a multi-regional study of the care of older person from a human rights perspective, this book will be of excellent use and interest, in particular to students and researchers of family and welfare law, long-term care, social policy, social work, human rights and elder law.

Helen Meenan is an expert on age discrimination and elder law and holds an Honorary Appointment at the Faculty of Business and Law, Kingston University, United Kingdom.

Nicola Rees is the Director of Studies and Principal Lecturer, Faculty of Business and Law, at Kingston University, United Kingdom.

Israel Doron is an Associate Professor and the Head of the Department of Gerontology at the University of Haifa, Israel.

Towards Human Rights in Residential Care for Older Persons

International perspectives

Edited by Helen Meenan, Nicola Rees, and Israel Doron

Routledge
Taylor & Francis Group

LONDON AND NEW YORK

First published 2016
by Routledge
2 Park Square, Milton Park, Abingdon, Oxon, OX14 4RN

and by Routledge
711 Third Avenue, New York, NY 10017

First issued in paperback 2017

Routledge is an imprint of the Taylor & Francis Group, an informa business

Library of Congress Cataloging-in-Publication Data
A catalog record for this book has been requested

ISBN 13: 978-0-8153-5537-3 (pbk)
ISBN 13: 978-0-415-72555-2 (hbk)

Typeset in Baskerville
by Apex CoVantage, LLC

Contents

Notes on contributors

Dr Isabella Aboderin is a Senior Research Scientist and Head of the Program on Aging and Development at the African Population and Health Research Center (APHRC) in Nairobi, Kenya, and an Associate Professor of Gerontology at the Centre for Research on Ageing, University of Southampton, UK.

She is the Regional Chair for Africa of the International Association of Gerontology and Geriatrics (IAGG), Technical Advisor to the Global Commission on Aging in Developing Countries, Member of the World Economic Forum Global Agenda Council on Ageing, Board Member of HelpAge International and the United Nations International Institute on Ageing (INIA), and Advisory Board member of the World Demographic and Aging Forum (WDA). She also serves on the African Commission on Human and People's Rights Working Group on the Rights of Older Persons in Africa.

Isabella holds a PhD from the School for Policy Studies from the University of Bristol, UK, an MSc in Health Promotion Sciences from the London School of Hygiene and Tropical Medicine, and a BSc in Cellular and Molecular Pathology from the University of Bristol.

Hilda Akinyi Owii is a Research Assistant (Ageing and Development Program), African Population and Health Research Centre, University of Oxford.

Takashi Amano, MSW is a PhD student at George Warren Brown School of Social Work, Washington University in St. Louis, St. Louis, MO. He was an Instructor at the Department of Health Policy and Management, Keio University School of Medicine, Tokyo, Japan.

Mohamed A. 'Arafa is Assistant Professor of Criminal Law and Criminal Justice at the Alexandria University Faculty of Law (Egypt); Adjunct Professor of Islamic Law and Middle Eastern Legal Studies at Indiana University Robert H. McKinney School of Law (USA); SJD, Indiana University Robert H. McKinney School of Law (2013); LL.M, University of Connecticut School of Law (2008); LL.B, Alexandria University School of Law (2006). Recently, he has been elected to act as a managing editor of the *Arab Law Quarterly Journal* in London. Professor 'Arafa served as an Associate Trainee Attorney and Executive Attorney Assistant at 'Arafa Law Firm (2007).

Israel (Issi) Doron is an Associate Professor and the Head of the Department of Gerontology at the University of Haifa, Israel. Professor Doron is also the Past President of the Israeli Gerontological Society, and the Founder of the Law in the Service of the Elderly association in Israel.

Carolyne Egesa is a Research Officer under the Population Dynamics and Reproductive Health Program. She holds a Master of Science degree in Gerontology from the University of Southampton, UK and a Bachelor of Arts degree from the University of Nairobi.

Sue Field is Adjunct Fellow in Elder Law at the University of Western Sydney, School of Law. Her current project addresses the policies and practices of financial institutions around substitute decision-making instruments and is funded by the National Health and Medical Research Council Partnership Centre on Dealing with Cognitive and Related Functional Decline in Older People.

Andy H. Y. Ho, PhD is an Assistant Professor at the Nanyang Technological University, Singapore, and an Honorary Lecturer at the Department of Social Work and Social Administration, The University of Hong Kong, Hong Kong Special Administrative Region.

Naoki Ikegami, MD, PhD is Emeritus Professor at Keio University and former Professor and Chair, Department of Health Policy and Management, Keio University School of Medicine, Tokyo, Japan.

Tomoaki Ishibashi, PhD is the Director of Research, the Dia Foundation for Research on Ageing Societies Tokyo, Japan.

Haris Kountouros, PhD has specialised in European and comparative labour law. From 1999 to 2004 he was a Visiting Lecturer in European Law at King's College London and has also taught Legal Theory at London Metropolitan University. Since 2006 he is an official of the European Parliament. His published work concentrates on EU law, labour law, equality and related themes.

Terry Y. S. Lum, PhD is an Associate Professor at the Department of Social Work and Social Administration and Director of the Sau Po Centre on Ageing, The University of Hong Kong, Hong Kong Special Administrative Region.

Hao Luo, PhD is a Lecturer at the Department of Sociology, School of Social Sciences, Tsinghua University, Beijing, People's Republic of China.

Cecilia Mbaka is Deputy Director of Gender and Social Development in the Ministry of Labour, Social Security and Services, Kenya.

Helen Meenan, BCL (UCD), LL.M (UvA), started her working life as a solicitor to the Irish Courts. She holds an Honorary Appointment at the Faculty of Business and Law, Kingston University, United Kingdom where she previously held the Jean Monnet Chair in European Law. She publishes and speaks widely on law and ageing particularly, on age discrimination and on the human rights of older people.

Richard J. Mollot, JD is the Executive Director of the Long Term Care Community Coalition, New York, NY, and the President of the Coalition for Quality Care, a US based NGO. He has written about and presented trainings on a variety of long-term care policy and legal issues, including: dementia care standards and practices; residential care law and regulatory oversight; and long-term care quality improvement.

Nicola Rees, PhD, National Teaching Fellow is the Director of Studies and Principal Lecturer, Faculty of Business and Law, at Kingston University, United Kingdom.

Michelle H. Y. Shum, JD is a PhD candidate at the Department of Social Work and Social Administration and a Research Fellow at the Sau Po Centre on Ageing, The University of Hong Kong, Hong Kong Special Administrative Region. Her research interests include social policy, third sector management, elderly, family and youth.

Jun Fang Wang, MSW is a PhD candidate at the Department of Social Work and Social Administration and a Research Fellow at the Sau Po Centre on Ageing, The University of Hong Kong.

Ying Wang, MA is a PhD candidate at the Department of Sociology, School of Social Sciences, Tsinghua University, Beijing, People's Republic of China.

Introduction

Helen Meenan, Nicola Rees, Israel Doron

This volume is a multi-disciplinary, international and multi-cultural reply to the often unheard voice of older people in residential care, whether in care homes or nursing homes. This is a unique group of concern to us. Their numbers are small but still significant amongst older people in most of the countries we have examined. China demonstrates that size is relative. It has 120 million people over the age of 65, and requires several million residential care beds already. Unique also because older people world-wide have entered or been placed in residential care for a variety of reasons but always in good faith. In most of the countries in our volume there is an agreement or contract between the older person or their guardian and the home. There is a basic understanding of what the bargain will entail. When a care home fails to deliver care safely or appropriately and fails to support the necessities of life at a minimum level, the results can be fatal or life-changing. Poor care is never part of the bargain. In some countries, the media is quick to seize on these stories and has played an important role in bringing them to public attention, where they cannot be ignored.

Residential care is also unique because it takes place behind closed doors, often away from the residents' own community and whether publicly or privately run, it is usually an environment which is not open to the public. It is likely a chosen final home and older people are transitioning through a number of challenging phases during their time there, perhaps from old age to decrepit old age, and for a growing number of older people this journey will involve dementia. This sector has often been characterised by a lack of voice, choice and control for older people. In a number of countries in this volume this is changing.[1] However, it will be shown that legislative efforts to improve this and other aspects of older peoples' lives can under-deliver in the implementation process, especially in a large country or federal system and further away from central government.[2]

---

1 England and Australia are examples where much effort has gone into improving the voice, choice and control of older people.
2 In different ways, the USA and China represent this viewpoint, the latter also for the vague and general rules and discretion vested in municipal governments, as described by Shum et al. herein.

The goals of this volume

At the planning stage, the focus of this volume was what role human rights, the constitutional rights of older people and dignity play in the regulatory systems for long-term residential care of older people. Where these features and principles exist, were they part of the foundations of the regulatory system or were they added on later? In our view this question was too narrow at such an early stage of exploration of the regulation of this sector. Our 'what' very quickly became 'how'. We set out to get a broader flavour of the characteristics of residential care, how and where it is delivered and how it is regulated, how regulation has emerged, where it is now and where it is going. Our over-arching question remains how is care delivered in terms of both quality and quantity? We believe that care must at least be sufficient in both of these respects to be truly effective. We also sought to discover what principles and practices guide the residential care of older people in other jurisdictions and the issues being faced by older people in residential care elsewhere. The question whether care home staff receive training and what it involves were important too. We also wanted to start to get a picture of the factors that affect quality in residential care in other countries. Thus, our initial emphasis on human rights and dignity became part of the journey rather than the entire journey or the sole destination. The timing of our book reflects a clear ongoing need for residential care (and in some countries more of it) for older people locally and across the globe.

A comparative approach

This volume aims to learn from comparisons between countries and what we learnt was humbling. Not least because every country in this volume has its own individual history of residential care for older people, its own path to regulation of that care and its regulation and supervisory systems have their own strengths and weakness. This volume reminds us that law reflects the values of the country and the times when and where it is enacted.[3] Very distinctive approaches and contexts are detailed throughout. Kenya is only starting its journey towards regulating long term care (LTC) facilities and, even with its small clutch of care homes, it cannot be dismissed, as it demonstrates a forward facing attitude to meet this issue head on. England with one of the longest histories of care for older people and detailed evolving regulation still faces stiff challenges but currently demonstrates considerable effort, a more rigorous inspection system and possibly the greatest public awareness when things go wrong.

China has a clear goal to provide sufficient numbers of care home beds and this is the central plank of its strategy. Japan currently has waiting lists and long waiting times for LTC beds and has by far the most comprehensive choice of pathways for training as a care giver, including the possibility of a four-year university degree. Shum et al. clearly assert the protective effect of a highly trained care work-force, stating that 'Japan has relied mostly on the training and qualifications

---

3 Note Thane, Whitton and Doron as cited by Terry Carney, 'Guardianship, "Social" Citizenship and Theorising Substitute Decision-Making Law', in Israel Doron and Ann M. Soden Eds, *Beyond Elder Law New Directions in Law and Aging* (Springer Verlag, Berlin Heidelberg, 2012) at p. 4.

of the direct care workers to protect the human rights of older people'.[4] Maintaining the quality of care workers may come under threat. Current shortages indicate difficulties in supplying care workers in future, making the need for strong legislation and enforcement more important.[5]

In Israel and the USA there has been considerable growth in assisted living facilities (ALFs), which vary greatly in variety and quality but typically offer more choice to those who can afford them. ALFs sometimes fall below the radar of federal regulation, for example in the USA where standards and regulation are developed at state level and unlike nursing homes they do not benefit from the rights and protections of the Nursing Home Reform Law. However, Israel now has a supervisory mechanism to inspect ALFs. Israel also has the benefit of successful court challenges to government contracts that reduced fees paid for publicly funded LTC beds. However, Doron writes that private nursing homes now prefer to accept only private patients which are charged higher rates than those paid by the government.[6] In the USA, a landmark Supreme Court decision on long-term care required states to place individuals in the least restrictive setting as appropriate for each person. Thus residential care may not be the best option for those who could live safely in the community.[7]

Australia emerges as a particularly stable example of LTC.[8] It has also embraced its status as one of the most culturally diverse countries in the world to ensure that older Australians receive care appropriate to their cultural, linguistic and religious beliefs.[9] Since July 2014 it has dispensed with the distinction between high care and low care facilities so that older people now have the right to 'age in place'. Above all, LTC facilities in Australia are subject to continuous monitoring of standards[10] by the Australian Aged Care Quality Agency and accreditation is an ongoing process where providers are approved for periods of two to three years. Importantly, the recent Quality of Care Principles[11] require that an approved provider demonstrate, '[T]he organisation's management has systems in place to identify and ensure compliance with all relevant legislation'.[12]

---

4 In this volume.
5 Ibid, according to Shum et al. herein, Japan is now debating relaxation of its strict immigration policy in order to attract more care workers from overseas.
6 In this volume.
7 Note Richard T. Mollot herein and his discussion of *Olmstead v. LC and EW* 527 US 581 (1999) and the challenges in implementing its parameters.
8 As highlighted by Field herein, there are still issues, for example, around the reporting of assaults in care homes, difficulties for providers in rural areas to hire appropriate staff and there is little evidence of staff training programmes being developed within a human rights framework, despite the AHRC advocating human rights training for all health care workers.
9 See Sue Field herein, who describes the Culturally and Linguistically Diverse Reforms in Aged Care (CALD), and how by 2012 more than 30% of Australians were born outside Australia.
10 However, Field herein refers to the possibility that assessment contact with a facility may be made over the telephone.
11 Commonwealth, 2014.
12 According to Sue Field, herein, approved providers must also demonstrate that they are engaged in a process of continuous improvement, which includes education and training of staff to ensure that staff remain accountable and the care and needs of residents are understood and met.

The role of regulation

This collection also continues along a pathway examining the type and role of regulation used to ensure that service providers deliver good quality care to older people in residential care. Wiener identified how different countries ensure that nursing homes, home care agencies and residential care facilities provide good-quality care as a 'key but neglected issue in long-term care' and, 'Although countries employ a number of strategies to accomplish this goal the most common approach is regulation' and, as we shall see, 'having a well-established regulatory system does not guarantee that all providers establish high quality'.[13] However, our authors represent a multi-disciplinary approach which crucially includes academic lawyers,[14] and is, therefore, broader than the important public health, health economics and medical-based approach. This enabled us to incorporate other strands in our examinations, a more critical assessment of the regulatory systems and consideration of the role (if any) of human rights and dignity.

We aimed to achieve a range of countries throughout the world, including some under-exposed ones in this field, a sample of cultural contrasts but also exemplars of more long-standing westernised models. Our eight country studies are Africa, the Arab World (with a focus on Egypt), Australia, China, England, Israel, Japan and the United States of America. It was critical that our selection incorporate a clear variety of regulatory approaches. Mor, Leone and Maresso proposed a framework for understanding regulation of long-term care quality with four categories.[15] They are: (1) long-term care quality systems based on 'professionalism', they included Japan; (2) long-term care quality systems based on regulatory inspection frameworks, they included Australia and England; (3) long-term care quality systems based on data measurement and public reporting, they included the USA; and (4) long-term care quality systems and developing regulatory systems, they included China and we would add Kenya and Egypt. Israel is interesting and may defy these clear demarcations. Doron believes it is a mixed system as there are elements of professionalism, but the core is still regulatory inspection.

Dignity

From the start we committed to a stand-alone chapter on dignity in addition to the country essays. Dignity is a universal principle and 'is arguably *the* universal principle'.[16] As a concept we struggle to define it but hold it very dear through individual yet overlapping understandings of what it means. Our inability to put

---

13 Joshua M. Wiener, PhD, Foreword to *Regulating Long-Term Care Quality: An International Comparison* (edited by Vincent Mor, Tiziana Leone and Anna Maresso, Cambridge University Press, 2014 at p. xvii).

14 Including the three editors.

15 Vincent Mor, Tiziana Leone and Anna Maresso, Eds, *Regulating Long-Term Care Quality: An International Comparison* (Cambridge University Press, 2014).

16 Foreword by Lord Justice Munby to Charles Foster, *Human Dignity in Bioethics and Law* (Hart, Oxford, 2011) at p. xiii.

it into words in no way detracts from its importance in our lives. We understand it in a place deeper than words. Win Tadd et al.'s 2010 multi-disciplinary study of the care of older people in the European Union reveals an important facet of older people's inter-action with dignity, 'in general, participants found it easier to identify situations when dignity was lacking than when it was present or what it meant'.[17] More positively, they also state that dignity 'was seen as a highly relevant and important concept that, when experienced, enhanced self-esteem, self-worth and well-being'.

The chapter on dignity explores dignity's role as a theoretical and legal construct specifically in the context of care for older persons. Kountouros and Rees highlight attempts to develop a human rights approach towards older persons and the idea that the protection of people in long-term care should be from a human rights perspective.[18] That we have a long way to go on the international part of this journey is brought home to us by attempts in 2012 to pass a UN Resolution on a comprehensive legal instrument to promote the rights and dignity of older persons, while supported by 53 states, 102 states abstained including all the Member States of the EU, Israel, Australia, China and Japan. Three states voted against the resolution, one of which was the USA. Kountouros and Rees also highlight that dignity does not have a single meaning but is a concept whose meaning is contextually variable and within the context of older people, the theoretical literature reveals it to be an explicitly multi-dimensional concept.

They report that successful claims based on dignity and violation of a human right are rare and are typically linked to the most serious cases of abuse, neglect, inhumane or humiliating treatment or discrimination. However, instruments such as AGE Platform Europe's *European Charter of rights and responsibilities of older people in need of long-term care and assistance* give hope. It is addressed directly to older people and includes rights to high quality and tailored care. Although non-legally binding, they demonstrate the rights of older people that are not compromised by reference to economic considerations. Kountouros and Rees consider *inter alia* that 'Dignity in care cannot be compromised by cost considerations'.

Dignity and the country studies

Throughout this volume dignity makes an appearance to greater and lesser extents. The dignity of human life is part of the curricula for care workers' certificates in Japan. The China chapter refers to examples of the deprivation of rights to self-determination, autonomy and dignity. But this is in addition to some surprising and rare examples of a sheltered place for older people's issues in Chinese society. For example, the People's Court gives priority to lawsuits concerning older persons' care and there are even some 'senior tribunals' to handle civil cases involving older

---

17 Note Kountouros and Rees herein.
18 In this volume, citing the Council of Europe, Age Platform Europe and also referring to the UN Convention on Rights of Persons with Disabilities.

persons. Sue Field writes that the concept of dignity remains constant through the aged care sector in Australia (and also that 'Aged care in Australia is without a doubt one of, if not the most, heavily regulated sector in our community'). In the USA, the Nursing Home Reform Law lists a right to dignity in a set of ten basic rights for residents. This is in addition to a requirement that each resident must be provided 'with care and services sufficient to attain and maintain his or her highest practicable physical, mental, and psycho-social well-being'.[19]

While dignity does not feature as such in the chapter on the Arab and Islamic world highlighting Egypt, the place and role of older people in the Islamic world and Egypt is almost unique in our collection. Islamic law, religion and teaching require a reverence and protection of older family members who enjoy 'a place of honor',[20] while at the same time allowing older people to remain a living part of the community with ongoing opportunities for active contribution.[21] So strong are the religious and cultural underpinnings that even where Arab constitutions and laws provide for older people, 'Arafa argues there are misapplications of these norms and domestic legislation must meet the lofty standards of Islamic law which provide an inclusive pattern of care for older people. This volume also reveals that even countries with robust cultural protections for older people are not immune to pressures felt in more westernised countries. Longer lives in Africa, the Middle East and China and rural to urban migration especially in China, are beginning to chip away at ancient family codes and the ability of families to continue to care for older people. Poverty plays a clear role in this trend in Kenya.

One of the two countries with the most pervasive presence for dignity in this volume is England. Dignity is prominent in many important reports and enquiries into the care of older people. It is prominent in the National Health Service as well as throughout social care. It is often chosen as a guiding principle by many professional and campaigning organisations for older people.[22] It features more significantly since 2014 as one of the dimensions of well-being that must be promoted by a local authority as part of its general duty to a person in its care.[23] It is now enshrined in law that service users must be treated with dignity and respect.[24] The other country is Australia, as stated above.

General contexts and key directions

Demographic ageing and the changing role of residential care

The most pressing context for the residential care of older people is the world-wide phenomenon of demographic ageing, which is currently underway. This

---

19 Richard T. Mollot, in this volume, who clarifies that this mandate and the rights for residents are individual rights that must be met by homes on an individual basis.
20 Mohamed Arafa in this volume.
21 For example, in politics or through the system of micro loans to older people to set up small businesses.
22 See, for example, the Dignity in Care Network, discussed in the chapter on England in this volume.
23 The Care Act 2014.
24 See Reg. 10 of the Health and Social Care Act 2008 (Regulated Activities) Regulations 2014.

project takes place at a time when global, European and national demographic structures are undergoing a similar process of considerable change, resulting in two phenomena in particular. People are leading significantly longer lives than previous generations did and the proportion of older people in the population is growing; this dual phenomenon is often described as demographic ageing. Average global life expectancy has grown by 20 years since 1950 and is expected to grow a further ten years by 2050.[25] The number of older people is also increasing by volume and percentage. As highlighted by the United Nations:

> the world is experiencing an unprecedented demographic transformation and that by 2050 the number of persons aged 60 years and over will increase from 600 million to almost 2 billion and that the proportion of persons aged 60 years and over is expected to double from 10 to 21 per cent. The increase will be greatest and most rapid in developing countries where the older population is expected to quadruple during the next 50 years.[26]

In the European Union, during the period from 2001 to 2050, the proportion of the population aged over 65 will grow from 16.1% to 27.5% and the proportion of the oldest, that is people aged over 80, will grow from 3.6% to 10%.[27] The increase in numbers of the older and the oldest old will also contribute to economic, health and social challenges. For example, one in five 20 year olds in the UK today are predicted to not only reach but surpass 100 years of age.[28] The growing number of centenarians in our population will add another dimension to elder care.[29] As will the emerging concept of the super centenarian,[30] that is someone who lives to 110 years or more.

While our ability to live longer world-wide is a symbol of man's success, the task now is to rise to meet the challenges this presents. Residential care has a continuing important role to play but this volume reveals that the role and nature of residential care is gradually changing. Some countries such as the USA, Israel and England are embracing more variety and more volume through assisted living facilities as an alternative to the traditional choice between a nursing home or residential care home. Some have pursued a policy of helping older people to

---

25 United Nations, *Report of the Second World Assembly on Ageing*, A/CONF.1979, Madrid, 8–12 April 2002, at p. 5.

26 UN, *Report of the Second World Assembly on Ageing*, A/CONF.1979, Madrid, 8–12 April 2002, at p. 1.

27 Communication from the Commission of 5 December 2001, The future of health care and care for the elderly: guaranteeing accessibility, quality and financial viability [COM(2001) 723 final. Not published in the Official Journal], available at http://eur-lex.europa.eu/legal-content/EN/TXT/HTML/?uri=URISERV:c11310&rid=1.

28 Michelle Mitchell, Age UK as quoted in Press Release, *ILC-UK Launch new report on centenarians, 'Living beyond 100' highlights key policy issues arising from growing numbers of people passing 100 year mark*, Tuesday 29 November 2011.

29 The number of centenarians in the UK population was estimated at 12,640 in 2010 and is projected to reach 100,000 by 2035, see ONS Statistical Bulletin, Older People's Day, 2011 Statistical Bulletin, http://www.ons.gov.uk/ons/dcp171778_235000.pdf.

30 This term refers to those who live to 110 or more, see http://www.livingsupercentenarians.com.

remain at home for much longer with the help of domiciliary support but this is not without its own set of challenges and concerns.[31] Some countries reveal trends towards entering it at older ages than in the past and also entering at a frailer stage. There is a gradual shift towards reducing the number of care home beds and increasing the number of nursing homes beds in England, for example. The private sector in some countries has embraced the provision of more luxurious, social homes but paying a high price is no guarantee of the quality of basic care delivered. In the main, there is evidence that residential care remains a fairly institutional and risk-averse experience.[32] Today, older people are also a more diverse group than ever before. New groups that have not featured before may grow into old age for the first time.[33] Some groups in society are ageing within structures that may not be ready for a larger older population, such as prisons.[34] Groups that may have hidden aspects of their identity in times past are currently entering old age and residential care more openly than before, such as LGBT, which has been positively embraced by Australia.

The physical and emotional landscape of ageing

It is not only the process of living longer that is important, this volume reveals that *where* a person ages is very relevant to their access to residential care and may have implications for the quality of care they receive. Both China and Australia reveal issues around finding appropriate staff to deliver care in rural settings whether as home care givers in Australia or as trained or even rudimentarily educated residential care givers in China. The majority of older Kenyans live in rural areas where poverty rates are significantly higher and affect more than three-quarters of them, in turn increasing demand for residential care.

'Arafa adds other dimensions when he refers to the fact that the comparatively small number of LTC facilities in Egypt are based in the larger cities and that the homeless in Egypt are mainly older people and children. Yet he asserts that Egypt has the highest number of LTC facilities in the Arab world. China in particular reveals the impact of rural to urban migration on care giving for older people, where older people are left behind when their families move to the city. England reveals the recent emergence of the severe loneliness of many older people as an issue, reflecting among other things the distant dispersal of family members and living alone at older ages. This contrasts with Kenya where only 7% of older

---

31 Note in England the report by the Equality and Human Rights Commission, *Close to Home: An Inquiry into Older People and Human Rights in Home Care*, 2011 which details some serious shortcomings, not least very rushed visits by home care workers. The Care Act 2014 now extends the protection of the Human Rights Act 1998 to the provision of care in a person's own home, when the care is partly or wholly publicly funded.

32 Note, in particular, England and the USA but note by contrast Kenya where residential care homes may lack even life-supporting amenities such as sanitation and water.

33 For example, thalidomide victims.

34 See for instance, J. Williams, 'Social Care and Older Prisoners', Journal of Social Work. 21 February 2012, doi:10.1177/1468017311434886, pp. 1–22.

people live alone. It may well be that those 7% are similar to the 'three no's category' described in the China chapter, 'those with no family support, no capacity to work, and no source of income',[35] although we are not certain if that is the case. Egypt too recognises an overlapping category. Arafa describes Ministerial Decrees providing *inter alia* a right to shelter welfare in shelter institutions for older citizens who have no family care providers.

Size and residential care

One of the striking features of this collection is the size of the residential care sector relative to each country's size. It will be shown that Kenya has only 18 recorded residential care homes at the time of writing and none of them is state owned. Egypt has only 300 for a relatively large country. The USA has approximately 15,465 nursing homes containing around 110 beds each against a national population of 318.9 million.[36] These figures contrast markedly with England, a medium-sized country by size and population in this study, which has 12,525 residential care homes and 5,153 nursing homes together catering for approximately 405,000 older people against a total population of around 53 million. The popularity of assisted living in the USA may partly account for the relatively small numbers of older people living in residential care there. Size of institution is also important. Positive correlations have been found between a small size of home and better quality of care, although small size is not in itself a guarantee of better care.[37]

Dementia

The demand for dementia care is one of the noticeable current trends as dementia patients grow in numbers in many countries. While there are estimated to be 36 million people worldwide with dementia today, this figure is set to double every 20 years and, by 2050, it is projected there will be 115 million people with dementia worldwide.[38] The chapter on England reveals some concerning findings on dementia patients, not least that they are likely to receive poor care at some point on their care journey. The scale of the dementia issue differs among our countries. For example, in China the number of people with dementia has almost tripled since the early 1990s and is now approximately 9.19 million people. Whether China's policy of creating vast numbers of care beds and a target of millions of new care workers takes into account the specialised needs of this particular group is not revealed herein.

---

35 Attributed therein to Wong & Leung (2012).
36 According to the World Bank.
37 Note England in particular.
38 The Alzheimer's Society http://www.alzheimers.org.uk/site/scripts/documents_info.php?docu mentID=412.

Staffing

By far the most telling revelation is the universal importance of just about every aspect of staffing. Whether it is insufficient numbers of staff, unsuitable staff, poorly trained or untrained staff, there is not a country in this book which does not have some staffing issues, even if as in Japan it is more likely the threat of future shortages of staff. The role of staff is paramount and sufficient numbers of staff are crucial. So too is the role of a manager. That well-trained staff proves to have a protective effect for residents will be demonstrated by Japan. In our concluding chapter we elaborate more fully on all relevant dimensions of staffing and their impact.

Regulation, inspection and enforcement

The countries in this book encompass the whole range of regulatory approaches to long-term care as at the time of writing. The country chapters will outline them, but by way of introduction there are common issues with enforcement whether through a persuasive approach (China, Japan where rectification might be preferred over revocation of licensure), the potential of England's escalating approach (which does not seem to produce strong deterrence), Australia's lack of complaints (apparently at least in part due to effective mechanisms). The importance of enforcement cannot be under-estimated as Wiener reminds us: 'Different countries have adopted varying strategies to enforce regulations. However, without enforcement, the standards are meaningless.'[39] There are also implementation gaps more readily identified at the international level but interestingly evident here in the larger or more federal countries (USA, China). The broad and vague regulation in China may be contrasted with very detailed and specific legislation in England. However, England may still have some gaps or areas of weakness as described in this volume.

The role of inspections varies greatly and comprises many forms such as announced and unannounced inspections, themed inspections for example in England and even the possibility of conducting an assessment contact by telephone in Australia. American state governments require that each nursing home is to be inspected at least once every 15 months and Australia only accredits homes for two to three years at a time. England has increasingly rigorous inspections but they take place within a risk-based system, thus there remains the possibility for now that some poorly performing homes may fall through the cracks. One of the most surprising discoveries was a role for volunteers in visiting LTC facilities in two countries, the USA and Egypt. In the USA, a quasi-governmental consumer advocate, the Long-Term Care Ombudsman Program plays an important role in protecting residents in nursing homes through monitoring, which includes their staff or trained volunteers visiting their assigned home on a weekly basis.[40] In Egypt, a number of agencies have a role in inspecting and overseeing care homes conducting monthly visits to them.[41]

---

39 In Mor, Leone and Maresso *supra* at p. xxii.
40 Richard T. Mollot describes other roles herein, but also highlights the wide variation in state approaches to this programme.
41 As described by Mohamed 'Arafa herein.

Human rights

An interesting question in these countries is whether older people have a right to residential care. The answer appears to be 'no' in Israel and it will be shown that in China the government appears to be proceeding on the basis that older people do and trying to provide enough physical beds to cope with upcoming demand. Another interesting question is how human rights can help in the care of older people. A human rights approach to caring for older people and human rights training for care-givers are two possibilities. The idea of a human rights approach to the care of older people is not new and finds its greatest exploration in this volume, in the chapter on England. However, it also finds expression in Australia where the Australian Human Rights Commission believes that the reforms of aged care 'easily accommodate a human rights approach'. Field advocates the education of Approved Providers and their staff stating: 'Until such time as a human rights approach underpins the philosophy of all aged care programs, and the fundamental principles associated with this approach become as commonplace as clinical skills, then we cannot really say we comply with our responsibilities in respect of human rights in aged care.' One of the messages in this book is that a human rights approach is very suitable for embedding in the care of older people.[42] Adoption of the right mind-set, infused with the right principles and a little knowledge, can help to avoid some of the issues highlighted throughout this collection. It can empower the individual in their unique role in the care of an older person, whether as direct carer, cleaner or cook, so that they feel personally responsible for their contribution to that care. Another message is that a shift towards person-centred care is conducive to a human rights approach. A human rights approach does not necessarily cost much to implement, however a very clear message from our authors is that insufficient staff in numbers, skills and attitude threaten the human rights and general experience of older people in residential care.

International human rights, global and regional contexts

This book was written at a time of hope for an international human rights instrument specifically to strengthen the protection of the rights of older people. Kountouros and Rees outline some of the history, suffice here to say that the UN established an open-ended working group on ageing in 2010 which includes members of the NGO community to examine the need for an international convention. Two different positions are present in the debate: (1) that older people already benefit from a variety of general human rights instruments and perhaps what is required is better implementation of existing instruments and, (2) greater protection can best be

---

42 When this field is more mature, monitoring human rights in residential care can form part of the future landscape and can benefit from other fields. See in this regard the ITHACA Toolkit, 2010, http://www.ithacastudy.eu which monitors human rights and general healthcare in mental health and social care institutions.

achieved through a specific instrument for older people. Interestingly, the fifth and most recent meeting of the OWA reports a growing number of delegates in favour of the second position: a convention for older people.[43] The need to bring visibility to older persons was also reported, which indeed would be a key advantage of a stand-alone convention. However, the OWA continues to pursue both tracks in its exploration of how to protect the rights of older people internationally.

Two world regions are also considering a regional convention. The Organization of American States, comprising 35 states including the USA, continues to consider a draft Inter-American Convention on the Human Rights of Older Persons.[44] Finally, the African Union Protocol on the Rights of Older People in Africa was passed in 2014 and is due for implementation in 2015. Aboderin et al. highlight that the Protocol commits Member States to '(i) Identify, promote and strengthen traditional support systems . . . to enhance the ability of families and communities to care for older family members but also to (ii) *enact or review legislation that ensures that residential care is optional for older persons' and "Ensure older persons in residential care facilities are provided with care that meets national minimum standards"'.*

The AU Protocol may well be the first regional instrument to be adopted. It and any others that follow will perform the invaluable function in their regions of making the rights of older people more visible and importantly more easily located by older people themselves. This book is not the last word but aims merely to be an early word on a specific and uniquely vulnerable group of older people, those in residential care. Our message to you is that we see, we hear and we are listening. Our authors, by coming together across nations and in the spirit of mutual respect, hope to produce something of value that will stimulate further thought in this field.

---

43 Open-ended Working Group on Ageing, Fifth working session New York, 30 July–1 August 2014. Report of the Open-ended Working Group on Ageing, A/AC.278/2014/2 at pp. 6 and 10, available at http://social.un.org/ageing-working-group/fifthsession.shtml.
44 Note *inter alia*, the Report on the Situation of Older Persons in the Hemisphere and the Effectiveness of Binding Universal and Regional Human Rights Instruments With Regard to Protection of the Human Rights of Older Persons, Permanent Council of the Organization of American States Committee on Juridical and Political Affairs, OEA/Ser.GCP/CAJP-3030/11 rev 2.

1 Human rights and residential care for older adults in sub-Saharan Africa

Case study of Kenya

Isabella Aboderin, Cecilia Mbaka, Carolyne Egesa, Hilda Akinyi Owii

Background and aims of the chapter

Debate on issues of ageing in sub-Saharan Africa (SSA) has intensified over the past decade (Aboderin, 2013). As part of the discourse, a nascent research focus on long-term care for dependent older persons has emerged in recent years (Aboderin & Hoffman, 2013). The interest in this area is fuelled, on the one hand, by a growing awareness of the considerable prevalence of functional impairments in SSA's older populations and, on the other hand, by long-standing concerns about impacts of rapid sociocultural and economic change on customary family care systems, which – in the absence of comprehensive formal services – provide the bulk of long-term care across most of SSA (Aboderin & Beard, 2014). One exception is South Africa, which has a long-established history of residential care, beginning under apartheid rule (Aboderin & Hoffman, 2013). For the most part, research on long-term care in SSA has, therefore, centred on 'informal' support provision by family members. A specific focus has been on examining the structure and content of family care arrangements and, to a lesser extent, the adequacy of care provided and its impacts on caregiver and recipient (Akinyemi, Adepoju & Ogunbameru, 2007; Ba-Gning, 2012; De Klerk, 2013; Gureje, Kola & Afolabi, 2006; Obrist, 2012; Odiambo, 2012; van der Geest & Frimpong-Nnuroh, 2013; van Eeuwijk, 2012, 2013; Aboderin & Hoffman, 2011). Within this context, a handful of small-scale empirical studies have begun to illuminate experiences of residential care in SSA, exploring contexts and underpinnings of, as well as pathways and attitudes to, its use (Pype, 2013; van Eeuwijk, 2013). At the research-practice interface, several studies in South Africa have investigated approaches for enhancing the quality of formal care provision (Stroebel, 2012; Brand, 2012; Du Toit, 2012; Clouston, 2012; Roos, 2012; Van Zyl, 2012).

In this chapter we aim to extend current perspectives on residential care in SSA by offering a situational analysis of such service provision and its human rights implications in Kenya, and reflecting on broader consequences for action in SSA and beyond. We do so by drawing on a critical appraisal of relevant regional and national policy, legal and human rights frameworks and debates, as well as on a narrative review of the small body of existing empirical evidence on contexts and realities of residential care in Kenya and other SSA countries. Following (i) a brief description of the geographic and socio-economic profile of Kenya, subsequent sections discuss (ii) key characteristics of Kenya's older population, (iii) Government responses to ageing in Kenya, (iv) the evolving policy discourse and frameworks on long-term care, (v) relevant national and regional legal and human rights instruments, (vi) emerging realities of long-term care in Kenya, and (vii) future perspectives for action on residential care in the country. The chapter concludes with reflections on possible implications of the developments in Kenya for action in other SSA States and globally.

Kenya – country profile

Home to close to 44 million people, Kenya is a multicultural country in Eastern Africa with a landmass of 582,642 km^2. It is bordered by Ethiopia, South Sudan, and Somalia in the North; Uganda and Tanzania in the West, and the Indian Ocean in the South East. Kenya's population comprises 42 distinct ethnic groups, and a spectrum of faiths. Approximately 71% of Kenyans are Christian (48% Protestant, 23% Catholic), 6% are Muslims and 23% are adherents of indigenous religions (Kenya National Bureau of Statistics, 2010). The country's population is predominantly rural, engaged in agriculture, with only 25% living in urban areas (United Nations Population Division, 2014a). With a per capita Gross National Income (GNI) of $870 (compared, for example, to $7,460 in South Africa and $35,800 in the UK) Kenya is classified as a low-income country (World Bank, 2014). Despite recording substantial economic growth over the past decade, income inequality is rising and poverty levels remain substantial. The most recent available figures suggest that 43% of the population live in extreme poverty, under $1.25 per day (World Bank, 2014).

Kenya's older population

Kenya's population is predominantly young, with over 60% aged below 25 years. However, the absolute number of older persons aged 60 years and above in the country is already considerable, and is projected to rise sharply over coming decades from 2.1 million today to 9.2 million by 2050. In the same time frame, the proportion of older people in the total population is set to double from 4.5% to 9.5% (United Nations Population Division, 2014b). Available national-level data suggests that a large majority (82%) of older Kenyans reside in rural areas, and that most, in both rural and urban settings, live in large households with five or more members. Only about 7% live alone. Analysis of per capita adult-equivalent household expenditure,[1] indicates that more than half (53%) of older persons in Kenya live in 'absolute' poverty and a quarter (25.6%) in hardcore poverty,

---

1 Calculations of such 'head-count' poverty rates are commonly used in analyses of household-based data. They divide total household expenditure (or income) by the number of adult equivalent household members, and compare per capita expenditure (or income) to arrive at the proportion of individuals below or above a pre-defined national or other poverty threshold/line.

with poverty rates significantly higher among rural dwellers. Evidence on older Kenyans' health status shows close to a third to have functional limitations and at least a quarter to suffer from chronic illness (Aboderin & Kizito, 2010).

Kenya – emerging responses to ageing

Prompted by a mounting awareness of the rapid growth in, and some of the profound challenges faced by its older population, Kenya – as one of a small but rising number of SSA States – has taken a series of substantial steps to respond to issues of ageing. In 2009 the country adopted a National Policy on Older Persons and Ageing (NPOPA) (Republic of Kenya, 2014a) in line with broad parameters set by the United Nations Madrid International Plan of Action on Ageing (MIPAA) (UN, 2002) and the African Union (AU) Policy Framework and Plan of Action on Ageing (AU Plan) (AU/HelpAge, 2003). Between 2012 and 2014, the NPOPA was reviewed to ensure concurrence with Kenya's new Constitution (2010) (Kenya National Council for Law Reporting, 2010). In its revised version, the policy now provides an overall direction for the future development of Government action on ageing. Its overarching goal is to foster an environment that empowers and facilitates older persons' participation in society and ensures their rights, freedoms and dignity. To this end, the NPOPA specifies key policy objectives and intended responses across ten thematic areas: older persons and the law; poverty and sustainable livelihood; health, HIV and AIDS; family, community and culture; food security and nutrition; infrastructure; education, training and ICT; employment and income security; social protection and services; and cross-cutting issues (Republic of Kenya, 2014a). In parallel to forging the National Policy, Kenya instituted a pilot cash transfer scheme for vulnerable older persons in 2006, as part of its overarching development strategy 'Vision 2030'. The programme has since been expanded to cover 164,000 older beneficiaries (Kenya Ministry of Labour, Social Security and Services, 2014).

In order to coordinate and further promote action on ageing across Government sectors, Kenya established in 2013 a 'Division on Older Persons and Social Welfare' (DOPSW) within the Department of Social Development in the Ministry of Labour, Social Security and Services. As part of its remit, DOPSW has begun to address questions of long-term care, seeking to engage with, and shape an emergent policy discourse on long-term, specifically residential, care in the country.

Long-term care: policy discourse and frameworks

The debate on long-term care has evolved over the past decade and, in recent years, has become characterised by a duality of views.

Rejection of residential care

On the one hand, a first perspective centres on a clear rejection of residential care. Taken as definitive in initial stages of the debate, this view is enshrined in early policy frameworks such as the AU Plan (2003), and exhorts a need to cement the role of the family in long-term care provision. Thus, while the Plan recognises that 'traditional' family care is 'under threat', it urges Member States to:

- Enact legal provisions that promote and strengthen the role of family and community in the care of older people
- Learn from traditional family values and norms to inform legislation about . . . care of older persons
- Discourage the institutionalization of older people and retain the cultural respect for older people

(AU/Help Age, 2003 p. 17)

Such opposition to residential care remains dominant in current popular and political discourse, which sees institutional service models as 'un-African' and, more specifically, as contrary to Kenyan cultural norms. This line of reasoning is exemplified in excerpts of a Kenya Senate debate in March 2014, which discussed – and subsequently rejected – a Member's proposal to 'initiate small small-scale residential homes in each county to enable [older people] access and necessary care and live dignified lives':

Traditionally or according to our society, our [elderly] people; men and women, would want to be supported while at their homes and not in a bondage house where they will think that they are being thrown away by their families. Traditionally, no one would want to leave their families to go and be caged in a place way from their home. Therefore I will not support any such idea.

(Parliament of Kenya, Senate Hansard,
20 March 2014 p. 27)

We need to delete the idea of establishing small-scale residential homes . . . That is un-African and it goes against our culture. I cannot imagine myself sending away my old mother to a home to be taken care of. I cannot imagine that. If we want to help these elderly people, let us help them while they are in their own homes. We should not send them to institutional homes. The idea of homes has worked in the developed world and European countries and even in the USA but I do not think we have reached that stage as a country. It is a taboo in . . . our cultures to send our parents away from home.

(Parliament of Kenya, Senate Hansard,
20 March 2014 p. 28)

As the last quotes expresses, and as Aboderin and Hoffman (2013) argue, the objections to institutional care should not be interpreted as reflecting a desire to limit public expenditure. Rather they reflect an assertion of African values and approaches vis-à-vis 'Western' models. In a broader sense, then, the 'centrality of the family' perspective must be understood as part of a wider critique of, and resistance to what have been seen as 'Africa-inappropriate' development modes imposed on the continent by European and American donor countries (Aboderin & Ferreira, 2008; Okumu, 2002).

Residential care as a necessary complement

On the other hand, a second more recently emerging perspective marks a clear departure from a blanket objection to institutional care. While upholding the importance of family support, this view posits a need to accept and engage with residential service provision as a necessary complement, or alternative, to family care. Expressed in the rejected Senate proposal mentioned above, this notion is captured most prominently in Kenya's revised National Policy on Older Persons and Ageing (Republic of Kenya, 2014a). Thus, the policy stipulates both (i) a need to 'strengthen . . . family and community support systems' and to 'promote and protect the family as a fundamental unit of the society, to provide care and assistance to Older Persons' (p. 10, sections 2.4.2 and 2.4.3i–ii) as well as (ii) the Government's intention to 'establish institutions to take care of Older Persons who are neglected, homeless and with special needs' and to 'regulate the establishment and the operations of institutions taking care of Older Persons' (p. 10. section 2.4.3viii–ix).

Legal and human rights frameworks

Crucially, a responsibility of Kenya's and other African Governments to embrace, and develop regulatory mechanisms for, residential care is also enshrined in a key extant human rights framework – namely the African Union Protocol on the Rights of Older People in Africa, which was passed by African Ministers of Social Development and is due to be adopted in 2015 (African Union, 2014). In its articles 11 and 12, the Protocol commits Member States to both '(i) Identify, promote and strengthen traditional support systems . . . to enhance the ability of families and communities to care for older family members but also to (ii) enact or review legislation that ensures that residential care is optional for older persons' and 'Ensure older persons in residential care facilities are provided with care that meets national minimum standards' (African Union, 2014).

Realities of long-term care: Organic expansion and human rights concerns

The emergent emphasis on a need for State regulation signals Governments' increased appreciation of, and readiness to address, two realities of long-term care in Kenya and SSA, broadly.

Organic expansion

The first is a slow, but significant 'organic' growth in the presence and use of formal, including institutional, care services for dependent older adults over the past few decades (Aboderin & Hoffman, 2013). As Kenya's National Policy on Older Persons and Ageing notes:

> The effectiveness of the traditional family and community structures to provide in-built support and caring for Older Persons is increasingly under

pressure. For instance, the emerging trend is for families to take older persons to institutions for elderly care. These institutions are not regulated by the state to ensure that they are Older Persons friendly.

(Republic of Kenya, 2014a p. 9)

An initial picture of extant formal service provision in Kenya was generated by a unique mapping exercise undertaken by DOPSW in 2014 (Republic of Kenya, 2014b). The initiative was motivated by accumulating anecdotal evidence, gathered by the Division in the course of its delivery of the older persons' cash transfer programme, which highlighted both (i) a frequent inadequacy of informal family care provision and (ii) the presence of formal providers in several counties in Kenya.

The survey revealed the existence of at least 18 residential care facilities, a majority of which were founded pre-1990. Three have been established post-2000. All of the identified care homes are run by charitable church-based or nongovernmental organisations, geared toward supporting poor or destitute older adults (Republic of Kenya, 2014b).

In addition to providing an insight into the profile of residential service provision at present, the results of the mapping exercise also provide pointers to the contextual factors and rationales that are key in driving its expansion. Indeed, they appear to support incipient analyses, which suggest that the growth of institutional care in SSA must be understood as a response to a very real need and demand on the part of both caregivers and recipients that is arising within contexts of poverty (Aboderin & Hoffman, 2011, 2013). Drawing on small-scale qualitative explorations in Nigeria and South Africa, this perspective suggests further that families' need for residential services reflects their multiple time, physical, economic and knowledge constraints (Aboderin & Hoffman, 2011, 2013). These capacity gaps are typically engendered in settings of: insecure incomes largely from informal sector work; lacking social security; inadequate housing; poor and costly basic services and amenities; and a dearth of accessible public education and training. Interestingly, anecdotal evidence from Kenya and Nigeria appears to point to the possible evolution of a two-tier system of formal care provision – with charitable residential services emerging as an only choice for the majority poor, while higher income strata choose – and are able to afford – private, home-based nursing care.

Human rights concerns

Closely related to the first, is a second reality specifically of long-term care in Kenya. This is the lack of regulatory oversight, and the documented poor condition of existing residential care facilities – which suggests deeply compromised standards of care within them (Republic of Kenya, 2014b). For all but one of the existing care homes, the DOPSW mapping highlighted: (i) major limitations in requisite infrastructure and basic amenities, such as sanitation, water, electricity, transport, (ii) a lack of essential supplies such as nutrition supplements, food or diapers, (iii) a dearth, or complete absence of relevant care skills and expertise among staff and (iv) serious personnel shortages given a typical reliance, in charity-run homes, on only few regular employees supplemented by volunteers with competing time obligations and often short-lived commitment to their care roles (Republic of Kenya, 2014b).

Taken together, the apparent constraints raise major concerns not only about the quality of current residential care in Kenya, but also about the extent to which basic constitutional rights of older residential care recipients – to live in dignity, to self-fulfillment and to participation (UN, 2002; Kenya National Council on Law Reporting, 2010) – are being safeguarded (Aboderin, 2014).

Residential care in Kenya: Future plans

In view of the emerging realities, a major priority of the DOPSW for the coming years is to promote a consolidation and development of the residential care sector in Kenya. As a first step, the Ministry of Labour, Social Security and Services plans to formulate, and enshrine in law, a set of robust and binding guidelines regarding the establishment, registration, management and operation of residential facilities, intended to effectively safeguard older people's rights vis-à-vis care providers and the State. Toward this end, DOPSW convened a first national 'brainstorming' consultation in November 2014 and is forging plans for further in-depth evidence generation on experiences and perspectives of residential care clients and personnel in Kenya. More importantly, however, given the absence of prior in-country experience with formal care coordination and regulation, DOPSW seeks to explicitly draw on relevant models, approaches and insights gained in countries that have an established, strong public oversight of residential care.

The chief country of interest in SSA is South Africa, which has made significant strides in strengthening standards in its long-established formal care sector. A civil society-led 'South African Older Persons Charter', which among others has articulated key rights of older people in residential care, was launched in 2011. In 2012, the South Africa Care Forum was established to provide a platform for private-sector exchange and collaboration on fostering best practice in care delivery (South Africa Care Forum, 2014). At a legislative level, South Africa ratified an Older Persons Act (2006), which became effective on 1 April 2010. The Act aims to (i) promote older adults' wellbeing, safety and security, (ii) protect the rights of older persons, (iii) enable older people to stay in their homes in the community for as long as possible, (iv) regulate services and residential facilities for older persons, and (v) recognise and combat elder abuse as a criminal offence. To these ends, the legislation sets out guiding principles and regulations to be observed by all State or other parties rendering services to older persons in national, provincial and, where applicable, local spheres of Government. The guidelines emphasise a principal need to (i) appreciate the social, cultural and economic contribution of older persons, (ii) promote the dignity of, and respect for older persons, (iii) recognise the multi-dimensional nature of older people's needs, (iv) enhance their participation in decision-making, (v) provide relevant education and training to ensure access to information, (vi) prioritise older persons in service provision, and (vii) further expand basic elder care provision in both urban and rural areas.

The Act's specific stipulations on formal care services centre on opportunities for State financial assistance to service providers, binding norms and standards for residential facilities, and the advancement of formal community-based care and training of workers. The latter – in contrast to current emphases in Kenya – reflects the Act's explicit endeavour to 'shift the emphasis from institutional care to community-based care' (Government of South Africa, 2006).

In addition to learning from the important legal and practice developments in South Africa, DOPSW also intends to draw on the expertise of other developing or developed countries, such as the United Kingdom, which are continuing to forge refined legal and human rights parameters as well as governing structures for their institutional care sectors (European Union, 2011; Welsh Government, 2014).

Concluding remarks: Implications for other countries

Kenya's perspectives and plans regarding residential care for dependent older persons evidently carry two important implications for other States.

First, is Kenya's potential role as a forerunner for other SSA countries that are yet to consider the realities of residential care in their societies. Pioneering activities in Kenya, such as the mapping of extant formal service provision, the embracing of residential care in national policy, and the steps taken to formulate a regulatory framework for the sector may, therefore, serve as models for adaptation and refinement in other national contexts in Africa. Second, of course, is the explicit opportunity for active, cross-country exchange and knowledge sharing – both at Africa-regional, South-South and North-South levels. The spectrum of experiences and insights presented in this volume will provide a valuable starting point for such dialogue.

References

Aboderin, I. (2014) 'Long-term Care for Older Persons in Sub-Saharan Africa: Realities, Discourses and Human Rights Implications'. Presented at the 5th Session of the United Nations Open Ended Working Group on Ageing, 29–31 July, United Nations, New York.

Aboderin, I. (2013) 'African Gerontology and Geriatrics: Strides and Crucial Next Steps'. *Journal of Nutrition, Health and Ageing*, 17 (Suppl. 1), p. 5.

Aboderin, I., Beard, J. (2014) 'Older People's Health in Sub-Saharan Africa'. *Lancet* online 6 November.

Aboderin, I. and Ferreira, M. (2008) 'Linking Ageing to Development Agendas in sub-Saharan Africa: Challenges and Approaches'. *Journal of Population Ageing*, 1, pp. 51–73.

Aboderin, I., Hoffman, J. (2013) 'Care for Dependent Older People in Sub-Saharan Africa: Recognizing and Addressing a "Cultural Lag"'. Paper presented in the symposium on 'Global Approaches to Policy Supporting Work and Care in Late Middle Age'; 20th IAGG World Congress of Gerontology and Geriatrics, 23–27 June, Seoul, South Korea.

Aboderin, I. Hoffman, J. (2011) 'Caregiving in Contexts of Poverty in Sub-Saharan Africa: Critical Perspectives on Debates and Realities'. Keynote paper presented at the Festival of International Conferences on Caregiving, Disability, Aging and Technology, 5–8 June, Toronto, Canada.

Aboderin, I., Kizito, P. (2010) *Dimensions and Determinants of Health in Old Age in Kenya and Nigeria. Report.* National Coordinating Agency for Population and Development (NCAPD), Kenya.

African Union (2014) Draft Protocol to the African Charter on Human and Peoples' Rights on the Rights of Older Persons in Africa. African Union, Addis Ababa, Ethiopia.

African Union/HelpAge International (AU/HelpAge) (2003) Policy Framework and Plan of Action on Ageing. HAI Africa Regional Development Centre, Nairobi.

Akinyemi, I.A., Adepoju, O.A., Ogunbameru, A.O. (2007) 'Changing Philosophy for Care and Support for the Elderly in South-Western Nigeria'. *BOLD*, 18 (1), pp. 18–24.

Ba-Gning, S. (2012) 'Older People in Senegal: Beyond Familial Acceptability'. Paper presented at the 1st IAGG Africa Region Conference on Gerontology and Geriatrics, 17–20 October, Cape Town, South Africa.

Brand, Y. (2012) 'Intergenerational Relationships – Using Telecommunications (Skype and Facebook) Within a Small Group Home to Build and Maintain Important Relationships'. Paper presented in the 1st IAGG Africa Region Conference on Gerontology and Geriatrics, 17–20 October 2012, Cape Town, South Africa.

Clouston, V. (2012) 'An Alternative to Conventional Institutional Care . . . Would Ageing-In-Place Work in South Africa?'. Paper presented in the 1st IAGG Africa Region Conference on Gerontology and Geriatrics, 17–20 October 2012, Cape Town, South Africa.

De Klerk, J. (2013) 'The Physicality of Relating: Negotiating Family Care for Advanced Old Age in the Context of HIV/AIDS, Tanzania'. Paper presented at the Invited international colloquium 'Ageing in Sub-Saharan Africa: Spaces and Practices of Care', 10 May, Catholic University of Leuven, Leuven, Belgium.

Du Toit, S. (2012) 'Occupation in Context – Exploring Meaningful Activities for Older Sesotho Persons Who Reside in Care Facilities in the Free State'. Paper presented in the 1st IAGG Africa Region Conference on Gerontology and Geriatrics, 17–20 October 2012, Cape Town, South Africa.

European Union (2011) European Charter of the Rights and Responsibilities of Older Persons in Need of Long-Term Care and Assistance, June 2010. Available at: http://www.age-platform.eu/images/stories/22204_AGE_charte_europeenne_EN_v4.pdf. Accessed 8 November 2014.

Government of South Africa (2006) Older Persons Act of 2006. Pretoria: Government of South Africa. Available at: http://www.justice.gov.za/legislation/acts/2006-013_olderpersons.pdf. Accessed 12 January 2015.

Gureje, O., Kola, L., Afolabi, E. (2006) 'Functional Disability Among Elderly Nigerians: Results from the Ibadan Study of Ageing'. *Journal of the American Geriatric Society*, 54 (11), pp. 1532–5415.

Kenya National Bureau of Statistics (KNBS) (2010) Kenya 2009 Population and Housing Census. KNBS, Nairobi, Kenya.

Kenya National Council for Law Reporting (2010) The Constitution of Kenya 2010. KNCLR, Nairobi, Kenya.

Kenya Ministry of Labour, Social Security and Services, 2014, personal communication Kenya National Senate, Hansard, 20 March 2014 p. 27. Available at: http://www.parliament.go.ke/the-senate/house-business/hansard?start=100. Accessed 20 October 2014.

Obrist, B. (2012) 'Who Cares for Frail Elderly People: A Rural-urban Comparison in Tanzania'. Paper presented at the 1st IAGG Africa Region Conference on Gerontology and Geriatrics, 17–20 October, Cape Town, South Africa.

Odiambo, S.W. (2012) 'From the Measure of Residential Arrangements to the Reality of Family Support and Care for Older Persons in Uganda'. Paper presented at the 1st

IAGG Africa Region Conference on Gerontology and Geriatrics 'Africa Ageing', 17–20 October, Cape Town, South Africa.

Okumu, W.A.J. (2002) *The African Renaissance. History, Significance and Strategy.* Africa World Press, Trenton, NJ.

Pype, K. (2013) 'Caring for People With and Without Value: Kinshasa's Retirement Homes between the Family, the State and the Church'. Paper presented at the Invited international colloquium 'Ageing in Sub-Saharan Africa: Spaces and Practices of Care', 10 May, Catholic University of Leuven, Leuven, Belgium.

Republic of Kenya, Ministry of Labour, Social Security and Services (MLSSS) (2014a) Draft National Policy on Older Persons and Ageing. Revised 2014. MLSSS, Nairobi, Kenya.

Republic of Kenya, Ministry of Labour, Social Security and Services (MLSSS) (2014b) Report on the establishment of a databank offering services to older persons. MLSSS, Nairobi, Kenya.

Roos, V. (2012) 'The Psycho-Social Experiences of Older Persons in an Economically Deprived and Culturally Diverse Residential Care Facility'. Paper presented in the 1st IAGG Africa Region Conference on Gerontology and Geriatrics, 17–20 October 2012, Cape Town, South Africa.

South African Care Forum (2014) [online] Available at: http://sa-careforum.co.za. Accessed 8 November 2014.

Stroebel, R. (2012) 'The Eden Alternative in South Africa'. Paper presented in the 1st IAGG Africa Region Conference on Gerontology and Geriatrics, 17–20 October, Cape Town, South Africa.

United Nations (UN) (2002) Madrid International Plan of Action on Ageing (MIPAA). United Nations, New York.

United Nations Population Division (2014a) World Urbanization Prospects: The 2014 Revision. United Nations, New York. Available at: http://esa.un.org/Unpd/Wup. Accessed 28 October 2014.

United Nations Population Division (2014b) World Population Prospects: The 2012 Revision. United Nations, New York. Available at: http://esa.un.org/Unpd/Wpp. Accessed 28 October 2014.

Van der Geest, S., Frimpong-Nnuroh, D. (2013) 'Will Families in Ghana Continue to Care for Older People? Comments from Two Case Studies'. Paper presented at the Invited international colloquium 'Ageing in Sub-Saharan Africa: Spaces and Practices of Care', 10 May, Catholic University of Leuven, Leuven, Belgium.

van Eeuwijk, P. (2012) 'Elderly Providing Elder Care. An Underestimated Commitment in Tanzania'. Paper presented at the 1st IAGG Africa Region Conference on Gerontology and Geriatrics, 17–20 October, Cape Town, South Africa.

van Eeuwijk, P. (2013) 'Elderly Providing Care for Elderly in Tanzania: Against Conventions – But Accepted'. Paper presented at the Invited international colloquium 'Ageing in Sub-Saharan Africa: Spaces and Practices of Care' 10 May, Catholic University of Leuven, Leuven, Belgium.

Van Zyl, M. (2012) 'A Public/Private Partnership: Ekuphumleni, Guglethu'. Paper presented in the 1st IAGG Africa Region Conference on Gerontology and Geriatrics, 17–20 October, Cape Town, South Africa.

Welsh Government (2014) Declaration of Rights for Older People in Wales. Welsh Government, Cardiff. Available at: http://gov.wales/docs/dhss/publications/140716olderen.pdf. Accessed 8 November 2014.

World Bank (2014) World Bank Open Data. Available at: http://data.worldbank.org. Accessed 28 October 2014.

2 What's new in the residential care of the elderly in the Arab and Islamic world? The case of Egypt

Mohamed A. 'Arafa

Let him be humbled into dust; let him be humbled into dust. It was said: Allah's Messenger, who is he? He said: He who sees either of his parents during their old age or he sees both of them, but he does not enter Paradise.[1]

The Prophet Mohammad (PBUH)

Part 1: Introduction and overview

The world's elderly population is rising quickly in developing countries especially in the Middle Eastern region. Though, in those countries with less progressive economic enlargement and advanced access to health care, it is problematic to cope with the economic, medical, and social needs of the elderly (Al-Heeti, 2007, pp. 205–206).[2] Real-world solutions to these challenges can be prompted by social awareness of the needs of ageing individuals. In the same vein, and as the older population grows in numbers, many cultural practices and norms have emerged and played a fundamental role in this area, as some cultural practices show that there is no easy way to change without offending the culture and teachings of that community (Kick, 2003).[3]

---

1 Aboû Al-Hussein, Muslim Ibn Al-Hajjaj Ibn Muslim Ibn Warat Al-Qushayri Al-Nisaburi, [Hadith No. 6189], [hereinafter Sahih Muslim], *available at* http://cmje.org/ translated in Univ So Calif, CENTER FOR MUSLIM-JEWISH ENGAGEMENT, http://www.usc.edu/org/cmje/religious-texts/hadith/.
2 See Roaa M. Al-Heeti, Note, *Why Nursing Homes Will Not Work: Caring for the Needs of the Aging Muslim American Population*, 15 ELDER L.J. 205, 206 (2007).
3 *Ibid. See generally* Ella Kick, *Health Care and the Aging Population: What are Today's Challenges? (Overview and Summary)* 8 J. OF ISSUES IN NURSING 2, May 31, 2003, http://www.nursingworld.org/ojin (last visited June 30, 2014) (providing nursing care to the elderly historically, ageing, the integration of the various disciplines that influence gerontology, steps to enhance the health of the ageing adult, and strategies to overcome the severe shortage of qualified gerontological nurses today) ("How the health care system addresses the needs of these frail elderly, who the formal and informal caregivers are, what health care costs in various settings, who pays for the care of these elders, and how these frail elderly persons impact the entire health care system are discussed. Issues that will impact the future care of frail elder are addressed by looking at today's delivery system, what is funded, and what is actually needed. Public and family responsibility for care of frail elderly is reviewed. Questions such as: How are the various community-based services used? Who uses them and what is their cost and effectiveness and how related to formal and informal caregivers in various minority groups. Creative solutions consider changing demographics, technological progress, and what nursing can do to enhance the care of the frail elderly").

It should be borne in mind that the spiritual and cultural background of Muslims and the teachings of Islamic intellectuals deter several Muslims from sending their older relatives to nursing homes (Gaspar, 2007).[4] In other words, this religious belief comes at a price, as Medical Insurance provides funds to cover stays in nursing homes for various family and ageing people, but still these programs do not afford the equivalent level of funding to individuals who live with family members at home, or at least not to all families who need upkeep and care (Clemetson, 2006).[5] The *Qura'nic* provisions explicitly give directions to care for elderly parents.[6] Additionally, the *Sunnah* (prophetic/*hadith*) traditions emphasize children's duty to care for parents as they were cared for as infants (Clemetson, 2006).[7] Traditionally, families and religious leaders have interpreted this as a duty to care for parents at home (Ajrouch and Fakhoury, 2003. pp. 353–372).[8]

Based on this succinct backdrop, this chapter examines what Islamic and Arab positive laws offer for the needs of the older population. Part 1 examined the Islamic attitude to the care of older people and their essential rights and Part 2 compares it with some Arab positive laws (various legal systems protecting the elderly in the Arab Middle East countries specifically, Egyptian laws). Part 3

---

4 *See generally* Claudia Gaspar, AGING MUSLIM COMMUNITIES, WORLD MUSLIM CONGRESS, Apr. 30, 2007, http://worldmuslimcongress.blogspot.com/2007/04/aging-muslim-communities.html (last retrieved June 30, 2014) ("Friday and holiday programming and bedside visitation must be provided by trained volunteers and congregational *imans* (faith) at nursing homes. The frequency of Friday programming depends on the number of residents and their level of acuity. *Imans* or trained volunteers could advise and counsel families on nursing home placements. Caring for the sick must become institutionalized in the Muslim community. Many communities had special societies which took responsibility for providing health care for the needy. These societies must be available to any community member or even a stranger who needed help").

5 *Ibid. See* Lynette Clemetson, *U.S. Muslims Confront Taboo on Nursing Homes*, THE N.Y. TIMES, June 13, 2006, http://travel.nytimes.com/2006/06/13/us/13muslim.html?pagewanted=print (last visited June 30, 2014) ("For generations, immigrant groups have grappled with the American concept of housing for the elderly, tailoring it to meet their ethnic, cultural and religious needs. But for many Muslims, the idea of placing parents in facilities is still unthinkable, seen as a violation of a K[Q]oranic obligation to care for one's elderly relatives").

6 The *Qur'an*, *Surat* (Chapter) Al-isra, 17: Verse 23 says: "Thy Lord has decreed you shall not serve any but Him, and to be good to parents, whether one or both of them attains old age with thee; say not to them 'Fie' neither chide them, but speak unto them words respectful."

7 *Ibid. See also* Clemetson, *supra* note 5.

8 Kristine J. Ajrouch and Nour Fakhoury, *Assessing Needs of Aging Muslims: A Focus On Metro-Detroit Faith Communities*, 7 J. CONTEMPORARY ISLAM 3, (SPRINGER LINK: September 2003), at 353–372. ("This study provides a critical perspective on the needs of aging Muslims by focusing on a diverse group of older adults including those with ancestry from African American, South Asian, Arab, and Albanian origins. Four focus group discussions were conducted with adults aged 60 . . ., strengths and challenges in the Muslim community, as well as suggestions for the way forward in addressing aging issues. Needs identified include quality of life and social relations. Strengths included references to tradition and scripture. The way forward consisted of the desire for options to support aging families within the community, often in small steps, though not necessarily only through mosques. In sum, this study uncovered areas of overlap and at times disagreement between and within groups, underlining the fact that there is no one kind of Muslim ageing, and that any approach to caring for Muslims must combine cultural sensitivity with flexibility in order to minimize anxiety and stress for both elders and their families").

highlights the international human rights instruments on the care of older people and how fair Islamic law in that field is much appreciated. Finally, it concludes that Islamic law is more than sufficient to generate an inclusive pattern for the care of elderly citizens, but domestic legislation must meet its lofty standards.

Part 2: Elder rights and care in Islamic (*Sharie'a*) legal theory: how far-reaching are they?

In this domain, the two introductory sources of Islamic law – the *Qur'an* and the *Sunnah* – encompass principles and instructions that construct family obligations to afford physical, psychological, and emotional comfort to ageing persons (Bassiouni & Badr, 2002, pp.138–139; Abdal-Haqq, 2002, p. 56; Khan, 1984).[9] Conventionally, the Muslim family organization is comprehensive rather than nuclear as extended family members may or may not occupy and reside in a common residential unit (Mahmood, 1989).[10] Professor Tahir Mahmood said that "A Muslim family primarily includes the self, the spouse and the immediate ascendants and descendants – the position of none of these constituents being inferior to any other" (Mahmood, 1989).[11]

Within the intergenerational roles prescribed by Islamic theory, older people have a place of honor in which the "security, protection, and comfort" of the elderly are "guaranteed by the behavioral norms and obligations" placed on younger members of the family (al-Sheha, p. 2).[12] Islamic law as a religious and socio-legal order is based on fairness and equality among individuals regardless of belief, religion, language, color, social status, race, gender, culture, or ethnicity as

9 The *Qur'an*, the holy book of Muslims, represents the first and the major source of *Sharie'a* law in which the word of God was revealed to the Prophet Mohammad (PBUH) verbally through the Angel Gabriel over a period of 22 years (610–632 C.E.). *Sunnah* is the collective word for the mass of texts which tell of the Prophet's spoken words, or are an account of acts or the absence of acts attributed to him. In other words, it is the oral or the habitual traditions – practice, life style, and conduct of Prophet Mohammad (PBUH). For further details on Islamic law and its sources, *see* M. Cherif Bassiouni and Gamal M. Badr, *The Shari'ah: Sources, Interpretation, and Rule-Making*, 1 UCLA J. ISLAMIC & NEAR E. L. 135, 138–39 (2002). *See also* IRSHAD ABDAL-HAQQ, *Islamic Law: An Overview of Its Origin and Elements*, 7 J. ISLAMIC L. & CULTURE 27, 56 (2002) (defining Islamic law, explaining the main elements and sources of the *Sharie'a*, and discussing the methodologies and schools of the Islamic jurisprudence). KHIZAR MUAZZAM KHAN, *Juristic Classification of Islamic Law*, 6 HOUS. J. INT'L. L. 23 (1983–1984).

10 Tahir Mahmood, *Law and the Elderly in the Islamic Tradition – Classical Precepts and Modern Legislation*, IX ISLAMIC & COMP. L. Q. 33, 33 (1989). In any event, however, family ties remain intact and family duties must be followed by all.

11 *Ibid.*

12 *See* Abdul-Rahman Al-Sheha, *Human Rights in Islam and Common Misconceptions*, DAR FOUNDATION, http:// www.darfoundation.com/Human%20Rights%20in%0Islam.pdf, at 2 (last retrieved June 30, 2014):

> Every society must ensure for its citizens the rights that guarantee for them their basic needs and security, and enable them to feel a sense of belonging and attachment to the larger social group. Individuals need to feel secure and a sense of belonging in order to perform their tasks and duties in a satisfactory manner . . . We firmly believe that the application of the individual and social principles of the third trend, when guided by the perfect revealed law from *Allah* in the *Qur'an* and *Sunnah*, will definitely make humanity happier and more prosperous. The

Islam forbids discrimination and racism and this is confirmed by the *Qura'nic* texts and the *hadith* teachings (*Qur'an* 49:13 & Ibn Hanbal, *no.* 24204).[13]

Regarding care rights for older people under the umbrella of the *Sharie'a* theory, it is generally well known that parents owe specific commitments to their own children and children likewise have certain responsibilities to their parents such as regard and respect are due to parents at all times, but extraordinary emphasis is sited on parents in old age.[14] "The most imperative burden next to that of faith (God worship) is the family . . . as parents are certainly motivated to look after their children, surrendering everything in the process, even when the sacrifice includes them personally . . . Thus, it is the children who need to be reminded of their sense of duty towards the generation that has become dry, in need of tender care, after having spent most of its vitality in bringing up their young" (Qutb, 2007, p. 119).[15] Hence, the deific and divinely command to take good care of parents in particular at older ages, comes in the form of an '*amr* (ruling) from God, following immediately after the command to worship God alone (Qutb, 2007, p. 120).[16] Furthermore, the *Qur'anic* texts treat the mother and father as equals and – with no doubt – these viewpoints are in contrast to some Muslim (incorrect, extreme and radical) interpretations that favor one parent over the other (Islam, 2012).[17] Accordingly, Islamic law is "absolutely clear that a person who is giving any kind

---

application of these principles will enable the society to achieve peace and security. These social rights and principles are not a result of previous experiences, social ideologies, temporary and immediate needs and/or political drives and motives; rather they are from the Beneficent and the Omniscient for man's progress to happiness in this life and salvation in the Hereafter. Mahmood, *supra* note 10, at 34.

13 In this sense, the *Qur'an* says "O mankind! We created you from a single (pair) of a male and a female, and made you into nations and tribes, that ye may know each other (not that ye may despise each other). Verily the most honored of you in the sight of *Allah* is (he who is) the most righteous of you. And *Allah* has full knowledge and is well acquainted (with all things)." Further, the Prophet Mohammad (PBUH) is reported to have said: "No Arab has superiority over a white person and no white person has superiority over an Arab; no black person has superiority over a white person and no white person has any superiority over a black person. The criterion of honor in the sight of *Allah* is righteousness and honest living." *See* Qur'an 49:13 & Ahmad ibn Hanbal (*hadith* No. 24204).

14 In this domain, the *Qur'an* reads at verses 17:23–24 "Thy Lord hath decreed that ye worship none but Him, and that ye be kind to parents. Whether one or both of them attain old age in thy life, say not to them a word of contempt, nor repel them but address them, in terms of honour. And, out of kindness, lower to them the wing of humility, and say: 'My Lord! Bestow on them thy mercy even as they cherished me in childhood'." *Ibid.*

15 Sayyid Qutb, 11 Fi Dhilal Al-Qur'an [In the Shade of the Qur'an] 119 (Adil Salahi trans. and ed., The Islamic Foundation, 2007); The *Qur'an* provides at 17:22 ("Take not with Allah another god; or thou (O man!) wilt sit in disgrace and destitution").

16 *Ibid.*, at 120. "The placement of parents at such a high pedestal . . . is aimed at providing a firm scriptural foundation for the formulation of detailed socio-legal principles in order to secure for the parents all possible material and emotional comfort that the children could afford to provide." Mahmood, *supra* note 10, at 35.

17 Therefore, the *Qur'an* "erects a system of material and moral protection for the elderly based on the family structure." Joseph A. Islam, *Parents*, Quran's Message, Apr. 2012, http://quransmessage. com/articles/parents%20FM3.htm (last visited June 30, 2014).

of material or emotional support to an elderly relative is in no sense doing a favour to him or her; he is only discharging his own sacred obligation and thereby acquitting himself well in the sight of God" (Mahmood, 1989, pp. 35–36).[18]

In summation, no maltreatment should be done to parents specifically in old age even if they commit any excesses (Ahmed, 2009).[19] They must be appreciated, loved, followed, and honored in speech and any other form of communication and this encompasses care and compassion to both parents, completely obeying and serving them in all performances allowable in *Sharie'a* (Ahmed, 2009).[20] In addition, several rights are due to parents after their death as *dua'a* and *istigfhar* (praying) for clemency and mercy for them; sending rewards to them in the form of charitable acts of worship and on their behalf; visiting their friends and relatives in a pleasant and humble way throughout life and supporting them wherever possible; settling their *al-diyoun* (unpaid debts) and fulfilling the permissible *wasiyyah* (bequests) they have made (Ahmed, 2009).[21]

Concerning the elderly's inheritance and financial rights, the pre-eminent pro-elderly principle in Islamic law is the doctrine of "absolute ownership of property" (Rahman, 1980, pp. 208–212).[22] Traditional property rights include the rights to exercise control over one's property, to use it for one's pleasure, and to extinguish rights in it by way of transfer (Rahman, 1980, pp. 209–210).[23] Additionally, under the Islamic law of inheritance, both parents are among the primary heirs of their children, and they cannot be excluded by each other or by any other heir (Ibrahim & Sihombing, 1989, p. 189) (Elsaman & 'Arafa, 2012, pp. 17–18).[24] In this

---

18 Mahmood, *supra* note 10, at 35–36. The Prophet of Islam said "Curse be on him who finds either of his parents in old age and does not attain eternal bliss by serving them well. On another occasion in a metaphoric warning he declared: None else but parents are their children's heaven or hell" and "There is no sin more fitted to have punishment meted out by *Allah* to its perpetrator in advance in this world along with what He stores up for him in the next world than oppression and severing ties of relationship." *See* Sunan Aboũ-Dawood, (*hadith* No. 4884) & *Sahih Muslim*, *supra* note 2 (*hadith* No. 6189).

19 See, e.g., Ahmed, *Rights of Parents*, HAQ ISLAM (Apr. 12, 2009), http://www.haqislam.org/rights-of-parents.

20 *Ibid*. If they are in need of funds, children should give them access to their own wealth, even if they are *kafirs* (unbelievers), and offer them the best of their food and drink.

21 *Ibid*. For example, visiting their graves and reciting the *Qur'an* in a loud voice, while abstaining from crying aloud, so that their souls will not be troubled.

22 Afzal-Ur-Rahman, MUSLIM EDUCATIONAL TRUST, ECONOMIC DOCTRINES OF ISLAM, Vol. II 208–12 (1980).

23 *Ibid*., at 209–10.

24 In the major schools of Islamic law, it is stated for instance that in the absence of the mother, a maternal grandmother becomes the heir and successor, and in the absence of both parents, a paternal grandfather becomes the heir and successor. Ahmad Ibrahim, *Islamic Concepts and Land Law in Malaysia*, *in* THE CENTENARY OF THE TORRENS SYSTEM IN 189 (Ahmad Ibrahim & Judith Sihombing, eds, 1989), at 189 ("While Islam therefore gives the right of benefit, sale and purchase and even inheritance of land to the individual, the absolute ownership of land is given to *Allah* and from Him to the State or the community"). For further discussion on this point, *see* Radwa S. Elsaman and Mohamed A. 'Arafa, *The Rights of the Elderly in the Arab Middle East: Islamic Theory versus Arabic Practice*, 14 MARQUETTE ELDER'S ADVISOR L. REV. 2 (2012), at 17–18 ("The Islamic law of inheritance takes remarkable care of elderly relatives by giving them shares in the deceased's property, even at the cost of excessive fragmentation").

respect, the provision of fiscal and emotional sustenance for the elderly is one motive why Islam extends adjacent familial relations beyond the nuclear family (Mahmood, 1989, pp. 184–185).[25] The rights to maintenance and emotional assistance are available regardless of whether any one of them is or are not a follower of Islam and, unlike with some inheritance practices, there is no order of priority between maternal and paternal ancestors – both have the same rights to maintenance (Mahmood, 1989, p. 186).[26] All in all, Islamic instructions create an environment that is extremely obsequious to elders (Elsaman & 'Arafa, 2012, pp. 24–26).[27] Additionally, respecting older leaders "is so important that the Prophet made it a part of respecting and venerating God . . . To ignore it is a gross misbehaviour" (Ahmed, 2010).[28] Likewise, Islamic law principles appreciate the value of work for everyone, comprising also the elderly, as the most significant teaching about labor in Islamic labor law is that work correlations are based on *brotherhood* collaborations (Zulfiqar, 2007, pp. 421–436).[29]

By the same token, the Prophet of Islam implied that the only acceptable norms of preference in employment are the workmanship, (merit), qualifications, and credentials an employee possesses – and not gender (sex) (Beekun, 2006).[30] *Sharie'a*, hence, provides for the right to equal management between males and females in occupation (or service) and in civic (society) participation (Elsaman & 'Arafa, 2012, p. 27).[31]

As for social insurance, solidarity, and security (collaterals), all the family duties towards the elderly, such as preservation and succession, are, consequently, enforceable by the State where *Sharie'a* law is effective (Elsaman & 'Arafa, 2012, p. 25).[32] Where an older person has no relative – near or distant – to take care of him or her, the community's apparatus or the public authorities must move to

---

25 Mahmood, *supra* note 10, at 184–85.

26 *Ibid.*, at 186. In this context, maintenance includes day-to-day needs, such as the provision of food, clothing, residence, and personal assistance, as well as respect. *See also* Elsaman & 'Arafa, *supra* note 24, at 18–20.

27 In this sense, the Prophet (PBUH) specified that the eldest in a group should lead the prayers if all in the group are equal in their knowledge and learning. He said "Being older in such a case merits leading the prayers." However, where all in the group are not equal in knowledge and learning, the person possessing the most knowledge should lead the prayer because knowledge is a higher honor than age. *See* Elsaman & 'Arafa, *supra* note 24, at 24–26.

28 Ahmed, *Social Manners with the Elderly*, HAQ ISLAM (Jun. 1, 2010), http://www.haqislam.org/social-manners-with-the-elderly (citing SHAYKH ABDLFATTAH ABU GUDDAH, ISLAMIC MANNERS (2001)) at 27.

29 Adnan A. Zulfiqar, *Religious Sanctification of Labor Law: Islamic Labor Principles and Model Provisions*, 9 U. PA.J. LAB. & EMP. L. 421, 436 (2007) (explaining employees' rights in Islamic labor law, the importance of having labor codes, and the development of a labor code from the sources of *Sharie'a*).

30 *See generally* Rafik Beekun, *The Leadership Process of Muhammad [PBUH] From Hadith Sources*, THE ISLAMIC WORKPLACE (2006), http://makkah.wordpress.com/leadership-andislam (last retrieved June 30, 2014).

31 Elsaman & 'Arafa, *supra* note 24, at 27 ("Historically, women could not only be present in Muslims' meetings during the era of the Prophet Mohammad (PBUH), but they could also discuss matters openly with the Prophet, argue and debate with men, defend and preserve their interests, take part in politics, and even serve in the military").

32 *Ibid.*, at 25.

contribute. This is important in light of the growing older population and deteriorating economic conditions especially after the Arab Spring uprisings. Such a problem is evident, in Egypt for instance, where the homeless are mainly older people, alongside children, who cannot find a proper place to take care of their needs. This is clarified where the Ministry of Social Solidarity declares that residential care facilities for older people in all of Egypt, amount to no more than 300 facilities (Elsaman & 'Arafa, 2012).[33] Such facilities are mainly allocated to the major cities of Cairo, Giza, and Alexandria where they house small numbers of older people. However, it should be borne in mind that political decisions and economic conditions have consequences on each and every aspect of life in a society. Thus, considering such circumstances, it is clear that the current tendency is more towards stabilizing the deteriorating economy and securing sufficient livelihood than providing proper care for older people (Elsaman & 'Arafa, 2012).[34] On the other hand, Islamic foundations alongside Non-Governmental Organizations ("NGOs") play a vital role in this framework where projects and activities are dedicated to the provision of assistance to the elderly in various areas of need.[35] One example of such foundations is "*Resalah* Charity Organization" which is actively involved in providing help to the elderly among other activities. One of these activities is "Righteous Son" where youth volunteers make visits to the elderly in their homes providing care and entertainment (Shehata, 2012).[36] In the same milieu, *zakāh* refers to "mandatory charity," a category of religious tax that is calculated "based upon a percentage of annual surplus wealth" (Bhala, 2011).[37] *Zakāh* occupies a vital position in the Islamic social and economic justice model as it is paid at the end of the year by Muslims whose earnings exceed *nisab* (amount), which is usually defined as the amount of money necessary to sustain one's family for one year and is neither a courtesy nor a gift, but a compulsory obligation (Elsaman & 'Arafa, 2012, pp. 28–29).[38]

33 *Ibid.*

34 *Ibid.*

35 *Ibid.*, at 27–28. ("For instance, the *waqf* is a religious endowment in Islamic law, typically denoting a building or plot of land used for Islamic religious or charitable purposes. *Waqf* is the permanent dedication of property for religious, pious, or charitable purposes and encourages private contributions to the public good"). *See generally* Tauqir Mohammad Khan, LAW OF WAQF IN ISLAM (2007) (analyzing "*waqf* as a special provision made under Islamic law. In Islamic religion, the concept of property, the laws, governing inheritance, donation, etc . . . are structured around a complex system of law").

36 *See generally* Dina Shehata, *Mapping Islamic Actors in Egypt*, THE NETHERLANDS-FLEMISH INSTITUTE IN CAIRO, AL-AHRAM CENTER FOR POLITICAL AND STRATEGIC STUDIES (Mar. 2012), http://media. leidenuniv.nl/legacy/mapping-islamic-actors − version-2.2.pdf. *See also* THE RESALA CHARITY ASSOCIATIONS' main page, at http://www.resala.org/.

37 *See generally* Raj Bhala, UNDERSTANDING ISLAMIC LAW (2011) (providing the essential foundational materials of Islamic Law, covers several other fields: banking and finance, *zakāh* as a policy model for developing countries as a means of redistributing income to the elderly poor, contracts, criminal law, family law, and property) (describing the *zakāh* system's various goals of providing economic rehabilitation for the employable, eliminating beggary and poverty, and redistributing wealth in society).

38 Elsaman & 'Arafa, *supra* note 24, at 28–29 ("Although *zakāh* is compulsory from a religious standpoint, it is voluntary from a legal standpoint, as it is not collected by State as a tax, but rather is paid directly by citizens to the charity of their choice.").

Part 3: The protection of older people's rights in the Middle Eastern region under international human rights law and Arabian domestic statutes: any reform following the Arab spring uprisings?

A mutual characteristic of care strategies and systems affording protection to older people in most Arab countries, is that older people in these regions are considered to be a source of spiritual dedication and wisdom, hence it is disgraceful to send them to a nursing home because it would interrupt the general religious and social feelings of obligation towards them (Abyad, 2006).[39] In this domain, the Arab (or Muslim) governments rely heavily on robust familial bonds as well as the private sector to take care of the seniors and this reliance may illuminate the deficiency of laws and regulations on elder rights in the Middle East.[40]

Arabian international human rights devices on (residential) care rights of older people: legal and institutional framework

Middle Eastern countries have taken key communal and cooperative actions in relation to the elder rights' field, by establishing various institutions dedicated to improving older people's status and lives. As these foundations believe that older people play an active and operative role in society – especially after the Arab Spring Uprisings – they aim to provide quality services to them while raising public, legal, and social awareness of older people's essential needs, so they can remain engaging and active in the surrounding community (Ward and Younis, 2013).[41] The main purposes of these care establishments are to:

(i) assist seniors to overcome complications in all economic, health, social, and rehabilitative aspects of life;

---

39 Abdulrazak Abyad, *Health Care Services for the Elderly in the Middle East*, 2 MIDDLE E.J. BUS. (July 2006), http://www.mejb.com/upgrade_flash/Vol2_Issue2/2_2_Healthcare.htm (last retrieved June 30, 2014).

40 *Ibid. See also*, Elsaman & 'Arafa, *supra* note 31.

41 *Id. See generally* William B. Ward and Mustafa Z. Younis, *Steps Toward a Planning Framework for Elder Care in the Arab World*, SPRINGER BRIEFS IN AGING, Vol: VII, 55 (2013) (reviews the elder care literature of the Arab world, offers steps toward planning a framework for improving elder health, quality life, training issues, and health care in the Arab world via (program assessment and planning), Arab world elder demographics; quality of life issues; demand for services; training issues and capacity). In this regard, Ward and Younis argued that:

> While the countries of the Arab world have the advantage of a unified language and culture that can be used to expedite development of area-wide approaches to a system of elder care, the lack of economic and political unification (such as common market and open trade) along with institutionalized age discrimination (some Arab countries restrict hiring for government and private jobs to persons younger than 45) present barriers to improving the health of older people. In addition, modernization and ease of transportation have resulted in a heavy focus on Western-style fast food, with an accompanying increase in chronic diseases such as hypertension, cardiovascular disease, diabetes, and cancer.

(ii)   promote their social status in society and engage them in family and community life;

(iii) educate the general public on matters facing seniors and provide guidance
and direction to older people's families; and

(iv)   advocate and campaign for their rights and endorse Islamic values on their
care and human treatment and maintenance.[42]

Arab (Muslim) countries including Egypt, have taken other vital steps by issuing various universal documents in the global human rights field comprising seniors' rights such as, the Cairo Declaration of Human Rights in Islam of 1993 ("CDHR"), the Universal Islamic Declaration of Human Rights of 1981 ("UIDHR"), and Arab Charter on Human Rights (2004) ("Charter").[43]

It should be noted that the UIDHR is based on the *Qur'anic* and *Sunnah* teachings as this tool offers diverse human rights such as "the right to life, equality, education, and freedom, [and] proscription against impermissible discrimination [racism], the right to justice, . . . the right and obligation to participate in the conduct and management of public affairs, . . . [among others]."[44] Most significantly this document specifies and confirms that everyone shall be materially supported and older people in particular, "shall be provided necessary care, [and elderly] mothers are entitled to special respect, care, and assistance from their families and communities."[45]

The CDHR, combines both Islamic and international formulations, and it was confused to some extent with the International Bill of Human Rights ("IBHR") (Mayer, 1994, pp. 407–429).[46] This agreement does not include precise or detailed

---

42 *Ibid.* For instance, Qatar Foundation for Elderly People Care ("IHSAN"), http://qatarcio.com/
organizations/other-organizations/qatar-foundation-for-elderly-people-care-ihsan/.

43 *See* Universal Islamic Declaration of Human Rights, 21 DHUL QAIDAH 1401, Sept. 19, 1981,
available at http://www1.umn.edu/humanrts/instree/islamic_declaration_HR.html [hereinaf-
ter UIDHR]; Cairo Declaration on Human Rights in Islam, Aug. 5, 1990, *available at* http://
www1.umn.edu/humanrts/instree/cairodeclaration.html [hereinafter CDHR], and Council of
the League of Arab States, Arab Charter on Human Rights, May 23, 2004, at http://www1.umn.
edu/humanrts/instree/arabcharter2.html [hereinafter "Charter"] (last retrieved June 30, 2014).

44 *Ibid.*, at UIDHR, *supra* note 43, at arts. I–XXIII.

45 *Ibid.*, at art. XIX(f)(g).

46 Ann Elizabeth Mayer, *Universal versus Islamic Human Rights: A Clash of Cultures or a Clash with a Construct?* 15 MICH. J. INT'L. L. 307, 329 (1994). In this regard, this bill declares that:

Everyone, as a member of society, has the right to social security and is entitled to realization,
through national effort and international co-operation and in accordance with the organization and resources of each State, of the economic, social and cultural rights indispensable for
his dignity and the free development of his personality. Everyone has the right to a standard
of living adequate for the health and well-being of himself and of his family, including food,
clothing, housing and medical care and necessary social services, and the right to security in the
event of unemployment, sickness, disability, widowhood, old age or other lack of livelihood in
circumstances beyond his control.

See International Bill of Human Rights (A/RES/3/217, Dec. 10, 1948), at arts. 22 & 25, http://
www.un-documents.net/a3r217.htm (last retrieved June 30, 2014).

rules for elder rights but rather has broad and common standards that apply to everybody, including the elderly, as equality between men and women and the proscription of discrimination.[47] On the other hand, the Arab Charter is in conformity with transnational human rights values and current human rights jurisprudence.[48] The Charter's preamble reads its intent to implement the "eternal principles" imparted by *Sharie'a* and other "divine religions."[49] The Charter establishes general rules on different aspects of human rights issues, such as "equality, health, work, education rights . . . [among others] and provides that each member country shall "ensure the necessary protection and care for mothers, children, older persons and persons with special needs."[50] Regrettably, the rules of these international covenants on the fortification of older people are few, broad, and not inclusive. Even those treaties that refer to *Sharie'a* as the focal source of their rules do not assure older people's indispensable rights which are so strongly advocated by the Islamic canons. This inconsistency represents a huge gap that exists between Islamic law theoretical principles and their correct legal (interpretation and) implementation in each country.[51]

Some applications from positive Middle Eastern (Arabian) legal systems on elder rights and the residential care of older people: any real reform?

Generally, various Arabian constitutions and laws include great rules to protect older people but have numerous misapplications of these norms such as the Algerian Constitution and the Algerian Family Codes.[52] Such misapplications represent, for example, a lack of residential care facilities and poor allocation of those that do exist. For example, the number of residential care facilities in Egypt do not exceed 300 – as stated above – they are allocated to the most important cities, which is not sufficient to face the needs of the growing older

---

47 *See generally* CDHR, *supra* note 43. By the same token, "every person has a right to be free from harm, to a healthy and clean environment, to marry, to knowledge and education, to freedom of religion (belief) and freedom of expression (thought and opinion), to own property, to privacy, to equality before the law, to fair criminal procedures and impartial trials, and to participate in public life."

48 *See generally* Charter, *supra* note 43. It should be noted that for every case of elder abuse or neglect that is reported to public authorities, human rights experts estimate that there may be many more as the real number of case have not been reported. Even in countries that are known for relatively stronger family structures, the elderly are increasingly getting short shrift. Far from the abuse that we see in the present day's community, the elderly have a protected and dignified status in Islamic law and any decline in this practice is concomitant with overall policy in adherence to Islamic norms.

49 *Ibid.*, at Preamble.

50 *Ibid.*, at arts. 33(b), 34, 38, 39, 41, 45, & 45.

51 Elsaman & 'Arafa, *supra* note 24, at 32.

52 People Dem. Repub. Algeria Const., Nov. 28, 1996, at arts. 29, 31, 50, 51, 54, 55, 56, 59, & 69. Furthermore, the Algerian Government has drafted a new statute punishing the maltreatment of elderly by youth in general, and children in particular, and discouraging placing the elderly in nursing homes. *See also* Code De la Famille, Jun. 9, 1984, at art. 36.

population. Even residential care, where it does exist, suffers either increasing costs or the continuous degradation of service quality (Mayer, 1994).[53] However, this number of residential care facilities is the highest in the Arab World. In addition to the rules of the contemporary Bahraini Constitution, which assure social security [solidarity] for its older citizens, by providing them with social coverage and health and medical insurance services, Bahrain has various employment and social insurance statutes that provide for older people and, a bill on the protection of the rights of older people and the creation of a national committee that would focus on ageing matters has been discoursed. According to an official governmental report in Bahrain, "The Kingdom of Bahrain is leading the list of the Arabic countries have set up national commissions for care of the elderly in decision No. 1 of 1984 establishing the National Committee for older persons to represent the jurisdiction to implement policy for care of the elderly in the Kingdom of Bahrain and the preparation of programs and projects in cooperation with the various actors involved in the development of services for the elderly."[54] This Ministry's role is reflected in inspiring civil society organizations to contribute to the operation of day-care parents' role in a positive community corporation program recognized by it several years ago.[55]

Another important example is that, according to the Kuwaiti Constitution, the government is in charge of providing assistance for older people against illness or incapability to work.[56] Kuwait also keeps inheritance rights of the elderly based on the Islamic law principles and other acts afford for social insurance and regulate pension and retirement compensation (Social Security Guide, Kuwait, 2009).[57] It should be borne in mind that Kuwait is considered to be one of the few and most developed Arab countries to have taken steps to enhance elder rights, in part because it has a wide-ranging health program whereby older people are provided with free in-home health services as well as a specialized (detailed) law concerning the social care of older people (Alrai Journal, 2010).[58]

---

53 Mayer, *supra* note 46.
54 Const. Kingdom of Bahrain, Feb. 14, 2002, at arts. 1, 2, & 4. For further information about the discussion of a law (Protecting Rights of the Elderly), *see* THE NATIONAL REPORT BAHRAINI HUMAN RIGHTS MINISTRY AND SOCIAL DEVELOPMENT (2009) (explaining the efforts regarding elderly issues and the residential care problems in Bahrain in addition to some legal regulations governing older people's development programs and harsh punishments in case of the maltreatment of older people), http://www.microsofttranslator.com/bv.aspx?ref=SERP&br=ro&mkt=en-US&dl=en&lp=AR_EN&a=http%3a%2f%2fwww.social.gov.bh%2fnode%2f697 (last retrieved Nov. 20, 2014).
55 *Ibid.*
56 Kuwait Cons., Nov. 11, 1962, at art. 11.
57 Pub. Inst. For Soc. Security, Social Security Guide in Kuwait, 3 (2009), *available at* http://www.pifss.gov.kw/upload/pifss_E_guide_eng_212.pdf (last retrieved June 30, 2014).
58 *Afasy: Kuwait is One of the World's Developed Countries in Protecting The Elderly*, ALRAI JOURNAL (Oct. 3, 2010), http://www.alraimedia.com/alrai/Article.aspx?id=229596&date=03102010 (*citing* Law

Elderly rights in Egyptian law after Egypt's uprisings: a way ahead and what's new?

Constitutional, legal, and regulatory elements

Following the Egyptian uprisings in 2011 and 2013 by the Egyptian people and the military, which exiled President Hosni Mubarak and overthrew the Islamist President Mohammad Morsi, respectively, the Egyptian Constitution of 2014 explicitly declares equality between men and women, criminalizes discrimination and provides for equal opportunity for all Egyptians, and the provision of cultural, social, and health services. In other words "All citizens are equal before the Law. They are equal in rights, freedoms and general duties, without discrimination based on religion, belief, sex, origin, race, color, language, disability, social class, political or geographic affiliation or any other reason. Discrimination and incitement of hatred is a crime punished by Law. The State shall take necessary measures for eliminating all forms of discrimination, and the Law shall regulate creating an independent commission for this purpose."[59]

With respect to rights of older people, Article 83 of the Egyptian Constitutional Charter guarantees elderly rights and stipulates "appropriate pensions to ensure them a decent standard of living" (Trager, 2013).[60] This constitutional provision reads:

> The State shall guarantee the health, economic, social, cultural, and entertainment rights of the elderly people, provide them with appropriate pensions which ensure a decent life for them, and enable them to participate in public life. In its planning of public facilities, the State shall take into account the needs of the elderly. The State shall encourage civil society organizations to participate in taking care of the elderly people. All the foregoing is to be applied as regulated by Law.[61]

Correspondingly, Article 17 provides the following constitutional norm:

> The State shall ensure that social insurance services are provided. All citizens who do not benefit from the social insurance system have the right to social

---

No. 11 of 2007, which establishes the National Committee for the Elderly). For further examples on elderly rights in various Arabian regions, *see* Elsaman & 'Arafa, *supra* note 24, at 34–45 (explaining the elderly legal and social status in Jordan, Morocco, Libya, Yemen, Palestine, United Arab Emirates, Iraq, Sudan, Tunisia, and others).

59 Constitution of the Arab Republic of Egypt, Jan. 18, 2014, at http://www.sis.gov.eg/Newvr/Dustor-en001.pdf, at art. 53.

60 *Ibid. See* Eric Trager, *Egypt's New Constitution: Bleak Prospects*, PolicyWatch 2183, Dec. 16, 2013, at 2 (explaining the main aspects of the new Egyptian constitution after the military had overthrown Morsi from power and how Egypt's transitional period will move forward to a democratic and stable condition according to the future roadmap).

61 Egypt Constitution, *supra* note 59, at art. 83.

security, in a manner that ensures a decent life in the event of being incapable to provide for themselves and their families, as well as in cases of incapacity to work, old age or unemployment. In accordance with Law, the State shall strive to provide suitable pensions to small farmers, agricultural workers and fishermen, and irregular labor. The funds of social insurance and pensions are deemed private funds that enjoy all aspects and forms of protection afforded to public funds. Those funds along with their returns are the rights of their respective beneficiaries; they shall be safely invested, and shall be managed by an independent entity in accordance with the Law. The State shall guarantee social insurance and pension funds.[62]

Accordingly, the rights of older people have great importance and a good deal under the Egyptian Constitution, within the frame of socio-economic justice ideals and the fair distribution of wealth. On the other hand, it should be noted that the most significant legislative framework on elder care rights, issued by the Ministry of Insurance and Social Affairs ("MISA") and other caring and official solidarity agencies are, as follows:

(a) Law No. 79 of 1975 [and its amendments] governs the establishment and operation of social insurance for civil servants, employees in private sector and in public enterprises.
(b) Law No. 54 of 1975 [and its amendments] on the establishment and operation of occupational voluntary private pensions plans in Egypt and its tax treatment (Specific bylaw regulates asset management of pension funds).
(c) Law No. 108 of 1976 regulates the creation and operation of a specific model for employers and self-employed-persons.
(d) Law No. 50 of 1978 prescribes regulations governing social insurance for migrant workers and Law No. 61 of 1981 on comprehensive social insurance issues.

---

62 *Ibid.* In the same vein, the same Constitution stipulates that:

Every citizen has the right to health and to comprehensive health care which complies with quality standards. The State shall maintain and support public health facilities that provide health services to the people, and shall enhance their efficiency and their equitable geographical distribution. The State shall allocate a percentage of government spending to health equivalent to at least 3% of Gross National Product (GNP), which shall gradually increase to comply with international standards. The State shall establish a comprehensive health insurance system covering all diseases for all Egyptians; and the Law shall regulate citizens' contribution to or exemption from its subscriptions based on their income rates. Refusing to provide any form of medical treatment to any human in emergency or life-threatening situations is a crime. The State shall improve the conditions of physicians, nursing staff, and health sector workers. All health facilities as well as health-related products, materials, and means of advertisement shall be subject to State control. The State shall encourage the participation of private and non-governmental sectors in providing health care services according to the law.

Ibid., at art. 18.

(e) Laws No. 64 and 112 of 1980 regulate the operation of alternative social insurance systems under the supervision of Ministry of Insurance and Social Affairs and social insurance for casual and informal workers.[63]

Likewise, Egyptian social insurance laws govern most social insurance issues and care rights for older people and provide for retirement pensions (social incomes).[64] Furthermore, the Egyptian Labor (employment) Law sets the retirement age at 60 and controls the employment relationship between employers and employees who reach 60 years of age while the Egyptian Inheritance Law regulates elders' inheritance rights according to *Sharie'a* principles and *fiqh* (jurisprudential) thought recognized values.[65]

Regarding the institutional and regulatory (supervisory) authorities for the rights of older people and their residential care, the Egyptian legislation singled out a number of agencies, authorities, and institutions to mobilize social security and the handling of health care issues for all citizens, including older people.[66] These multiple agencies and organizations are intended to address older people's human rights issues; none of these are politically independent and most of them are closely linked to the executive authority (President, Prime-Minister, or the Minister of Social Solidarity) (Boggatz *et al.*, 2009, p. 33).[67] However, the law grants certain privileges to most of these agencies to help guarantee their independence. The most important agencies in Egypt in this area are presented here in brief.

i   The Ministry of Insurance and Social Affairs ("MISA"), in charge of effective operation of the insurance and social security systems, manages some pension programs within social assistance strategies and is part of the national poverty alleviation program.

ii   The General Authority for Health Insurance ("GAHI") oversees the provision (status) of health care and medical insurance and treatment of all individuals including older people in cases of injury (harm and damage) and sickness.

iii The National Social Insurance Authority ("NSIA") is responsible for managing and handling the pension and insurance policies of both public (government officials) and private sector's subscribers.

---

63 *See* IOPS Country Profile: Egypt, (Jan. 2011), *available at* http://www.oecd.org/site/iops/researchandworkingpapers/egypt-pensionsystemoverview.htm, at 7.

64 Law No. 79 of 1975 (Social Insurance Law), AL-JARIDA AL-RASMIYYAH [THE OFFICIAL GAZETTE], Aug. 28, 1975.

65 Law No. 12 of 2003 (Labor Law), AL-JARIDA AL-RASMIYYAH [THE OFFICIAL GAZETTE], Apr. 7, 2003, at art. 125 & Law No. 77 of 1943 (Inheritance Law), AL-JARIDA AL-RASMIYYAH [THE OFFICIAL GAZETTE] (1943).

66 *Ibid.*, at *IOPS Country Profile: Egypt, supra* note 63.

67 *Ibid. See also* Thomas T. Boggatz *et al.*, *Attitudes of Older Egyptians Towards Nursing Care at Home: A Qualitative Study*, 24 J. CROSS CULT. GERONTOL. 33 (2009) (elaborating the elderly status in nursing care).

iv The Egyptian Insurance Supervisory Authority ("EISA") deals with licensing, supervising, and controlling the private pension funds.[68]

In practice, most of these agencies have been proven to be efficient in undertaking their role in enhancing rights of older people. In addition all of these agencies, especially GAHI have a role regulating care homes, inspecting and overseeing them by conducting actual monthly visits to the older peoples' homes, to make sure that they are suitable and sufficient for their needs.[69] Furthermore, these agencies work to provide several services for older people, including service requests, prosthetic strategies and services of life and health, psychological, entertainment and cultural activities, social services, permanent and temporary accommodation and physical therapy and treatment work.[70] Moreover, these establishments, according to their legal responsibilities identified by social solidarity and labor laws, provide different activities that contribute to assisting and facilitating older people to practice certain crafts and hobbies and encourage them to recover motor skills naturally and urge them to rely upon themselves, and provide training for older people to do simple crafts that help them.[71]

On the other hand, they also voluntarily might ask willing Egyptian physicians and nurses to volunteer in various disciplines, to examine and treat those in need of medical services such as weekly examination of diabetes and blood pressure, as well as numerous trained social workers to deliver lectures to guide seniors.[72] Despite privileges granted to these institutions to protect them from interference or ensure their independence, as mentioned above, even after those privileges, they still suffer from weaknesses in terms of their freedom and lack of complete political independence. Therefore, one of the main weaknesses of these governmental organizations is their subordination to the executive branch. Accordingly, it is highly recommended to shield these agencies from political interference, by enhancing their independence and ensuring that no political interference takes place in their decisions, as the neutrality in presenting the findings of these agencies adds to their credibility and impartiality.

---

68 *Ibid.*, at *IOPS Country Profile: Egypt, supra* note 63, at 4–7. ("Voluntary occupational pension plans have been established in Egypt since 1975 known as 'Special Insurance Funds' (SIF). In addition to pension payments, SIFs could provide a range of other benefits (marriage disbursement, disability, decease of the member, etc.) in accordance with the decision of a Fund's board of directors and approval by the Egyptian Insurance Supervisory Authority (EISA)").

69 Boggatz *et al., supra* note 67.

70 *Ibid.* ("Also, these bodies have to oversee the financial perspective of the elderly places and give monies like grants, donations, gifts, etc . . . coming from businessmen and several individuals for this purpose").

71 *Ibid.*

72 *Ibid.* In addition to working on following up older people and recording all changes to the conditions for better adjustment between them and their family members, and to managing the correlation between older people and the outside community via visits, trips, and foreign tours, along with a program of daily living services and identifying the social and recreational activities period, in cooperation with NGOs.

The state of affairs of older men's and women's rights in the Egyptian socio-legal system

Practically speaking, employees retire at the age of 60 with some exceptions where personnel retire at the age of 70 or, a bit earlier such as members of the judiciary, university faculty, members of the military and police retire *before* the age of 60, for example retirement at the age of 50 or 55.[73] It should be noted that based on the Islamic notion of equality, Egyptian laws and regulations do not discriminate between older men or women when passing any policy related to older people's welfare and development (Abulkheir, 2011, p. 3).[74] Thus, the transformation in the age profile of the population constitutes the basis for planning programs.[75] According to numerous official statistical data and surveys issued by the Central Agency for Public Mobilization and Statistics ("CAPMS"), there is a systematic growth in older people in the population and this is predicted to rise methodically starting from 2011 to reach 11,500,000 (11%) in 2025 and, about 24,000,000 (21%) in 2050 (Abulkheir, 2011, p. 4; Eldeeb, 2003).[76]

In this regard, Law No. 112 of 1980 on comprehensive social insurance, resolves to pay security pensions from the Social Insurance Fund ("SIF") for public officials and the public and private sectors in cases of, "aging, disability and death, work injuries, sickness, unemployment, and social welfare for pension beneficiaries and the top of this pension beneficiaries' list come senior citizens."[77] The same law "enforces employers to pay 15% of the insured monthly wages to the Social Security System ('SSS')" and also designates, "terminating the insured service upon reaching the retirement age stipulated upon in the current employment law or, for reaching the age of 60."[78] Moreover, several Ministerial Decrees such as, No. 218 of 1990, No. 90 of 1997 establish a right for senior citizens to recreational welfare services through day care clubs for older people and a right to shelter welfare for those who have no family care providers, through senior citizens' sheltering institutions based on his/her economic and social circumstances.[79]

---

73 There are various retirement systems like the early retirement system due to the privatization policy and retirement upon the completion of 20-year service period. Accordingly, there is no unified age norm for retirement valid for all the public bodies and governmental authorities.

74 *See* Ahmed Abulkheir, NATIONAL REPORT ON SENIOR CITIZENS' RIGHTS IN THE ARAB REPUBLIC OF EGYPT, *Ministry of Solidarity and Social Justice: Seniors' Division*), Feb. 3, 2011, at 3, http://www.ohchr.org/Documents/Issues/OlderPersons/Submissions/Egypt.pdf.

75 From the demographic indicators' perspective, rates and statistical indicators of the Central Agency for Public Mobilization and Statistics designate that the long-lived resident's phenomenon in Egypt is the result of a demographic transition process associated with the mortality and fertility rates.

76 Abulkheir, *supra* note 74 at 4. ("from 1.100.000 in 1947 Census to 3.400.000 in 1996 census and then to 3.4 million at present – the proportion of seniors to the total population ranged between 6.1% in 1947 and 5.8% in 1996 to 6.3% today . . . confirms the upsurge in elderly rate to 7% or more of total population"). *See also* Bothiana Eldeeb, SOCIAL STATISTICS IN EGYPT, UNITED NATIONS STATISTICS DIVISION, Apr. 28, 2003, http://downloadpdfebook.herokuapp.com/tag/social-statistics-in-egypt-united-nations.

77 *See generally* Law No. 112 of 1980 (Comprehensive Social Insurance), *AL-JARIDA AL-RASMIYYAH* [THE OFFICIAL GAZETTE] (1980).

78 *Ibid.*, at arts. 17 & 18 (Part III, Chapter I on Aging, Disability, and Death Insurance) (Chapter II on Pensions and Compensations).

79 *See generally* Ministerial Decrees No. 218 of 1990 and 90 of 1997.

Other laws allow "seniors access to free medical and therapeutic care, providing services and concessions for elderly on the transportation, ticket-airways, theaters, markets, and exhibitions, . . . etc., aggregating the reduction rate on railway tickets for retirees, access to the services of physiotherapy and physical fitness at cut-rate fees in comparison to other places, and in case that elders who are not entitled for social security annuities can benefit from the aging allowance."[80]

In that light the Egyptian legal system permits all citizens to contribute to political and parliamentary life without excluding certain age assemblies, henceforth, the law allows older people to participate in public elections with no age barrier or discrimination based on gender.[81] Also, the creative families' project assists older people to access small and micro soft loans and social resources through public national banks (e.g. National Bank of Egypt and Nasser Social Bank) with inconsequential interest rates and payment facilities, to support them to launch their own small initiatives (entrepreneurs) (Abulkheir, 2011, p. 7).[82] By the same token, exploiting pensioners' acquisitive and professional experiences, plays a fundamental role in contributing to the social development process.[83] Law No. 84 of 2002 on governing the work of NGOs and private institutions, endorsed senior citizens to share in the NGOs' administration, run plans and projects, using their professional skills and abilities.[84]

On the other hand, Egyptian laws forbid and condemn committing any violent acts or abuse against all citizens including older people, as they attain an honored and privileged status within their families in Egyptian society based on the religious (Islamic) values and ethical and moral traditions (strengthening ties among family members).[85] In other words, Egyptian culture considers older individuals

---

80 *See* Law No. 75 of 1964 (Issuance of Health Insurance); Law No. 30 of 1977 (*amended by* Law No. 87 of 2000) (Social Security), at art. 6 (this law entitles seniors to receive financial assistances in lump-sum system in some cases); Republican Decrees No. 77 of 1981, 40 of 1997, and 591 of 1982 on the same issues.

81 For instance, most peoples' representatives in the local/public councils and departments are elderly. Seniors' welfare activities such as the sheltering/accommodation houses and day care clubs, which train seniors who have no occupation or profession on some handicrafts with financial revenue, as well as allowing him/her to play a role in developing his/her community. It should be noted that elder exploitation is an emergent problem in Egypt. It is a multifaceted phenomenon that comprises numerous risk factors and found in a diversity of sorts. Higher percentages of neglected elderly people suffer from depressive indications and psychological pain.

82 Abulkheir, *supra* note 74, at 7. For example, creating specific departments for elders' care and treatment by some public universities such as the Senior Care Center at Cairo University and the Social and Health Care at Helwan University and these centers works through the assistance of volunteer students and alumni. See, e.g., Cairo University's Center for the Care of the Elderly, http://enia.cu.edu.eg/ (last retrieved June 30, 2014).

83 *Ibid.* For example occupying their free time with a positive paid job (*i.e.* hiring those with teaching experience in wiping out illiteracy and remedial classes for the diverse school periods).

84 *Ibid. See generally* Law No. 84 of 2002 on (Non-Governmental Organizations), http://www.bu.edu/bucflp/files/2012/01/Law-on-Nongovernmental-Organizations-Law-No.-84-of-2002.pdf.

85 Seniors in Bedouin (rural) areas also enjoy an outstanding position in their societies and families as this is considered a sort of esteeming of values and ethical traditions. Also the work of institutive councils is usually based on the elders' efforts, as they enjoy a judicial authority, their rulings

as the voice of history, deep experience and knowledge, and heritage (Elsaman & 'Arafa, 2012, p. 34).[86]

In this regard, under the new Egyptian Constitution and the current laws (such as labor law and Social Solidarity) and others concerning older people's rights and their residential care, all sorts of abuses are prohibited and punished. The current laws state that "physical abuse against a senior citizen entails any use of physical force (e.g. hitting, striking, beating, pushing, shaking, pinching, kicking, slapping, and burning) likely to result in injury, physical pain or impairment will be punished by the Egyptian Penal Code regarding the penalties of serious bodily injuries or manslaughter."[87] Emotional and/or psychological abuse typically is defined by the laws as "an act that causes emotional pain, distress or anguish (assaults, intimidation, humiliation, threats, insults, harassment, etc. . . .)" (Belal, 2004).[88] It should be noted that an abuser can be a spouse, partner, relative, a friend or neighbor with the intent to deny a vulnerable older individual their resources (Jackson and Hafemeister, 2012).[89] In Egypt, perpetrators of elder abuse can comprise anyone in a position of trust, control or authority as family connections, neighbors and friends, are all communally considered as relationships of confidence, whether

are mandatory to all the younger age groups and they take the duty of implementing the effective norms in such regions. Social customs and moral traditions play an imperative role in crystallizing elder's status within the Egyptian culture. So far, social and economic changes, cost of living, and narrow houses formed a sort of virtual negligence to these doctrines.

86 *See* Elsaman & 'Arafa, *supra* note 24, at 34. ("Lately, civil society organizations have started to endorse programs for taking care of the elderly. The vast majority of elder Egyptians are taken care of by their families, but an increasing number residing in large cities are provided with in-home care by non-family members or are placed in nursing homes").

87 *See* Law No. 58 of 1937 (Egyptian Penal Code) (*reformed in* 1952), *Al-Jarida Al-Rasmiyya* [THE OFFI-CIAL GAZETTE], (Egypt), arts. 234–240. Physical abuse may include seemingly minor acts of physical contact. For instance, if used inappropriately; and holding someone against their will, referred to as false arrest. Additionally, any non-consensual sexual relation with an elderly person is considered sexual abuse. Also, sexual contact with an older person who is incapable of giving consent or who is too confused to fully understand what is happening is considered to be a sexual act. Neglect is included as a new concept on the draft laws and defined as "the failure to provide a dependent senior citizen with life necessities, such as food, clean water, shelter, personal hygiene, clean clothing medicine, safety, basic comfort." On the other hand, financial abuse includes a broad spectrum of fraud, outright theft, and other methods of extracting financial or material gain from vulnerable older persons. Finally, abandonment happens when a designated caretaker or legal guardian leaves an older individual to fend for himself or herself and this is defined by law as well.

88 *Ibid. See generally* AHMAD 'AWAD BELAL MABAD'E KANUN AL-'UQUBAT AL-MASRY: AL-KESM AL-'AMM [PRINCIPLES OF EGYPTIAN CRIMINAL LAW, PART I: THE THEORY OF CRIMINAL OFFENCES] (2004).

89 For example, in Hybrid Financial Exploitation ("HFE") abusive individuals are more likely to be a relative, chronically unemployed, and dependent on the elderly person. *See* Shelly L. Jackson and Thomas L. Hafemeister 2 *Pure Financial Exploitation Vs. Hybrid Financial Exploitation Co-occurring With Physical Abuse And/Or Neglect Of Elderly Persons* 3, PSYCHOLOGY OF VIOLENCE [SERIAL ONLINE] (July 2012), at 285–296, http://www.researchgate.net/publication/232568717_Pure_financial_exploitation_vs._Hybrid_financial_exploitation_co-occurring_with_physical_abuse_andor_neglect_of_elderly_persons ("compar[ing] pure financial exploitation (PFE) of an elderly person – financial exploitation that occurs independently of another form of elder abuse – with hybrid financial exploitation (HFE) – financial exploitation that co-occurs with physical abuse and/or neglect").

or not the older adult truly thinks of the people as "honest and trustworthy."[90] Furthermore, institutional abuse is a very recognizable phenomenon in Egypt and Middle Eastern regions as a result of mutual practices or processes that are part of the governing of a care institution or service (Garner and Evans, 2000).[91]

It should be noted that the Ministry of Solidarity and Social Justice ("MSSJ") in cooperation with the National Centre for Social and Criminological Research ("NCSCR") are responsible for conducting social, legal, physical, and philosophical research and field studies on older people's behaviors, to ascertain the most substantial difficulties and issues they may face, as well as, recognizing their needs, welfare services, and legal rights so that decision and policy makers can study the contemporary status of institutional welfare to pinpoint any negative features (Abulkheir, 2011, p. 11).[92] In addition, these foundations along with some NGOs, are in charge of creating training programs and the preparation of professional skills and courses for elder-caregivers.[93]

Last but by no means least, concerning existing statutes, strategies, and programs to realize justice and attain practical and legal solutions to transgression and misuse of older people's rights, some NGOs are committed to defending older people in judicial settings when they are exposed to defilement of their rights in a collective manner, such as the Post-Retirement Welfare Society ("PRWS") and Pensioners Welfare Society ("PWS") (Abulkheir, 2011, p. 12).[94]

---

90 *Ibid.* The most popular of abusers are blood relatives, normally the older adult's spouse/partner or sons and daughters, although the sort of exploitation fluctuates according to the relationship. In some circumstances the abuse is "domestic violence grown old" or "advance inheritance" of property, valuables, and money.

91 This sort of abuse is referred to as "poor practice," though this concept replicates the motive of the culprit rather than the impact upon the older being. *See generally* Jane Garner and Sandra Evans, *Institutional Abuse of Older Adults*, COUNCIL REPORT CR84 (June 2000), ROYAL COLLEGE OF PSYCHIATRISTS (London [Review 2005]), http://www.ibrarian.net/navon/paper/Institutional_abuse_of_older_adults.pdf?paperid=4825803.

92 *See generally* Hanaa Kheir-El-Din, *The Egyptian Economy: Current Challenges and Future Prospects: Toward a More Efficient and Equitable Pension System in Egypt*, CAIRO SCHOLARSHIP ONLINE (2008) & Abulkheir, *supra* note 74, at 11.

93 *Ibid. See also generally* Patrick Clawson and Michael Eisenstadt, *Demography in the Middle East: Population Growth Slowing, Women's Situation Unresolved*, THE WASHINGTON INSTITUTE (2009), http://www.washingtoninstitute.org/policy-analysis/view/demography-in-the-middle-east-population-growth-slowing-womens-situation-un (last retrieved June 30, 2014). ("Fifty years of rapid population growth in the Middle East is coming to an end. The Middle East is experiencing the same 'demographic transition' to slow population growth that other areas have gone through. The immediate reason for the slower population growth is a fall in the number of children born to the average woman over her lifespan, known as the 'total fertility rate' (TFR). While contraception availability and urbanization played a part in the declining TFR, the main factor was the empowerment of women. In recent decades, Middle Eastern women have made great progress at gaining more equal access to education, but that has not yet translated into more access to employment outside the home. The demographic transition through which the Middle East is passing presents an opportunity that is also a challenge. The opportunity is several decades in which the economy faces a relatively light burden in caring for children and the elderly").

94 *Ibid. See also* Abulkheir, *supra* note 74 at 12.

Part 3: Future trends on older people's rights and residential care following the Arab spring revolts: conclusions and policy (practical) considerations

In conclusion, though Islamic (*Sharie'a*) law offers an inclusive system for caring for and defending the care of older people, including their residential care and human rights through numerous categories, real and genuine practice has often failed to live up to its standards and ethical notions. Still, this scheme could be used as a vehicle for the reallocation (or redistribution) of wealth in Middle Eastern society, or to construct a consistent source of survival and sustenance for the older people, especially the elderly poor, by providing a modest safety net for the most vulnerable.

The autonomous risk factors for maltreatment and oppression of older people, were mainly older age, inadequate pension and a caregiver other than spouse but include also factors such as memory problems (such as dementia), physical disabilities, depression, mental health difficulties, loneliness, lack of social support, abuses alcohol or other substances, history of abusing others, unemployment, criminal history or record. Where dependent, the number of children being three or less and, a caregiver other than a spouse were significant independent attributes for "neglect" as a form of elder mistreatment.[95]

Notwithstanding this extremely decent, moral, and comprehensive Islamic socioeconomic justice system, the elderly are not entirely protected by domestic labor, employment, corporate, and social security legislation and protocols, nor are the Islamic (Arab) elderly completely protected by international human rights techniques. The deficiency or absence of legal protection of older people is due to the failure of most Arab Middle Eastern nations, to apply and put into force laws that identify the Islamic responsibilities and obligations their citizens are presumed to already follow.

In view of that, an Islamic classical ideal cannot be secured unless we inaugurate an influential and large State, strong in its economy, social bodies, educational agenda, and other necessities; that is, a country that creates adequate resources to permit and help all its citizens to enjoy a sound and decent life without poverty. As a result, developing Muslim regions should advance Islamic legal standards and classical (traditional) models concerning older people's maintenance and care via social insurance and security, and should stimulate their rights to food, drink, shelter, clothing, medicine, and appropriate jobs. This will entail inspiration, creativity, and long term vision in using up-to-date perceptions and practices to form a comprehensive social system. Moreover, social public awareness needs to be spread throughout the Arab Middle East on the complications or harms facing older people and how to fix them.

Governments may, for instance, afford tax inducements to administrations that offer home nursing care. Providing appropriate employment prospects for older

95 *See generally* M.T. Yasamy, T. Dua, M. Harper, and S. Saxena, *Mental Health of Older Adults, Addressing a Growing Concern*, WORLD HEALTH ORGANIZATION, DEPARTMENT OF MENTAL HEALTH AND SUBSTANCE ABUSE, http://www.who.int/mental_health/world-mental-health-day/WHO_paper_wmhd_2013.pdf.

people and removing any labor market obstacles to them are also indispensable procedures. Public pension structures should be supplemented and technologically advanced, and prevailing pension amenities should be upgraded and enriched for a better quality of life. Furthermore, safe and comfortable life style programs for disabled older people should be delivered. These proposals cannot be applied and be in effect without dedicated statutes and legal regulations that systematically provide for the fortification of older people in the Arab World.

Education and training programs for those in the criminal justice system, such as police forces, prosecuting attorneys, and the judiciary, on elder manipulation as well as amplified lawmaking to protect and guard older people, will also assist to minimize elder abuse and will also provide enhanced and developed support to victims of this sort of abuse. Likewise, community participation in responding to elder exploitation can contribute to older individuals' safety. Communities can advance programs that are structured around meeting the essential needs of older people such as creating the Financial Abuse Specialist Teams ("FAST") as in the United States, which are multi-disciplinary assemblies that entail public and private professionals who volunteer their time to advise Adult Protective Services ("APS"), law enforcement, and private counsels on problems of susceptible adult financial misuse.

Recent events show that the time for fulfilling and employing such drastic action plans is now. The modern Arab Spring rebellions, mainly the two big Egyptian Uprisings have given rise to much legal and political chaos. This turmoil could be moderately improved by restructuring and remodeling laws in various sectors, to strengthen a sense of community in Arab Middle Eastern nations, older people's residential care and advancing their human rights is a sector ripe for transformation.

Bibliography

Irshad Abdal-haqq (2002), *Islamic Law: An Overview of Its Origin and Elements*, 7 J. ISLAMIC L. & CULTURE 27, 56.

Abdulrazak Abyad (2006), *Health Care Services for the Elderly in the Middle East*, 2 MIDDLE E.J. BUS. (July 2006), http://www.globalaging.org/health/world/2008/healthoverview.pdf

Ahmed Abulkhcir (2011), *National Report on Senior Citizens' Rights in the Arab Republic of Egypt*, MINISTRY OF SOLIDARITY AND SOCIAL JUSTICE: SENIORS' DIVISION), Feb. 3, 2011, at 3, http://www.ohchr.org/Documents/Issues/OlderPersons/Submissions/Egypt.pdf

Afasy: Kuwait is One of the World's Developed Countries in Protecting The Elderly, ALRAI JOURNAL (Oct. 3, 2010), http://www.alraimedia.com/alrai/Article.aspx?id=229596&date=03102010

Ahmad 'Awad Belal (2004), Mabad'e Kanun Al-'Uqubat Al-Masry: Al-Kesm Al-'Amm [Principles of Egyptian Criminal Law, Part I: The Theory of Criminal Offences] (on file with author).

Ahmed (2009), *Rights of Parents*, HAQ ISLAM (Apr. 12, 2009), http://www.haqislam.org/rights-of-parents

Ahmed (2010), *Social Manners with the Elderly*, HAQ ISLAM (Jun. 1, 2010), http://www.haqislam.org/social-manners-with-the-elderly

Kristine J. Ajrouch and Nour Fakhoury (2003), *Assessing needs of aging Muslims: A Focus On Metro-Detroit Faith Communities*, 7 J. CONTEMPORARY ISLAM 3, (SPRINGERLINK: September 2003).

Roaa M. Al-Heeti (2007), Note, *Why Nursing Homes Will Not Work: Caring for the Needs of the Aging Muslim American Population*, 15 ELDER L.J. 205, 206.

Aboū Al-Hussein Muslim Ibn Al-Hajjaj Ibn Muslim Ibn Warat Al-Qushayri Al-Nisaburi, http://cmje.org/

Abdul-Rahman al-Sheha, *Human Rights in Islam and Common Misconceptions*, DAR FOUNDA-TION, http://www1.umn.edu/humanrts/research/Egypt/HumanRightsinI-slam.pdf

Rafik Beekun (2006), *The Leadership Process of Muhammad [PBUH] From Hadith Sources*, THE ISLAMIC WORKPLACE, http://makkah.wordpress.com/leadership-andislam

Raj Bhala (2011), *Understanding Islamic Law*.

Thomas T. Boggatz *et al.* (2009), *Attitudes of Older Egyptians Towards Nursing Care at Home: A Qualitative Study*, 24 J. CROSS CULT. GERONTOL 33.

Cairo Declaration on Human Rights in Islam, Aug. 5, 1990, http://www1.umn.edu/humanrts/instree/cairodeclaration.html

M. Cherif Bassiouni & Gamal M. Badr (2002), *The Shari'ah: Sources, Interpretation, and Rule-Making*, 1 UCLA J. ISLAMIC & NEAR E. L.

Patrick Clawson and Michael Eisenstadt (2009), *Demography in the Middle East: Population Growth Slowing, Women's Situation Unresolved*, THE WASHINGTON INSTITUTE, http://www.washing toninstitute.org/policy-analysis/view/demography-in-the-middle-east-population-growth-slowing-womens-situation-un

Lynette Clemetson (2006), *U.S. Muslims Confront Taboo on Nursing Homes*, THE N.Y. TIMES, June 13, 2006, http://travel.nytimes.com/2006/06/13/us/13muslim.html?pagewanted =print

Constitution of the Arab Republic of Egypt, Jan. 18, 2014, at http://www.sis.gov.eg/Newvr/Dustor-en001.pdf

Constitution of Kingdom of Bahrain, Feb. 14, 2002, at http://www.wipo.int/wipolex/en/details.jsp?id=7264

Council of the League of Arab States, Arab Charter on Human Rights, May 23, 2004, http://www1.umn.edu/humanrts/instree/arabcharter2.html

Egyptian Penal Law No. 58 of 1937 (*reformed in* 1952), *Al-Jaridah Al-Rasmiyyah* [THE OFFI-CIAL GAZETTE], http://www1.umn.edu/humanrts/research/egypt-constitution.html

Bothiana Eldeeb (2003), *Social Statistics in Egypt, United Nations Statistics Division*, Apr. 28, 2003, http://downloadpdfebook.herokuapp.com/tag/social-statistics-in-egypt-united-nations

Radwa S. Elsaman (2011), *Corporate Social Responsibility in Islamic Law: Labor and Employment*, 2 YONSEI L.J. 64.

Radwa S. Elsaman and Mohamed A. 'Arafa (2012), *The Rights of the Elderly in the Arab Middle East: Islamic Theory versus Arabic Practice*, 14 MARQUETTE ELDER'S ADVISOR L. REV. 2.

Jane Garner and Sandra Evans (2000), *Institutional Abuse of Older Adults*, COUNCIL REPORT CR84 (June 2000), ROYAL COLLEGE OF PSYCHIATRISTS (London [Review 2005]), http://www.ibrarian.net/navon/paper/Institutional_abuse_of_older_adults.pdf? paperid=4825803

Claudia Gaspar (2007), *Aging Muslim Communities, World Muslim Congress*, Apr. 30, 2007, http://worldmuslimcongress.blogspot.com/2007/04/aging-muslim-communities.html

Ahmad Ibrahim (1989), *Islamic Concepts and Land Law in Malaysia, in* THE CENTENARY OF THE TORRENS SYSTEMS IN 189 (Ahmad Ibrahim & Judith Sihombing, eds).

International Bill of Human Rights (A/RES/3/217, Dec. 10, 1948), http://www.un-documents.net/a3r217.htm

IOPS Country Profile: Egypt, (Jan. 2011), http://www.iopsweb.org/researchandworking papers/42952582.pdf

Joseph A. Islam (2012), *Parents*, QURAN'S MESSAGE, http://quransmessage.com/articles/parents%20FM3.htm

Shelly L. Jackson and Thomas L. Hafemeister (2012), *2 Pure Financial Exploitation Vs. Hybrid Financial Exploitation Co-occurring With Physical Abuse And/Or Neglect Of Elderly Persons* 3, PSYCHOLOGY OF VIOLENCE [SERIAL ONLINE] (July 2012), http://www.researchgate.net/publication/232568717_Pure_financial_exploitation_vs._Hybrid_financial_exploitation_cooccurring_with_physical_abuse_andor_neglect_of_elderly_persons

Khizar Muazzam Khan (1983–1984), *Juristic Classification of Islamic Law*, 6 HOUS. J. INT'L. L. 23.

Hanaa Kheir-El-Din (2008), *The Egyptian Economy: Current Challenges and Future Prospects: Toward a More Efficient and Equitable Pension System in Egypt*, CAIRO SCHOLARSHIP ONLINE.

Ella Kick (2003), *Health Care and the Aging Population: What are Today's Challenges?* (Overview and Summary) 8 J. OF ISSUES IN NURSING 2, May 31, 2003, http://www.nursingworld.org/ojin

Tahir Mahmood (1989), *Law and the Elderly in the Islamic Tradition – Classical Precepts and Modern Legislation*, IX ISLAMIC & COMP. L. Q. 33, 33.

Ann Elizabeth Mayer (1994), *Universal Versus Islamic Human Rights: A Clash of Cultures or a Clash with a Construct?* 15 MICH J. INT'L. L. 307, 329.

Tauqir Mohammad Khan (2007), LAW OF WAQF IN ISLAM.

National Report Bahraini Human Rights Ministry and Social Development (2009), http://www.microsofttranslator.com/bv.aspx?ref=SERP&br=ro&mkt=en-US&dl=en&lp=AR_EN&a=http%3a%2f%2fwww.social.gov.bh%2fnode%2f697

Pub. Inst. For Soc. Security, SOCIAL SECURITY GUIDE IN KUWAIT, 3 (2009), http://www.pifss.gov.kw/upload/pifss_E_guide_eng_212.pdf

Sayyid Qutb (2007), 11 Fi Dhilal Al-Qur'an [In the Shade of the Qur'an] 119 (Adil Salahi trans. and ed., The Islamic Foundation).

Afzal-Ur-Rahman (1980), Muslim Educational Trust, Economic Doctrines of Islam, Vol. II, 208–12.

Dina Shehata (2012), *Mapping Islamic Actors in Egypt*, THE NETHERLANDS-FLEMISH INSTITUTE IN CAIRO, AL-AHRAM CENTER FOR POLITICAL AND STRATEGIC STUDIES (Mar. 2012), http://media.leidenuniv.nl/legacy/mapping-islamic-actors---version-2.2.pdf

Eric Trager (2013), *Egypt's New Constitution: Bleak Prospects*, POLICYWATCH 2183, Dec. 16, 2013.

Universal Islamic Declaration of Human Rights (1981), 21 Dhul Qaidah 1401, Sept. 19, 1981, http://www1.umn.edu/humanrts/instree/islamic_declaration_HR.html

William B. Ward and Mustafa Z. Younis (2013), *Steps Toward a Planning Framework for Elder Care in the Arab World*, SPRINGERBRIEFS IN AGING, Vol. VII, 55.

M.T. Yasamy, T. Dua, M. Harper, and S. Saxena (2013), *Mental Health of Older Adults, Addressing a Growing Concern*, WORLD HEALTH ORGANIZATION, DEPARTMENT OF MENTAL HEALTH AND SUBSTANCE ABUSE, http://www.who.int/mental_health/world-mental-health-day/WHO_paper_wmhd_2013.pdf

Adnan A. Zulfiqar (2007), *Religious Sanctification of Labor Law: Islamic Labor Principles and Model Provisions*, 9 U. PA. J. LAB. & EMP. L. 421, 436.

3 Human rights and residential care for older persons – an Australian perspective

Sue Field

Introduction

This chapter will provide an overview of the human rights of residents in Australian Residential Aged Care Facilities (RACFs).

Population demographics

According to the Australian Bureau of Statistics, and based on the estimated population in December 2013,[1] the current Australian population is 23,528,260 persons (Australian Bureau of Statistics, 2014b). Of these persons, 3.22 million were over the age of 65 years as at June 2012, accounting for approximately 14% of the total population (Australian Bureau of Statistics, 2014b). The greatest density of older persons can be found in Tasmania and South Australia with certain areas of high density to be found on the New South Wales coast. The impact on governments of these large areas of persons over 65 years of age will be felt as those baby boomers[2] reach 'older' age and may require assistance with activities of daily living, particularly if they require admission to a RACF.[3]

'How old is old?' Whereas the test for beauty is a subjective one,[4] the test for old age is objective and based on a person's birth certificate. In 2015, a person that is 65 years of age is eligible for the Age Pension (providing, of course, that they meet the income and assets tests prescribed by the Commonwealth Government). However, from 1 July 2017 the qualifying age for the Age Pension will increase to 65 and one half years. From then on every two years the qualifying age will rise by six months so that by 2023 the qualifying age for the Age Pension will be 67 years of age (Australian Government, Department of Human Services, 2014).

---

1 The last census undertaken in Australia was 2011 the next is due in 2016.
2 In Australia, Baby Boomers are generally defined as those persons born between the years 1946 to 1965.
3 Notwithstanding that it has been fact, and common knowledge, that Australia has an ageing population, the Australian Government still expresses 'surprise' at this fact and the impact this older demographic cohort will have on the resources of the Government!
4 Usually considered to be in the eyes of the beholder.

In an unprecedented move in May 2014, the Federal Treasurer announced that by 2035 the qualifying age for the Age Pension would rise to 70 years of age.[5] If eligibility for the Age Pension is the determining factor in deciding whether a person is 'old' it would appear, based on these proposed changes, that old age is being redefined.

Cultural attitudes towards residential aged care

Culturally, Australians in the past have not experienced extended families living together in the one residence. Young people grew up and left home.[6] Parents stayed on in the family home and eventually died at home or after a brief hospitalisation. However, as life expectancy is now 78.4 years for males and 84.6 years for females (Australian Bureau of Statistics, 2014a), ill-health and absence of family or community support leads to situations where some people have no option but to move into residential care. Whilst some cultures may consider it shameful to 'put their parents in a home', the increasing number of ethnic specific aged care facilities would belie the fact that all aged persons within a particular community are cared for at home by their offspring.[7]

Demographics of aged care

Evidently, not every older person requires admission to a RACF. The Commonwealth Government has a commitment to providing home care packages to enable older people to stay in their homes for as long as possible. Recent changes to Home Care have seen the introduction of Consumer Directed Care whereby the consumer can choose how they would like the money that is allocated for their care to be spent. Before receiving any government subsidised care, an assessment must be made by the Aged Care Assessment Team (ACAT) to determine the level of care required by the person to assist them to stay at home.

Statistical data reveals that the number of persons residing in aged care facilities was only 132,420 in 1999, increasing to 165,032 in 2011 (Australian Institute of Health and Welfare, 2012, p. 60). More recent figures indicate that in the 2012–2013 period, 226,042 persons received permanent care in RACFs (Department of Social Services, 2012–2013, p. 8). However, these increases must be considered in the light of an overall increase in the Australian population and the increased number of places available in RACFs.

Of note though, is the increase in the number of residents who are over the age of 85 years. In 1999 there were 64,638 residents aged 85 years or older, but by 2011 the number of these older persons had increased to 93,841 (Australian

---

5 This change has yet to pass in the Senate, which has the ability to block legislative changes.

6 Though there is a growing trend of younger people now living at home with their parents or returning home. This change has not occurred for cultural reasons, but for economic reasons as many young people cannot afford the current rents/house prices in the larger cities.

7 Government recognition of this fact is explored later in the chapter when strategies addressing this issue are outlined.

Institute of Health and Welfare, 2012, p. 60). Once again, these figures are representative of the ageing population generally. However, in real figures while the percentage of people over 80 years of age residing in care accommodation is 15%, only 1.1% of those in the 60–79 age bracket live in RACFs (also known as 'cared accommodation') (Australian Bureau of Statistics, 2011).

Legal context of residential aged care

Australia has a federal system of government, comprising six states and two territories. Legislation is, therefore, both Commonwealth (Cth) and State/Territory-based. However, both residential care and 'Home Care' (formerly known as 'Community Care') are governed by Commonwealth legislation, namely the *Aged Care Act 1997* (Cth) (the '*Aged Care Act*') and the associated Principles. Although there is no direct constitutional power for the federal government to legislate on residential aged care, according to the Australian Law Reform Commission:

> There are a number of heads of constitutional power that support aged care legislation. They include the appropriations power, the power to make grants to the States, the Territories power, the corporations power and the external affairs power. Perhaps the strongest source of constitutional power is the social welfare power, which provides that the Commonwealth may make laws regarding the provision of maternity allowances, widows' pensions, child endowment, unemployment, pharmaceutical, sickness and hospital benefits, medical and dental services . . . benefits to students and family allowances. This would include providing services for people who, because of their age, experience some degree of incapacity or an inability to provide adequately for their own health care needs.
>
> (Australian Law Reform Commission, 1995, p. 30)

At the outset it should be noted that, pursuant to the *Aged Care Act*, the Commonwealth only has the power to regulate aged care where the 'Approved Provider'[8] is in receipt of subsidies pursuant to the Act.

Admission to a RACF can only occur when the person seeking admission is assessed by an ACAT as requiring care that cannot be met within the community. Pursuant to s 96–2(5) of the *Aged Care Act* the Secretary can delegate certain powers and these include delegating power to the ACAT for the purpose of assessing someone as eligible to receive the various types of aged care available.

Residential aged care services

As mentioned above, Commonwealth Government aged care subsidies can only be provided to an Approved Provider. Approved Providers are assessed *inter alia*

---

8 The term 'Approved Provider' refers to those persons who have been approved by the Secretary of the Department to provide aged care services and who are in receipt of the government subsidies.

in respect of factors such as suitability to provide care, the experience of their key personnel, their history of financial management, previous experience in aged care and their ability to meet the standards imposed by the Government (Department of Social Services, 2012–2013, p. 58). The complete criteria used for assessing individuals as Approved Providers is addressed in Part 2, section 6 of the *Approved Provider Principles 2014* (Cth).[9] These services may be offered through charitable and/or religious organisations, for-profit bodies, community organisations or the government sector. At 30 June 2013 there were 2,718 RACFs in Australia with a total of 216,477 places available for those in need of residential care (Department of Social Services, 2012–2013, p. 59). Whilst it would appear that there are more residents than places (see above), this figure takes into account residents who may have deceased or been admitted to hospital, or moved out of aged care and been replaced by another resident. It is interesting to note that at the same time 58.3% of the care places were offered by not-for-profit organisations (these are considered to be the religious, charitable and community-based providers), 36.2% were conducted by for-profit organisations and government providers were only 5.5% of those offering residential care (Department of Social Services, 2012–2013, p. 59).

RACFs can be found throughout Australia and vary in size depending on their location and type of facility. There are a number of RACFs that are culturally specific reflecting not only the impact of migration particularly post-World War II but also recognising the needs of Aboriginal and Torres Strait Island peoples (ATSI). Prior to 1 July 2014, RACFs were generally divided into 'High Care' (previously known as 'Nursing Homes'), 'Low Care' (previously known as 'Hostels'), a combination of both High and Low Care, 'Dementia Specific Facilities', and some facilities offered 'Dementia Secure' 'beds' within their facilities.[10]

Reforms to aged care

In April 2012 the Commonwealth Government introduced a number of reform packages[11] to aged care, marking the start of a ten-year programme aimed 'to create a flexible and seamless system that provides older Australians with more choice, more control and easier access to a full range of services, where they want it and when they need it' (Commonwealth of Australia, 2012, p. 29) – a truly remarkable initiative!

To date the Government has: changed Community Care to Home Care Packages, and provided supplements to both home care and residential care; developed a national website entitled 'My Aged Care';[12] established a national contact centre; established the Australian Aged Care Quality Agency to oversee the quality

---

9   The authority for the Principles can be found in the *Aged Care Act 1997* (Cth) s 96–1.

10   These changes are elaborated on further in the chapter.

11   Known as 'Living Longer. Living Better'.

12   See Australian Government, Department of Social Services. (n.d.) My Aged Care. Commonwealth of Australia. Retrieved 13 August 2014, from http://www.myagedcare.gov.au/.

of aged care; established the Aged Care Pricing Commission, the role of which is to examine fees associated with extra services, and accommodation fees that are higher than those determined by the Minister (Australian Government, Department of Social Services, 2014b).

Over the next two years, the Government aims to further increase access and choice for consumers of aged care and establish a framework to undertake a five-year review. Over a five-year period it is the Government's intention to work with the aged care sector to identify and develop further reforms. (Australian Government, Department of Social Services, 2014b).

It appears that the changes to be developed over the final six years will be determined in consultation with the sector (Australian Government, Department of Social Services, 2014b).

Culturally and linguistically diverse reforms in aged care

The reforms to aged care also include the 'National Ageing and Aged Care Strategy for People from Culturally and Linguistically Diverse (CALD) Backgrounds'. This Strategy was launched by the Commonwealth Government in December 2012 in recognition of the differing needs of people from CALD backgrounds, who constitute a growing proportion of the Australian population over 65 years of age. This reflects Australia's status as one of the most culturally diverse countries in the world – by 2012, more than 30% of Australians over 65 will have been born outside Australia (Department of Health and Ageing, 2012a, p. 4).

The purpose of the Strategy is to ensure that older Australians from CALD backgrounds can receive residential care appropriate to their cultural, linguistic and religious beliefs. To achieve this, the Government has set six strategic goals and detailed actions to realise the goals:

- Goal 1 – CALD input positively affects the development of ageing and aged care policies and programmes that are appropriate and responsive.
- Goal 2 – Achieve a level of knowledge, systems capacity and confidence for older people from CALD backgrounds, their families and carers to exercise informed choice in aged care.
- Goal 3 – Older people from CALD backgrounds are able and have the confidence to access and use the full range of ageing and aged care services.
- Goal 4 – Monitor and evaluate the delivery of ageing and aged care services to ensure that they meet the care needs of older people from CALD backgrounds, their families and carers.
- Goal 5 – Enhance the CALD sector's capacity to provide ageing and aged care services.
- Goal 6 – Achieve better practice through improving research and data collection mechanisms that are inclusive of cultural and linguistic diversity in the ageing population (Department of Health and Ageing, 2012a, p. 1).

To this end the Government encourages aged care providers to meet the needs of specific groups, and, as mentioned earlier, there are discreet facilities that cater to the various CALD groups within Australian society (Australian Government, Department of Social Services, 2014a).

Lesbian, gay, bisexual, transgender and intersex reforms to aged care

A further Strategy was also developed and launched by the Government at the same time as the CALD Strategy. This Strategy, known as the 'National Lesbian, Gay, Bisexual, Transgender and Intersex (LGBTI) Ageing and Aged Care Strategy', was announced in July 2012 and addresses the needs of another group that has previously been marginalised within aged care due to historical discrimination. This historical discrimination has led many LGBTI people to hide their sexual orientation, and there has been serious neglect of LGBTI issues in Australian gerontology until recently (Department of Health and Ageing, 2012b, p. 6–7). The Government's aim in developing this Strategy is to better support the aged care sector to deliver care to LGBTI people that is sensitive and appropriate.

The goals, set by Government, to achieve this are as follows:

- Goal 1 – LGBTI people will experience equitable access to appropriate ageing and aged care services.
- Goal 2 – The aged care and LGBTI sectors will be supported and resourced to proactively address the needs of older LGBTI people.
- Goal 3 – Ageing and aged care services will be supported to deliver LGBTI inclusive services.
- Goal 4 – LGBTI-inclusive ageing and aged care services will be delivered by a skilled and competent paid and volunteer workforce.
- Goal 5 – LGBTI communities, including older LGBTI people, will be actively engaged in the planning, delivery and evaluation of ageing and aged care policies, programmes and services.
- Goal 6 – LGBTI people, their families and carers will be a priority for ageing and aged care research (Department of Health and Ageing, 2012b, p. 1).

Funding of residential care

As a result of the Commonwealth Government's 'Living Longer. Living Better' Strategy, funding of residential care has, since 1 July 2014, undergone the most far-reaching changes since the introduction of the *Aged Care Act* in 1997.

Residential aged care is not free, although there are provisions in the *Aged Care Act* to assist persons who have little if any income.[13] Prior to entering a RACF the prospective resident or their legal representative (such as their attorney pursuant to a power of attorney, or their financial manager pursuant to a financial management order) can request to have an income and asset assessment test. This test is undertaken by the Government. Even if the prospective resident does not request

---

13 Both Residential Care and Home Care are subject to means testing.

the assessment prior to entering a facility, the Government will assess their income and assets on admission. The test is designed to determine the amount of fees and accommodation charges that the resident will be charged whilst residing in the facility.

It should be noted that the family home is exempt from the determination of assets, provided that it is occupied by a spouse or another 'protected' person.[14]

Essentially there are three different financial payments to be met by an incoming resident, and four for those residents requiring extra services.[15]

The first of these financial payments is a basic daily fee which covers food, heating etc. This fee equates to 85% of the Age Pension (single). As the Age Pension is currently $766.00 per fortnight, this equates to $651.00 a fortnight.

The second fee is a means-tested fee, which covers some of the care received by a resident. This is the fee that is calculated on the individual's income and assets and is determined by the Government. It is capped at $25,000.00 per annum with a life cap of $60,000.00.

The third fee is an accommodation payment. Since 1 July 2014, residents can now choose to pay for their accommodation either through a Daily Accommodation Payment or a Refundable Accommodation Deposit or they can choose a combination of both. This latter payment is also means tested (Australian Government, Department of Social Services, 2014c).

Should residents require extra services then additional fees apply. These fees must be approved by the new Aged Care Pricing Commissioner.[16]

Since 1 July 2014, the distinction between facilities offering high care or low care has been removed and residents will now have the right to 'age in place'.[17] The actual impact of how this will work, both for the Approved Provider and the resident, is not quite clear at this stage. Agreements between the resident and the Approved Provider will require very careful consideration to take into account various issues that may arise. These might include, for example, where a resident who requires little assistance in the first instance moves into a facility, then perhaps develops greater clinical needs such as dementia, but residents and/or families still want the resident to remain in the same room, which from a care perspective may not be realistic.

As mentioned earlier, classification of the care recipient's needs for residential care is undertaken by the ACAT prior to admission to the facility.[18] Based on the care needs of the recipient, the RACF receives a government subsidy for that resident. This subsidy is in addition to the fees paid by the resident.

---

14 A protected person is someone who is a dependent child, a carer eligible for income support payment (and has lived in the home for two years) or a close relative who is eligible for income support payment (and has lived in the home for five years).

15 Extra services may include a greater choice of meals, wine and other ancillary benefits.

16 The authority for this can be found in the *Extra Service Principles 2014* (Cth).

17 The Security of Tenure provisions under the *Aged Care Act* and *User Rights Principles* will be outlined later in the chapter.

18 See the *Classification Principles 2014* (Cth).

The concept of dignity in residential aged care

The seminal legislation governing aged care is the *Aged Care Act* and the new/ amended *Aged Care Principles*.[19] To ensure that Aged Care Providers meet their responsibilities under the legislation and subsequently maintain accreditation[20] RACFs are subject to continuous monitoring by the Australian Aged Care Quality Agency to ensure that they meet the prescribed Standards.[21] Accreditation is an ongoing process with Approved Providers assessed by the Aged Care Quality Agency and receiving accreditation (or re-accreditation) for periods of one to three years (this process is discussed later in this chapter). The Standards that are to be met by the Approved Provider are to be found in Schedule 2 of the *Quality of Care Principles 2014* (Cth) and cover four specific areas, namely: management systems, staffing and organisational development; health and personal care; care recipient lifestyle; and physical environment and safe systems. Within each of these domains is a set of 'expected outcomes', one of which is that the Approved Provider is compliant with the legislation. The Approved Provider must, therefore, demonstrate that:

> [T]he organisation's management has systems in place to identify and ensure compliance with all relevant legislation, regulatory requirements, professional standards, and guidelines, about physical environment and safe systems.
>
> (*Quality of Care Principles 2014* (Cth))

Compliance with the relevant legislation includes compliance with the various Principles, set out above.

Prior to admission the 'care recipient'[22] is offered an agreement to sign (or be signed by their representative). The agreement contains, *inter alia*:

(a) the care recipient's rights and responsibilities;
(b) the services to be provided to the care recipient;
(c) the fees and other charges to be paid under the agreement.

> (*User Rights Principles 2014* (Cth) cl 14(2))

---

19 See the *Accountability Principles 2014* (Cth), *Aged Care (Transitional Provisions) Principles 2014* (Cth) – made under the *Aged Care (Transitional Provisions) Act 1997* (Cth), *Allocation Principles 2014* (Cth), *Approval of Care Recipients Principles 2014* (Cth), *Approved Provider Principles 2014* (Cth), *Certification Principles 1997* (Cth), *Classification Principles 2014* (Cth), *Committee Principles 2014* (Cth), *Grant Principles 2014* (Cth), *Information Principles 2014* (Cth), *Quality of Care Principles 2014* (Cth), *Records Principles 2014* (Cth), *Sanctions Principles 2014* (Cth), *Subsidy Principles 2014* (Cth) and *User Rights Principles 2014* (Cth).

20 Once approved by the Secretary of the Department, Approved Providers may offer aged care services, however, this is subject to the facility being accredited by the Quality Agency, pursuant to the *Quality Agency Principles 2013* (Cth).

21 This agency derives its powers under the *Australian Aged Care Quality Agency Act 2013* (Cth) and the *Quality Agency Principles 2013* (Cth).

22 The term 'care recipient' is used in the *Aged Care Act 1997* (Cth) to describe a resident in a RACF (or someone receiving home care).

The concept of dignity is enshrined within the *User Rights Principles*. Included in these rights is the right that each resident is:

> . . . to be treated with dignity and respect, and to live without exploitation, abuse or neglect . . .
>
> (*User Rights Principles 2014* (Cth) Sch 1 cl 1(d))

To ensure that aged care providers are meeting their responsibilities, including treating residents with dignity and respect, each facility is subject to an assessment contact, on an annual basis. The contact onsite visit, which may be an announced, or unannounced, is conducted by assessors from the Quality Agency. The role of the assessors is to measure the quality of care against the Standards mentioned previously. On occasions the assessment contact may be conducted by telephone.

A further safeguard is the review audit, which is a complete review of the performance of the facility, measured against the Standards. As with the assessment contact, a review audit may also be announced or unannounced.

Failure of an Approved Provider to meet the required Standards can lead to a decision by the Quality Agency not to accredit or to re-accredit a facility (*Quality Agency Principles 2013* (Cth) div 4).

Complaints and compliance in respect of aged care

Notwithstanding that all Approved Providers must meet the required Standards, the care of residents can vary within different facilities. However, the concept of dignity remains constant throughout the aged care sector. Furthermore, the regulations under which the Providers operate ensure that residents are treated well and with respect.

Should a care recipient/resident or their representative have a complaint about an Approved Provider that cannot be resolved through the facility's internal complaints mechanism, then pursuant to the *Complaints Principles 2014* (Cth) a complaint may be made to the Secretary of the Department.[23] The complainant can request that the Secretary keep confidential:

(a)   the identity of the complainant;
(b)   the identity of a person identified in the complaint;
(c)   any other details included in the complaint.

> (*Complaints Principles* 2014 (Cth) cl 6(3))

As can be imagined, in some circumstances it can be problematic for an Approved Provider to respond to certain complaints. On the other hand, when dealing with a complaint the Secretary can do one of three things: dismiss the

---

23 A reference to the Department is a reference to the Department of Social Services, the Department which has amongst its responsibilities, Ageing and Aged Care.

complaint,[24] resolve the complaint (which may include providing assistance to either the complainant or the Approved Provider), or refer the matter for resolution (*Complaints Principles 2014* (Cth) cl 10). Should the matter be referred for resolution, the Secretary may: undertake an investigation, refer the issue to mediation, request the Approved Provider to further examine the issue and attempt to resolve it, or require the parties to participate in a conciliation process (*Complaints Principles 2014* (Cth) cl 7).

In certain circumstances, both the Approved Provider and the complainant may apply to the Aged Care Commissioner[25] for a review of the Secretary's decision (*Complaints Principles 2014* (Cth) cl 24).

Some of the functions of the Commissioner are:

(a) to examine decisions that are made under the *Complaints Principles* and are identified by those Principles as being examinable by the Aged Care Commissioner, and make recommendations to the Secretary arising from the examination;

(b) to examine complaints made to the Aged Care Commissioner about the processes for handling matters under the *Complaints Principles*, and make recommendations to the Secretary arising from the examination;

(c) to examine, on the Aged Care Commissioner's own initiative, the processes for handling matters under the Complaints Principles, and make recommendations to the Secretary arising from the examination . . .

(*Aged Care Act 1997* (Cth) s 95A-1)

However, should the Secretary determine that an Approved Provider has not complied with their responsibilities pursuant to Parts 4.1, 4.2 and 4.3 of the *Aged Care Act*,[26] sanctions may be imposed on them by the Secretary (*Aged Care Act 1997* (Cth) s 65–1; *Sanctions Principles 2014* (Cth)). In determining whether or not to apply sanctions to the Approved Provider the Secretary must take into consideration a number of factors which include whether the non-compliance is of a minor or a serious nature, if it has occurred before, whether the health, welfare or interests of future care recipients would be threatened, and whether the Approved Provider has failed to comply with any earlier undertakings to remedy the non-compliance (*Aged Care Act 1997* (Cth) s 65–2; *Sanctions Principles 2014* (Cth) cl 14).

The most serious sanction that may be imposed by the Secretary is the revocation or suspension of an Approved Provider's approval as a provider of aged care

---

24 There are several grounds for dismissing the complaint and these include the Secretary is of the belief that the complaint was not made in good faith, the matter is subject to a coronial inquiry, the issue concerning the complaint occurred more than a year before the complaint was made to the Secretary.

25 The Aged Care Commissioner is a statutory officer appointed under Part 6.6 of the *Aged Care Act 1997* and is authorised to investigate complaints about the decision of the Secretary and the Aged Care Quality Agency.

26 Pt 4.1 relates to Quality of Care, 4.2 relates to User Rights and 4.3 relates to Accountability.

services.[27] However, before sanctions are imposed the Secretary must undertake certain steps which include a notice of non-compliance to the Approved Provider setting out the Secretary's intention of imposing sanctions. Notwithstanding this, the Secretary does not have to issue a notice of non-compliance if he/she is satisfied that 'there is an immediate and severe risk to the safety, health or well-being of care recipients to whom the Approved Provider is providing care' (*Aged Care Act 1997* (Cth) s 67–1(2)).

In some instances the Secretary, rather than impose a sanction on the Approved Provider, may appoint an adviser to assist the Approved Provider remedy the issue (*Aged Care Act 1997* (Cth) s 66A-2), or an administrator to administer the Facility for the period determined by the Secretary (*Aged Care Act 1997* (Cth) s 66A-3).

A sanction may not be imposed upon an Approved Provider if the Secretary specifies in the letter of imposition that the sanction will not be imposed if the Approved Provider meets certain conditions which may include the appointment of an administrator or adviser, further training for staff or allocation of some of the places[28] to another Approved Provider (*Aged Care Act 1997* (Cth) s 66–2(1)). A list of facilities, with sanctions imposed upon them, is found on the Government website.

As a result of the stringent requirements to be met by Aged Care Providers there is little case law in this area as most matters are dealt with under the *Aged Care Act* and its *Principles* as well as the mechanisms within the legislation. Should a situation arise where there may be criminal negligence involved, then the matter is pursued through the Court system as with any criminal matter.

Whilst Elder Law in itself is emerging as a speciality in Australia and certainly includes accommodation issues, in particular residential aged care, the focus is on advice on the agreements between the Approved Provider and the care recipient and issues that may arise over payments, security of tenure and provision of care, rather than litigation.

Provision of care and a human rights approach

Australia has a number of Commonwealth Acts that recognise and address the issue of human rights. These include:

- *Australian Human Rights Commission Act 1986* (Cth);
- *Age Discrimination Act 2004* (Cth);
- *Disability Discrimination Act 1992* (Cth);
- *Racial Discrimination Act 1975* (Cth);
- *Sex Discrimination Act 1984* (Cth) (Australian Human Rights Commission, n.d.).

Furthermore, Australia is a party to the following key human rights treaties:

- *International Covenant on Civil and Political Rights* (ICCPR);
- *International Covenant on Economic, Social and Cultural Rights* (ICESCR);

---

27 *Aged Care Act 1997* (Cth) s 66–1 includes the full range of sanctions that the Secretary can impose.
28 Meaning residents/care recipients of the facility.

- *Convention on the Rights of the Child* (CRC);
- *Convention on the Elimination of all Forms of Discrimination against Women* (CEDAW);
- *Convention on the Rights of Persons with Disabilities* (CRPD);
- *Convention on the Elimination of All Forms of Racial Discrimination* (CERD);
- *Convention Against Torture* (CAT) (Australian Government, Attorney-General's Department, n.d.).

From the reforms instituted by the Government and the overall objects of the *Aged Care Act*, which include:

> (e) to facilitate access to aged care services by those who need them, regardless of race, culture, language, gender, economic circumstance or geographic location;
>
> (g) to encourage diverse, flexible and responsive aged care services that:
>
>> (i) are appropriate to meet the needs of the recipients of those services and the carers of those recipients; and
>>
>> (ii) facilitate the independence of, and choice available to, those recipients and carers . . .
>
> (*Aged Care Act 1997* (Cth) div 2 s 2–1(1))

it could be argued that Australia does promote a human rights approach when providing residential care. However, the practicalities of providing care with the limited resources available to providers – a fact which is acknowledged in the objects of the *Aged Care Act*[29] – would indicate that Australia still has some way to go before really adopting a human rights approach to aged care on a daily basis. An examination of some of these issues will demonstrate where the shortfalls lie in this regard.

The issues surrounding substitute decision-making in aged care

As with any federal system of government,[30] tensions can, and do, arise between the powers of the various jurisdictions. This tension is of particular concern to aged care providers, as whilst aged care is governed by Commonwealth legislation, substitute decision-making is governed by State/Territory legislation. For example, the *Quality of Care Principles* define a representative of a care recipient as:

> (a) a person nominated by the care recipient as a person to be told about matters affecting the care recipient; or

---

29 *Aged Care Act 1997* (Cth) div 2 s 2–1(2) states that 'due regard must be had to: (a) the limited resources available to support services and programs under this Act; and (b) the need to consider equity and merit in accessing those resources'.

30 Australia has six states and two territories.

(b) a person:

 (i) who nominates himself or herself as a person to be told about matters affecting a care recipient; and

 (ii) who the relevant Approved Provider is satisfied has a connection with the care recipient and is concerned for the safety, health and well-being of the care recipient.

(2) Without limiting subparagraph (1)(b)(ii), a person has a connection with a care recipient if:

(a) the person is a partner, close relation or other relative of the care recipient;

or

(b) the person holds an enduring power of attorney given by the care recipient;

or

(c) the person has been appointed by a State or Territory guardianship board (however described) to deal with the care recipient's affairs;

or

(d) the person represents the care recipient in dealings with the Approved Provider.

Note: Nothing in this section is intended to affect the powers of a substitute decision-maker appointed for a person under a law of a State or Territory.

(*Quality of Care Principles 2014* (Cth) Pt 1 cl 5)

Although the 'Note' to this definition should clarify that in relation to the operation of this particular section, preference is given to the State/Territory appointed decision-maker, this leaves open to interpretation what happens when a substitute decision-maker is not appointed by the older person, but where instead reliance is placed on a 'person responsible' pursuant to the State/Territory legislation. It also pre-supposes that staff caring for a resident, the 'person responsible' under the State/Territory legislation, and the resident themselves are familiar with the 'nuances' of the legislation.[31]

While some jurisdictions define 'mental capacity',[32] others such as New South Wales refer instead to a 'person in need of a guardian', which is defined as 'a person who, because of a disability, is totally or partially incapable of managing his or her person' (*Guardianship Act 1987* (NSW) s 3(1)).

---

31 A 'person responsible' is someone who can make health decisions for a person whose mental capacity is impaired. There is a hierarchical structure starting with a spouse in a close continuing relationship, a person who has care of the person, or a close friend or family member.

32 Most notably Queensland – see *Guardianship and Administration Act 2000* (Qld) Sch 4 s 3.

In s 3(2), the Act further defines 'reference to a person who has a disability as a reference to a person:

(a) who is intellectually, physically, psychologically or sensorily disabled,
(b) who is of *advanced age*, [emphasis added]
(c) who is a mentally ill person within the meaning of the *Mental Health Act 2007*, or
(d) who is otherwise disabled,

and who, by virtue of that fact, is restricted in one or more major life activities to such an extent that he or she requires supervision or social habilitation.

As mentioned above, problems arise when aged care workers are confronted with various legislative instruments based on different definitions of mental capacity and substitute decision-makers. In the worst case scenarios, there is a misinterpretation by the substitute decision-maker of their powers, and when combined with a knowledge deficit on the part of the health worker this may lead to the older person not being consulted in the decision-making process and/or conflict arising between family members as to who the decision-maker is, or even if one is required.

Accreditation standards and ongoing training: skills, knowledge and human rights

The Accreditation Standards require 'management and staff [to] have appropriate knowledge and skills to perform their roles effectively' (*Quality of Care Principles 2014* (Cth) Sch 2 pt 1 item 1.3, pt 2 item 2.3, pt 3 item 3.3 and pt 4 item 4.3). Furthermore, if specialised nursing care is required then under the Standards these needs must be 'identified and met by appropriately qualified nursing staff' (*Quality of Care Principles 2014* (Cth) Sch 2 pt 2 item 2.5). Should the care recipient require palliative care then '[t]he comfort and dignity of terminally ill care recipients is maintained' in aged care (*Quality of Care Principles 2014* (Cth) Sch 2 pt 2 item 2.9).

Although RACFs employ registered nurses, much of the clinical work is undertaken by enrolled nurses or aged care workers.[33] The aspects of training and education, as with any educational organisation, vary between the education providers of the qualifications. The Australian Human Rights Commission (AHRC) is of the belief that the recent (and ongoing) reforms instituted by the Government 'easily accommodate a human rights approach' (Australian Human Rights Commission, 2012, p. 1).

The AHRC advocates human rights training for health workers 'to ensure they are culturally competent, respect difference and diversity in the older Australian population and understand and respect human rights' (Australian Human Rights Commission, 2012, p. 2).

---

33 Registered nurses undertake a three-year undergraduate degree, enrolled nurses undertake a diploma in nursing and aged care workers usually have a Certificate 3 or 4 in aged care.

In particular, the AHRC advocates that the implementation of advance care training programmes includes not only general practitioners, but also health workers in both the acute health sector and the aged care sector (Australian Human Rights Commission, 2012, p. 2). Although there are programmes already in existence addressing substitute decision-making, including advance care planning, assisted decision-making is still in its infancy in many jurisdictions.

Accreditation of a RACF is an ongoing process and Approved Providers must demonstrate that they are engaged in a process of continuous improvement, which includes education and training of staff to ensure that staff remain accountable and the care needs of residents are understood and met. For this to occur, however, aged care facilities require sufficient staff and the financial resources to fund both the staff and their ongoing education needs.

This is problematic on two counts. Working in aged care has not always been viewed as a 'first choice' by both qualified and unqualified health care workers, though this negative attitude towards working with older people is gradually changing, perhaps, in part, as gerontology becomes a more integral part of health curricula to meet our changing demographics. The introduction of post-graduate courses, for registered nurses, in aged care and the recognition that aged care is in itself a speciality has seen an increase in the number of qualified staff seeking employment in this area. Nevertheless some Approved Providers may have difficulty in recruiting appropriate staff, a situation that is often exacerbated in rural areas because of the paucity of people available to engage in the workforce. Furthermore, as the financial remuneration of health workers increases this places an extra burden on the Approved Provider to find the funds to meet an increase in expenditure, or find more innovative ways to provide the care, while still meeting the Standards.

Further issues of concern

One particular area of concern, not only to aged care providers, but also to residents relates to what the Act refers to as 'reportable assaults'.[34] The introduction of this amendment in July 2007,[35] while in theory attempting to reduce elder abuse in RACFs, has in fact reduced the rights of older persons to determine what action they want taken in respect of the incident. Whilst elder abuse in any form is to be deplored and mechanisms should be implemented to protect vulnerable people, the vulnerable person should have the right to decide what should happen in the circumstances. The provisions in the legislation remove that right.

Section 63–1AA(2) of the *Aged Care Act* states that:

> If the Approved Provider receives an allegation of, or starts to suspect on reasonable grounds, a reportable assault, the Approved Provider is responsible

---

34 *Aged Care Act 1997* (Cth) s 63–1AA(9) defines a reportable assault as 'unlawful sexual contact or unreasonable use of force'.

35 The amendments were introduced following allegations of sexual abuse in an aged care facility.

for reporting the allegation or suspicion as soon as reasonably practicable, and in any case within 24 hours, to:

(a) a police officer with responsibility relating to an area including the place where the assault is alleged or suspected to have occurred; and

(b) the Secretary.

(Aged Care Act 1997 (Cth) s 63–1AA(2))

Should the Approved Provider not comply with this requirement, then sanctions can be applied.

Whilst the aim of this section is designed to protect vulnerable people, it is of interest to note that clause 53 of the *Accountability Principles* outlines the circumstances in which an Approved Provider is not required to report alleged or suspected reportable assaults. These include if:

(a) within 24 hours after the receipt of the allegation, or the start of the suspicion, the Approved Provider forms an opinion that the assault was committed by a care recipient to whom the Approved Provider provides residential care; and

(b) before the receipt of the allegation or the start of the suspicion, the care recipient had been assessed by an appropriate health professional as suffering from a cognitive or mental impairment; and

(c) within 24 hours after the receipt of the allegation or the start of the suspicion, the Approved Provider puts in place arrangements for management of the care recipient's behaviour; and

(d) the Approved Provider has:

 (i) a copy of the assessment or other documents showing the care recipient's cognitive or mental impairment; and

 (ii) a record of the arrangements put in place under paragraph (c).

(Accountability Principles 2014 (Cth) cl 53)

The concern is, should the 'reportable assault' occur in a situation where both residents are in a domestic relationship and the 'offender' is suffering from a cognitive impairment, in some situations the arrangements (*Accountability Principles 2014* (Cth) cl 53(1)(c)) may include the removal of one resident to another facility, with little expectation of a continued relationship between the couple. This raises the issue of whether the resident is actually protected from physical abuse or whether it merely highlights the need for further resources to be provided to aged care providers to care for residents with cognitive impairment.

Such resources could include further specialised training for aged care workers.

Conclusion

This chapter, while providing an overview of the residential care sector within Australia, has highlighted changes in Government policy relating to the rights of those persons residing in aged care facilities. In particular this change can be found in the two strategies addressing the specific needs of previously marginalised individuals. The 'National Lesbian, Gay, Bisexual, Transgender and Intersex (LGBTI) Ageing and Aged Care Strategy' and the 'National Ageing and Aged Care Strategy for People from Culturally and Linguistically Diverse (CALD) Backgrounds' if successfully implemented, should see Australian aged care further complying with its obligations in respect of human rights.

The more recent changes relating to Ageing in Place should provide a greater degree of autonomy and security for older persons, who previously may have found themselves moved within a particular facility (to better cater for their increasing care needs) or transferred to a different facility offering care specific to their needs.

The continual monitoring of residential aged care facilities by the Aged Care Quality Agency and the provision (by the Agency) of self-assessment tools to assist Approved Providers monitor their performance against the Standards, should also ensure that the improvement process is an ongoing one.

The harmonisation of substitute decision-making legislation to ensure consistency between the States/Territories would also assist individuals in understanding the rights and responsibilities of individuals when making decisions. Such a harmonisation would remove much of the confusion experienced not only by aged care workers but by the substitute decision-maker themselves, who as mentioned earlier, often do not understand the extent (and limitation) of their powers.

Aged care in Australia is without a doubt one of, if not the most, heavily regulated sector in our community. Whilst we acknowledge that some older persons are vulnerable and require assistance, education of staff as to the rights of the individual to make their own informed decisions should be adopted in all situations. If the Federal Government really does want to:

> . . . create a flexible and seamless system that provides older Australians with more choice, more control and easier access to a full range of services, where they want it and when they need it . . .
>
> (Commonwealth of Australia, 2012, p. 29)

then they will need to provide assistance to aged care providers to ensure that the resources are available to implement the changes successfully and ensure that on a daily basis the care requested by the resident, and provided by the Approved Provider is delivered.

In theory, the 'Living Longer. Living Better' reforms recognise the need for change and a more transparent approach to aged care in Australia. However, for these reforms to be successful and the rights of older people embedded in their daily care, the education of the Approved Providers (and their staff) is essential. Although the AHRC has advocated human rights training for health workers many education programmes appear to focus solely on clinical skills, and there is scant evidence of programmes developed within a human rights framework.

Until such time as a human rights approach underpins the philosophy of all aged care education programmes, and the fundamental principles associated with this approach become as commonplace as clinical skills, then we cannot really say that we comply with our responsibilities in respect of human rights in aged care. Positive changes are happening – albeit slowly. Perhaps the impetus for change will come through the Standards themselves and the monitoring process conducted by 'the Agency'!

What is not required, however, is legislation that protects *all* older people from making bad decisions – in that regard Australia is certainly defending the rights of older people.

Bibliography

Legislation

Accountability Principles 2014 (Cth)
Age Discrimination Act 2004 (Cth)
Aged Care Act 1997 (Cth)
Aged Care (Transitional Provisions) Act 1997 (Cth)
Aged Care (Transitional Provisions) Principles 2014 (Cth)
Allocation Principles 2014 (Cth)
Approval of Care Recipients Principles 2014 (Cth)
Approved Provider Principles 2014 (Cth)
Australian Aged Care Quality Agency Act 2013 (Cth)
Australian Human Rights Commission Act 1986 (Cth)
Certification Principles 1997 (Cth)
Classification Principles 2014 (Cth)
Committee Principles 2014 (Cth)
Complaints Principles 2014 (Cth)
Disability Discrimination Act 1992 (Cth)
Extra Service Principles 2014 (Cth)
Fees and Payments Principles 2014 (No 2) (Cth)
Grant Principles 2014 (Cth)
Information Principles 2014 (Cth)
Quality Agency Principles 2013 (Cth)
Quality Agency Reporting Principles 2013 (Cth)
Quality of Care Principles 2014 (Cth)
Racial Discrimination Act 1975 (Cth)
Records Principles 2014 (Cth)
Sanctions Principles 2014 (Cth)
Sex Discrimination Act 1984 (Cth)
Subsidy Principles 2014 (Cth)
User Rights Principles 2014 (Cth)

Strategies

Department of Health and Ageing. (2012a). *National ageing and aged care strategy for people from culturally and linguistically diverse (CALD) backgrounds*. (Publications No. D0982) Retrieved from http://www.fecca.org.au/images/stories/cald-aged-care/national-cald-aged-care-strategy.pdf

Department of Health and Ageing. (2012b). *National lesbian, gay, bisexual, transgender and inter-sex (LGBTI) ageing and aged care strategy*. (Publications No. D0981) Retrieved from http://www.acon.org.au/sites/default/files/lgbti-strategy.pdf

Treaties

International Covenant on Civil and Political Rights (ICCPR)
International Covenant on Economic, Social and Cultural Rights (ICESCR)
Convention Against Torture (CAT)
Convention on the Elimination of All Forms of Racial Discrimination (CERD)
Convention on the Elimination of all Forms of Discrimination against Women (CEDAW)
Convention on the Rights of Persons with Disabilities (CRPD)
Convention on the Rights of the Child (CRC)

Reports

Australian Human Rights Commission. (2012). *Respect and choice: A human rights approach for ageing and health*. Retrieved from http://www.humanrights.gov.au/sites/default/files/document/publication/human_rights_framework_for_ageing_and_health.pdf

Australian Institute of Health and Welfare. (2012). *Residential aged care in Australia 2010–2011: A statistical overview* (Aged care statistics series no. 36, Cat. no. AGE 68). Retrieved from http://www.aihw.gov.au/WorkArea/DownloadAsset.aspx?id=10737422896

Australian Law Reform Commission. (1995). *The coming of age: New aged care legislation for the Commonwealth* (Report No. 72). Retrieved from http://www.austlii.edu.au/au/other/lawreform/ALRC/1995/72.html

Commonwealth of Australia. (2012). *Living Longer. Living Better* (Publications No. D0769). Retrieved from http://library.bsl.org.au/jspui/bitstream/1/3244/1/Literature%20Review%20and%20Description%20of%20the%20Regualtory%20Framework.pdf

Department of Social Services. (2012–2013). *Report on the operation of the Aged Care Act 1997*. Retrieved from https://www.dss.gov.au/our-responsibilities/ageing-and-aged-care/tools-and-resources/ageing-and-aged-care-research-and-statistics/general-ageing-and-aged-care/report-on-the-operation-of-the-aged-care-act-1997

Productivity Commission. (2011). *Caring for older Australians: Overview* (Report No. 53). Retrieved from http://www.pc.gov.au/__data/assets/pdf_file/0016/110932/aged-care-overview-booklet.pdf

Websites

Australian Bureau of Statistics. (2014a). *3302.0 – Deaths, Australia, 2013*. Retrieved 21 November 2014, from http://www.abs.gov.au/ausstats/abs@.nsf/Latestproducts/3302.0Main%20Features32013?opendocument&tabname=Summary&prodno=3302.0&issue=2013&num=&view

Australian Bureau of Statistics. (2014b). *Population clock*. Retrieved 12 July 2014, from http://www.abs.gov.au/ausstats/abs@.nsf/0/1647509ef7e25faaca2568a900154b63?OpenDocument

Australian Bureau of Statistics. (2011). *4914.0.55.001 – Age Matters, Jun 2011*. Retrieved 18 August 2014, from http://www.abs.gov.au/ausstats/abs@.nsf/Latestproducts/4914.0.55.001Main%20Features3Jun%202011?opendocument&tabname=Summary&prodno=4914.0.55.001&issue=Jun%202011&num=&view

Australian Government, Department of Human Services. (2014). *Age Pension – Department of Human Services*. Retrieved 12 July 2014, from http://www.humanservices.gov.au/customer/services/centrelink/age-pension

Australian Government, Department of Social Services. (2014a). *Culturally and linguistically diverse people – My Aged Care*. Commonwealth of Australia. Retrieved 12 July 2014, from http://www.myagedcare.gov.au/eligibility-diverse-needs/culturally-and-linguistically-diverse-people

Australian Government, Department of Social Services. (2014b). *Overview – Australian Government Department of Social Services*. Retrieved 13 August 2014, from http://www.dss.gov.au/our-responsibilities/ageing-and-aged-care/aged-care-reform/overview

Australian Government, Department of Social Services. (2014c). *Residential care – Australian Government Department of Social Services*. Retrieved 13 August 2014, from https://www.dss.gov.au/our-responsibilities/ageing-and-aged-care/overview/advice-to-the-aged-care-industry/aged-care-entry-record/aged-care-reform-implementation-update

Australian Government, Department of Social Services. (n.d.). *My Aged Care*. Commonwealth of Australia. Retrieved 13 August 2014, from http://www.myagedcare.gov.au/

Australian Human Rights Commission. (n.d.). *Legislation – Australian Human Rights Commission*. Retrieved 13 August 2014, from http://www.humanrights.gov.au/our-work/legal/legislation

Complaints to the Commissioner – Aged Care Commissioner. (n.d.). Retrieved 13 August 2014, from http://www.agedcarecommissioner.gov.au/complaints/

4 Protecting the rights of Chinese older persons in need of residential care

The social justice and health equity dilemma in the People's Republic of China

Michelle H. Y. Shum, JD, Andy H. Y. Ho, PhD, Hao Luo, PhD, Jun Fang Wang, MSW, Ying Wang, MA, Terry Y. S. Lum, PhD

Introduction

China, often portrayed as an ageing giant due to policy-driven fertility decline and increasing life expectancy, is facing unprecedented challenges in the care of its fast-growing older population. Since its market-based reforms of the late 1970s, the country has experienced profound demographic and socio-economic transformations, most prominently marked by the shrinkage of family size and the upsurge of rural-to-urban migration. Both of these phenomena have gradually undermined and jeopardized the traditional role of the family as the principle care-providing unit for the aged. In an ambitious attempt to address the increasing demands of services for older people while balancing the growing disparity between formal and informal care, the central Chinese Government has launched a number of national-level policies to push forward a prodigious expansion of residential care services across the country. Though these are admirable efforts, they are established upon a fragmented health and social care system without recourse to a mature legal foundation based on human rights. As a result, residential care services in China are often poorly planned, lack regulation and governance, and fail to provide quality and dignified care to older people in need.

In this chapter, we begin by examining the various developmental challenges of China's long-term care system in the context of an ageing population and rapid demographic change. Next, we critically discuss the constitutional and legal-regulatory frameworks for the provision of residential care, and investigate the violations of human rights cases in Chinese residential care homes are facilitated by an underdeveloped legislation system. Finally, since the quality of care for older persons hinges to a great extent on the balance between social justice and health equity, we argue that the only way to protect the dignity and personhood of Chinese older persons in residential care is to strengthen the foundation of human rights, enhance regulatory monitoring and compliance, and cultivate professional responsibility and competence.

Population ageing and long-term care in China

Over the past three decades, the number of persons aged 65 and above has risen from 68 million in 1980 to 120 million in 2010, accounting for 8.9% of the total population (Sixth National Population Census of State Council, 2010). This trend of expansion will continue at an amplified rate for the number of older persons is projected to double within the next 30 years to account for 22.6% of the population; in particular, the number of those aged 80 and above is predicted to grow from 1.4% in 2010 to 5.0% in 2040 (Kinsella & He, 2009). These statistics mark the beginning of an accelerated trend of population ageing because the people of China are living much longer, with an average life expectancy of 73.5 years (State Council, 2011b). Unfortunately, this increased longevity is also associated with greater prevalence of chronic life-limiting illnesses and declining psychological health (Feng, Pang, & Beard, 2014; Zhang, 2013). It is estimated that the number of people with dementia in China was around 9.19 million in 2010, while it was only 3.68 million in 1990 and 5.62 million in 2000 (Chan et al., 2013). Furthermore, China's old-age dependency ratio will surge, increasing more than threefold, from 11 older persons aged 65 or over per 100 people aged 15–64 in 2010 to 39 in 2050 (United Nations, 2013), and the demand for long-term care is also expected to rise in the foreseeable future.

In the face of population ageing, the central government heavily emphasized the need to expand senior care services in the State Council's 12th five-year developmental plan for 2011–2015 (State Council, 2011a). Specifically, the plan outlined an overarching framework for a three-tier care model for older people to be implemented across all of China by the year 2020; the first, bottom, tier involves the 'foundation' of home-based care; the second, middle, tier involves the 'backing' of community-based care; and the third, top, tier involves the 'support' of institutional care. This model is also known as '9064, since 90% of the older people are expected to spend the last stages of their life at home and be cared for by their family (*foundation*), 6% are expected to spend the last stages of their life at home with community support services (*backing*), and 4% are expected to reside in long-term care institutions (*support*). Based on this national framework, many provincial governments have begun to formulate and implement local policies to expand home care and community care services, while insistently giving developmental priority to residential care (Zhan, Luo, & Chen, 2012). These efforts, though commendable, are not without challenges and issues as the long-term care system in China remains largely undeveloped.

Traditionally, the responsibility for providing care and support to older people in China has rested primarily with the family, as the cultural principle of filial piety dictates caregiving obligations between adult children and their ageing parents (Chow, 2006; Chow & Lum, 2008; Chan, Ho, Leung et al., 2012). Filial piety is the bedrock upon which earlier care policies for older people were founded, and the Chinese Government long ago adopted a socialist system of welfare and only provided care to destitute older persons who fall into the 'three no's' category, particularly those with no family support, no capacity to work, and no source of income (Wong & Leung, 2012). However, with vast modernization and the social changes highlighted by radical fertility reduction resulting from the one-child policy, smaller family size, longer life expectancy, decreases in intergenerational co-residence, as well as rapid expansion of internal migration, families' ability to support and care for older persons is drastically reduced (Wu, Mao, & Xu, 2008; Cheung & Kwan, 2009). Inevitably, responsibility for care of older persons has increasingly fallen upon the government in the modern era, causing enormous pressure to develop and expand long-term care for the aged. However, most provincial governments in China have little or no experience of providing such services, and consequently many have begun a process of welfare socialization (Ding, 2011), outsourcing long-term care services to the private sector, and relying heavily on the marketplace to make available the numbers of residential care beds required under the State Council's developmental plan. Yet one must recognize that the marketplace is too inexperienced and untested, and its ability to build suitable residential homes providing excellent care is highly questionable.

Developmental overview of residential care in China

Before the 1990s, residential care was rare and very limited in China. The few facilities that catered to older persons were state-run social welfare institutions serving those without children, the mentally ill, and the destitute with no family (Gu & Liang, 2000; Ikels, 1993; Wu et al., 2008). Given the traditional emphasis on filial piety, older people who were institutionalized were also highly stigmatized for having no children, or none willing to provide care, which is a source of shame in Chinese culture (Chen, 1996; Shang, 2001). Thus, it was not until the late 1990s that residential care began to emerge as a solution to the ageing population and the declining availability of family care. Specifically, the government enacted the *Provisional Measures for the Management of Social Welfare Institutions* in 1999 to allow state-run institutions as well as private enterprises, non-government organizations (NGOs), and individuals to invest in and operate not-for-profit social welfare units for the aged (Ding, 2011). These regulations officially permitted the market and NGOs to engage in the provision of residential care, marking the beginning of welfare socialization in China.

Despite its consistent growth since the early 2000s, there is no clear and definitive definition of residential care. While there are various names ascribed to residential care units, such as social welfare institutions for the aged, homes for the aged, hostels for older persons, nursing homes, and homes for older persons in rural areas, they all adopt a mixed model of care to provide a limited range of services to older persons with varying degrees of functional capacity and cognitive acuity. No objective or standardized assessment has been developed to accurately determine the care and support needs of older persons in these care facilities, and there are no clear eligibility criteria for entering residential care. Nonetheless, a recent national survey shows that over half of the current homes for the aged rejected residents who could not look after themselves, and only 20% accepted older persons with disabilities or dementia (State Council, 2011b). Notwithstanding such restrictions and limitations, recent evidence suggests that increasing numbers of older persons intend and desire to live in a residential care facility, due mainly to the fact that their children cannot care for them, they wanted more autonomy and do not want to become a burden on their family (Guan, Zhan, Liu, 2007).

Provincial governments across China have incessantly pushed the development and expansion of residential care so as to meet the '9064' objectives as imposed by the national care policy for older people. Between 2000 and 2012, more than 3.9 million residential care beds were made available. This is an astonishing figure when compared to the 901,000 beds provided after Modern China was founded in 1949. But in order to reach the target number of 30 beds per 1,000 older persons by 2015 as demanded by national policy, several million new nursing home beds would need to be added quickly (Ministry of Civil Affairs, as cited by Wu & Dang, 2013). While governments have unveiled different policies to subsidize and encourage NGOs and private institutions to be even more involved in the provision of residential care in a frantic attempt to meet this huge target, there is a lack of clear guidelines and regulatory standards ensuring the quality of care provided. Most privately run residential homes are poorly equipped in terms of both facilities and professional support (Wong & Leung, 2012). Shortage of qualified care workers is one of the biggest challenges faced by all residential care service providers. In sum, the underdeveloped state of residential care in China is marked by an overt emphasis on quantity over quality, an acute shortage of competent staff, and a lack of regulatory standards, posing a great threat to the rights, dignity, and personhood of older persons in need of residential care.

Balancing residential care provision and human rights protection

Although the provision of residential care to destitute older persons has long been endorsed by the central Chinese Government as part of its human rights goals. In 1991, China issued its first official document on human rights, the White Paper – Human Rights in China, to express to the international community its determined interest in human rights protection. Its commitment to guarantee older persons' right to access residential care was further affirmed through the publication of another White Paper, The Development of China's Undertakings for the Aged, in 2006 (Information Office of the State Council, 2006). Such commitments were put into practice through the Government's pledge to increase the number of beds in day care facilities and nursing homes, as well as to extend support to the establishment of not-for-profit nursing homes by private enterprises (National Human Rights Action Plan of China [NHRAP], 2009–2012). While these valuable developments affirm China's constitutional principle that the 'state protects and respects human rights', China, on the other hand, is still lacking a robust legal-regulatory framework to protect the institutionalized older persons from risk of maltreatment and abuse due to its late development and inexperience in providing residential care services, particularly in partnership with a large number of private enterprises.

Legal protection of human rights

Recognition and protection of elders' rights in China is founded upon its reform and opening-up in the 1970s, marked by the progressive development and promotion of human rights. Learning from the bitter lessons of the Cultural Revolution, which left the country lawless and its citizens deprived of basic freedoms and rights, China entered into a new era of socialist governance and established a renewed constitution appropriate to the political and economic reality. China also shifted its approach to human rights from the blind rejection of the Mao era to active engagement with international laws and norms (Qu, 2009). When China first promulgated its supreme law, the *Constitution of the People's Republic of China* (the *Constitution*) in 1982, it guaranteed Chinese citizens fundamental rights compatible with international standards. Older persons, as ordinary Chinese citizens, are thus assured of their equality before the law with inviolable personal dignity and freedom, alongside their political, social, economic, and cultural rights. Insulting and unlawfully depriving older persons of their freedom are effectively prohibited. The *Constitution* shaped the basis of other laws and regulations for older persons, and became the fundamental code of conduct for all state organs, social organizations, and citizens. In 2004, the status of older persons' human rights were further transformed from a 'deserved right' to a 'legitimate right' (Sun, 2014), when China declared without qualification that 'the state respects and protects human rights' in the fourth amendment to the *Constitution* (1982).

Yet, along the path of China's progressive human rights development, the state gave priority to accomplishing 'the right to subsistence' as a prerequisite over all other human rights, as it aimed to feed its 1.3 billion citizens and improve their living standards (Information Office of the State Council, 1991). Economic and social rights evidently have clear precedence over civil and political rights in China (Information Office of the State Council, 2000, 2005, 2013). This distinctive priority was made explicit when China adopted different approaches to addressing and implementing the two most important international human rights treaties (Delisle, 2013). Specifically, although China is a signatory of both the *International Covenant on Civil and Political Rights* (ICCPR) and the *International Covenant on Economic, Social, and Cultural Rights* (ICESCR), only the ICESCR was ratified.

Legal-regulatory framework for residential care homes in China

Against the backdrop of the state's exclusive prioritizing of guaranteeing social and economic rights to its citizens, older persons in China undeniably have the right to adequate living standards as well as services to support and maintain their physical health and mental well-being. Nonetheless, institutionalized older people are at particular risk of mistreatment due not only to their functional dependency (Spector, Fleishman, Pezzin, & Spillman, 2001). Rules and regulations to safeguard the rights, dignity and uniqueness of older persons in residential care homes are irrefutable. In China, before the state's heightened concern to push the national '9064' care agenda for older persons in 2011, according to the *Provisional Measures for the Management of Social Welfare Institutions* promulgated by the Ministry of Civil Affairs in 1999, a prospective service provider must first apply for approval and obtain a 'Certificate of Approval to Open a Social Welfare Institution' before establishing a residential care home. Nonetheless, the *Provisional Measures* is a non-specific rule to regulate the approval and licensing of all forms of social service institutions, including those catering to the needs of the deprived, the disabled, orphans, and of course residential care for the older persons. In general, residential care homes at that time were mainly governed by three departmental rules promulgated by ministries under the State Council at the national level, namely 'Two gui fan, One biao zhun' (Ministry of Civil Affairs, 2009). The two gui fan are the *Code for the Design of Buildings for Elderly Persons* (1999) and the *Basic Standard for Social Welfare Institutions for the Elderly* (2001). While the former regulates the brickwork and construction of all residential care homes, the latter sets out guidance on basic service standards in residential care homes, including meals, personal care, rehabilitation, and psychological services. The one biao zhun is the *National Standards for Old-Age Care Workers* (2002), which sets out the qualification requirements for persons who provide nursing care and assistance to the older persons. The standards of old-age care workers are classified into four ranks according to training and skill levels. It is at least 180 hours for entry-level workers and ethical values in treating older persons are included though not at the heart of the training. Additional training hours of 150, 120 and 90 are required for promotion to intermediate, advanced, and technician level respectively.

Yet, the two gui fan are insubstantial and written only in the briefest of terms, merely stipulating an outline of 'what' should be done, without laying down a clear quality standard. In effect, these rules mainly serve to ensure the quality of the built environment of residential care homes, the equipment and facilities they house as well as the provision of basic living needs of older persons; they neglect the protection of the dignity, rights, and well-being of institutionalized older persons. Moreover, although the one biao zhun sets certain training standards for a qualified old-age care worker, there are no mandatory requirements that only certified old-age care workers were responsible for taking care of older persons. While there were 322,703 old-age care worker positions in the public residential care sector at the end of 2012 (Ministry of Civil Affairs, 2013a) and the state projected a need of 6,000,000 old-age care workers for the whole country by 2020 (State Council, 2010), only 10,967 people received the old-age care workers' training and 9,491 received the qualification within 2010–2013 under the government promotion (Vocational Skill Assessment and Guidance Centre of Ministry of Civil Affairs, 2014). Such significant discrepancy between demand and supply of old-age care workers in the market implies older persons in residential care homes are not taken care of by the state recognized worker. Due to a serious shortage of certified old-age workers, some municipal governments, such as Guangzhou, provide brief training of around seven days to persons who provide care and assistant to older persons. Furthermore, thorough implementation of the 'Two gui fan, One biao zhun' was also an issue as the number of accidents in residential care homes kept rising. In 2009, the Ministry of Civil Affairs issued a circular requesting all municipal governments to conduct inspections and ensure all residential care homes meet the standards set forth in the 'Two gui fan, One biao zhun' (Ministry of Civil Affairs, 2009).

It was not until 2012, when the Standing Committee of the National People's Congress (NPCSC) revised its national *Law on Protection of the Rights and Interests of the Elderly* (*LPRIE*) and enforced in 2013, that a new chapter was added to safeguard older persons' right to obtain residential care and provide some regulations to inform service quality in residential care homes. Specifically, *LPRIE* 2012 conferred upon the Civil Affairs Department of the People's Government at the county level or above, the power to guide and supervise residential care homes and to approve and issue licences for their establishment. Subsequently, in 2013, and in accordance with *LPRIE* 2012, the Ministry of Civil Affairs promulgated *Rules for the Permission of the Establishment of Elderly Service Institutions* (the *Permission Rule*) and *Rules for the Administration of Elderly Care Institution* (the *Administration Rule*) to standardize the registration and management of residential care homes at the national level specifically for older persons.

Notwithstanding this progress, the recently amended and enacted laws inherited the generally ineffectual characteristics of most Chinese laws, which are written in general, broad, and vague terms, for they are simply principles to 'suggest' the duties that residential care homes should perform without providing a comprehensive framework to 'govern' their performance. Clearly, supplementary rules are required to fill the gap regarding execution (Ministry of Civil Affairs, 2013b). Though the Ministry of Civil Affairs is determined to form a list of supplementary rules to standardize the provision and quality of residential care homes by 2017 (Ministry of Civil Affairs, 2013c), before those rules are actually formed, it is subject to municipal governments' discretion to develop temporal-local rules or remain merely reliant on the old 'Two gui fan, One biao zhun' to regulate the operation of residential care homes. While this may allow flexibility as individual municipalities can develop rules that suit their needs, China is still left without a comprehensive and unified regulatory standards and supervision mechanism at national level to ensure proper governance in residential care homes. Nonetheless, the following sections will critically examine the recent revised or enacted laws and rules that aim to protect the rights of institutionalized older persons.

Law on Protection of the Rights and Interests of the Elderly 2012

The *LPRIE* was first enacted by the NPCSC in 1996 to stipulate the state's undertaking to develop policy on protecting older persons in accordance with the *Constitution*. It is applicable to all citizens aged 60 and above. At that time, the protection focused only on elders' rights to obtain material assistance from the state (social security), receive maintenance and support from families, and participate in social development. It was only in 2012 that the right to residential care was included to advance care for older persons.

Older persons' right to residential care is now endorsed in 15 provisions of *LPRIE*, specifically in the chapter on social services. Yet these provisions are nothing more than simple directives to command various government departments, through incentive-driven policy, to competently equip the state with sufficient professional, technological, and regulatory standards to provide residential care. Under *LPRIE*, the registration requirements for establishing a residential care home are only specified in the briefest of terms while the scope and the methods of supervision by the Civil Affairs Department of the People's Government are unclear and abstruse. Without any detailed specifications, it simply invests the 'relevant departments' of the State Council with the power, and their own discretion, to formulate rules to regulate the construction of care service facilities for older persons, to form category regulations for residential care homes, and to assess and maintain the provision and quality of service (Article 42).

China has missed the propitious opportunity to take advantage of the inherent legal authority bestowed upon *LPRIE* as a piece of national legislation to establish mechanisms for protecting the fundamental rights of older persons in need of and living in residential care homes. As a result, only a catch-all term is being enacted – 'the residential care institution and their staff shall not in any way infringe the rights and interests of the older persons' (Article 47). Residential care homes that fail to comply will attract civil or criminal liability according to the law (Article 79) and the person in charge will be subject to disciplinary action (Article 80), but nothing more. The ambiguity and incomprehensibility of *LPRIE* inevitably means that it fails to serve as a robust backbone for formulating the regulatory standards in the *Permission Rule* and the *Administration Rule*.

Rules for the Permission to Establish Elderly Service Institutions 2013

The *Permission Rule* is applicable to all institutions that provide both 'accommodation' and 'care services' to older persons, but does not include day care centres or mutual aid service centres. Nor does the rule provide clinical care classification for older persons with varying degrees of functional dependencies, as all residential care homes are seen as a unified category of service provider. There are six eligibility criteria for establishing a residential care home: (1) a proper name, address, institutional charter, and management system; (2) basic living spaces that comply with national environmental protection, fire safety, health, and epidemic prevention requirements; (3) administrative, technical, and frontline staff who can provide care; (4) adequate financial capital and resources; (5) a minimum of ten care beds; and (6) adherence to other laws and conditions. Clearly, the *Permission Rule* is not an adequate regulatory standard, as no further elaborations or stipulations are offered as to how to achieve each criterion. Before other supplementary standards are formed, the execution of the *Permission Rule* is subject to the discretion of municipal governments to set their own standards, and such inadequacies have led to unpredictable enforcement of the approval and renewal of licences, and the forfeiting of those granted to service providers that do not comply with the legal standards.

China seems to have deliberately set low establishment criteria in order to accelerate the provision rate of residential care services and thereby fulfil the national '9064' care agenda for older persons (State Council, 2013). Without comprehensive supervisory standards, however, some of the low requirements may become mere expediencies for a prospective service provider, and not necessarily benefit the older persons. For instance, the *Permission Rule* does not explicitly state the required composition of the residential care team in terms of number and ratio, the required level of training for each category of care worker, or the required tasks that individual care staff should undertake. Only limited and vague workforce standards can be found in the *Basic Standard for Social Welfare Institutions for the Elderly* formed earlier in 2001, which declares that facilities serving older persons with special nursing needs (i.e. totally dependent or paralyzed older persons) should have one doctor and a 'corresponding number' of nurses and support staff, where the 'corresponding number' depends solely on the capabilities needed to fulfil the required standard of care. Without a standardized ratio composition for residential care teams, means that it is highly doubtful that institutionalized older persons are being cared for by qualified, professional, and ethical staff. Undoubtedly, the *Permission Rule* was enacted with the purpose of driving up service provision rates by allowing service providers with limited experience, capital, resources, and personnel to enter the residential care home market (Cheung, 2013). The absence of well-defined workforce requirements and clear quality standards jeopardizes the safety and lives of those dependent on residential care.

Rules for the Administration of Elderly Care Institutions 2013

The *Administration Rule* was promulgated on the same date as the *Permission Rule* in 2013. It only contains 36 short articles, but aims at standardizing the operation, maintenance, and management of residential care homes. The scope generally includes service provisions, maintenance of service standards, record keeping, regulations for safety, fire, and health, the employment of qualified staff, and the provision of training in professional ethics and internal management. Not surprisingly, and similar to other regulatory laws and rules, the *Administration Rule* is written in broad and vague terms, and includes a wide variety of regulations in a short piece of legislation. Like *LPRIE*, it states only the functions of residential care homes without providing proper provisional guidelines and standards.

With no stipulation of a specific standard or guideline, municipal governments have great discretion to devise their own supplementary rules to establish their own form of service monitoring. Even though the *Administration Rule* devotes a chapter to inspection and supervision, it does not set out a standardized means of inspection. Individual inspecting authorities are left with options to choose between written inspection, inspection on the spot, or other means (Article 28). Although the *Administration Rule* also endows the Civil Affairs Department with the role of ombudsman to receive and handle complaints about residential care homes, the stipulated monitoring mechanism is written in vague terms. Generally, it states that the Civil Affairs Department should establish reporting and complaint systems for the management of service institutions for older persons (Article 31). Without precise rules to set up various service standards and a comprehensive inspection mechanism, the regulation of residential care homes depends solely on municipal governments' judgment and decision to implement the rules. No standardized control of service quality exists at national level that can safeguard older persons from mistreatment and abuse. Yet, one merit is to mandate publishing the inspection report to the public (Article 28) and recommend involvement of older persons in supervision of the management and services rendered by residential care homes (Article 26).

In terms of enforcement strategies, China tends to adopt a compliance model categorized by Day and Klein in 1987 (Day & Klein, 1987). Instead of strict adherence to the 'black letter law' for punishing wrongdoing, the government would negotiate and bargain with the service providers to improve the situation. Rectification of a situation takes precedence over punishment and revocation of licence. Under the ascendency of *LPRIE*, the *Permission Rule* provides no punishment for service providers who establish a residential care home without proper licensing or compliance to licensing standards. The licensing authority will only instruct service providers to rectify the situation, unless the violation constitutes a crime, affects the administrative provisions of public security, or causes personal injury or property damage. The same is applied in treating discovery of wrongdoing stipulated in the *Administration Rule*, such as failure to provide a service in compliance with the standards and regulations of the state and discrimination against, insult, abuse, or abandonment of the aged, as well as other violations of their legitimate rights and interests (Article 33 of the *Administration Rule*). Rectification of the situation is again the first consideration. A fine up to CNY 30,000 can be imposed if the situation is serious. And of course service providers would receive punishment if an act constitutes a criminal offence. There is, however, nothing about making the revocation of licence as punishment for discovered non-compliance of regulations during the inspection under the *Administration Rule*. Definitely, the *Permission Rule* reserves the licensing department power to withdraw the permission licence of a residential care home for certain stipulated situations, such as obtaining a licence in improper ways and permission has been given to a residential care home in non-compliance with regulations (Article 23 of the *Permission Rule*). In fact, there is no further specification as to when the revocation mechanism will be invoked. The licensing authorities are vested with discretion to decide upon the circumstances. While negotiation and collaboration may consequentially assist the growth of residential care service, without clear guidelines, improper exercise of such discretion may put older persons at risk of mistreatment and abuse.

Other remedies for maltreatment

In situations where an institutionalized elder's rights have been infringed upon, apart from filing a complaint to the Department of Civil Affairs, according to the recently enacted *Tort Law of the People's Republic of China*, the individual can also file a private lawsuit for compensation. Adopted by the NPCSC on 26 December 2009 and in force since 1 July 2010, this legislation provides another level of protection for older persons against medical malpractice, negligence, and any other form of maltreatment. According to the White Paper – The Development of China's Undertakings for the Aged 2006, the People's Court gives priority to lawsuits concerning seniors' support and medical care, and takes seriously the handling of cases of mistreatment, abandonment, and harm of seniors, as well as crimes infringing upon senior citizens' rights of person and property. Some grassroots people's courts have set up 'senior tribunals' to handle civil cases involving older persons. Furthermore, the Supreme People's Court of China has formulated regulations on judicial assistance, and on postponement, reduction, or exemption from court costs for poor senior citizens (Information Office of the State Council, 2006). In appropriate cases, individuals can launch administrative reconsiderations or administrative litigation to launch a retrospective review of the conduct of an administrative organ.

Incongruity between protection and action in residential care

As the previous sections have shown, broad and vague regulatory rules prescribing no unified regulatory standards and supervision mechanism at national level in turn assume the municipal government's responsibility to formulate its own rules for implementation. Incomprehensive guidelines as well as the vested discretion leave a loophole for superficial implementation of the aforesaid laws and rules, which sequentially put older persons in residential care homes at risk of mistreatment of abuse. Our clinical field observations of the management and service provisions of residential care homes in the city of Xiangyang – the second biggest city in the province of Hubei, together with various reports of neglect and abuse in residential care homes in other major cities in China, provide illustrations of the deprivation of older peoples' rights to appropriate care, self-determination, autonomy, and dignity during life's most vulnerable moments.

Deprivation of rights to appropriate care

The loose legal-regulatory framework of residential care, and the qualification of care workers, or lack thereof, pose an immense challenge to the safeguarding of older persons' right to appropriate care. According to a 2005 survey that investigated the educational background of administrators and frontline workers of 28 residential care homes in Shanghai (Wu, Carter, Goins *et al.*, 2005), most administrators had only basic general education with no specialized training in social work, nursing, or geriatrics; while most frontline workers were laid-off workers of state-run factories and migrant workers from rural villages, who similarly had no training in care for older persons. The shortage of qualified care staff is common and widespread. Feng *et al.* (2011) reported that less than one-third of all residential care facilitates in Nanjing employed a professional nurse or a qualified physician, and that in Beijing most residents of government-sponsored nursing homes experienced great dissatisfaction with their care due to the lack of adequately trained staff.

It is important to note that this evidence is taken from major developed cities in China. One can only imagine the deprived state of residential care in smaller cities with lower levels of economic development. Our in-depth interview with the owner of a 20-bed private nursing home in Xiangyang showed the worrying reality. We were told that though she had not even completed primary school, she was the staff member most competent to manage and prepare her residents' daily medication because all the other workers had difficulties sorting and counting the pills. Limited by their education as well as their lack of general knowledge in care for older persons, these workers even assigned nicknames to residents to facilitate care coordination. An old man was named 'little lobster' given the Chinese harmonic that means short, blind, and deaf. Clearly, the right to appropriate care for this gentleman and many other nursing home residents is seriously undermined by the shortage of qualified care workers for older persons.

Apart from an incompetent workforce, dependent older people are further deprived of appropriate care due to the lack of an adequate health assessment and care management system. In 2011, a lawsuit was brought in the city of Lechang, Guangdong Province, where the son of a nursing home resident accused the home of medical negligence, which had resulted in his mother wandering in the woods and dying of hypothermia on the mountain (Chinanews, 2013). The nursing home refuted the accusation and claimed that the son should take full responsibility as he had concealed his mother's history of mental illness. Regardless of who was at fault, this lawsuit clearly illustrates that the nursing home did not conduct a thorough assessment of the resident's psychological health or cognitive acuity before admission, failed to provide regular checkups and assessments, and lacked competent staff to identify mental health risks. In fact, among most residential care homes in China, residents are usually asked to do nothing more than fill out simple forms that elicit their health conditions and care needs, and are not required to provide formal proofs of physical and mental fitness by a licensed physician.

The Lechang incident, and many other similar ones, unveil systemic discrimination against frail and highly dependent older persons, who are often denied residential care. The service agreements between care homes and their residents usually contain unfair clauses that allow homes to refuse or terminate care to older persons who are diagnosed with mental illness or exhibit any signs of behavioural problems. Older persons in poor health are usually excluded from waiting lists for residential care, and this is especially the case for government-owned homes, the two biggest government-owned residential care homes in Beijing clearly state that they only accept older persons who are 'independent in self-care'. According to Feng *et al.* (2011), the percentage of residents who are independent in daily functioning comprised 61% of all government facilities and only 36% among non-government facilities. In addition, they observed no significant differences in staffing across different types of home, indicating that non-government facilities have a higher case mix but fewer resources. Such inequality due to health discrimination clearly deprives older persons of their right to physical and psychological well-being as well as access to adequate residential care.

Deprivation of rights to self-determination, autonomy, and dignity

As it is stated in the *European Charter of the Rights and Responsibilities of Older People in Need of Long-term Care and Assistance* despite increasing functional dependency, the right of older persons to make their own life choices and care decisions should always be respected and never undermined, unless they become mentally incapacitated. While the *General Principles of Civil Law of the People's Republic of China* (2009) permit granting guardianship of an older person to his or her family, the law is only applicable when one is mentally incapacitated. However, upon examining the articles of numerous residency agreements provided by several government-owned residential care homes in Xiangyang, our team has identified numerous loopholes that clearly violate elders' right to self-determination and autonomy even though they are of sound mind. A consistent finding across different residency agreements is the non-negotiable requirement of a third-party guarantor as a condition of admission. The guarantor, usually a statutory maintenance promisor or a family member, functions eerily similarly to the custodian of a minor: they can make major decisions about the care of an older person resident through consultation with the nursing home, without first consulting the resident. In the agreement used by a major government-owned residential care home with 850 beds, one article clearly states that 'the resident, *with the permission of his/her guarantor*, has the right to go out'. Our field observation team met Mrs Wu, who, despite being cognitively eloquent and physically able, was not allowed to take part in the spring outing organized by her nursing home because her guarantor did not approve it. The nursing home told her that they did not want to be held responsible if she accidently fell or became ill during the outing since she was already over the age of 85. Mrs Wu was devastated and found crying in her room, writing a poem to express her sorrow and grief: '*Time, like a knife for slaughtering a pig, has turned me from an energetic young girl to an old witch covered with wrinkles. I am alone.*' In the name of safety, institutionalized older persons are often deprived of their freedom as their right to life choices is transferred to a third party to ensure that residential care homes are released from responsibility for potential consequences.

Furthermore, older persons who are dependent on residential care have no right to make their own care decisions or to engage in advance care planning, as such decisions are made between the guarantor and the residential care home in accordance with most residency agreements. While advance care planning and advance directives are increasingly popular in the West and among most developed countries, because they serve to empower older persons with dignity by respecting their choices and preferences for end-of-life care (Ho, Chan, Leung *et al.*, 2013; Ho, Leung, Tse, *et al.*, 2013), no effective action has been taken to establish similar legislation in China. Although the Beijing Living Will Promotion Association was established in 2013 to promote the ideals of 'living and dying with dignity', advance care planning and advance directives are still new concepts that have yet to be widely recognized. Our field observation team met Mrs Liu, who, having witnessed the pain and suffering of aggressive treatments that temporarily maintained the survival of her fellow nursing home residents, desired to set up her own advance directive so that she would not need to suffer from futile treatments if she fell seriously ill and unconscious. Mrs Liu told the nursing home that she could not bear the idea of being hooked up to machines and wished for a peaceful and dignified death. In response, the nursing home told her that if 'that day' came, they would consult her son in making such decisions. Mrs Liu turned to her son to express her will, but was told not to be paranoid because 'that day' was not coming anytime soon. Mrs Liu persisted in writing her own living will, but the nursing home affirmed that by convention they would still follow her son's wish.

To die in peace and with dignity is a basic and universal human right, and everyone should be able to engage in advance care planning and to establish their own advance directives. Under current practices, institutionalized older persons who are cognitively astute are denied this fundamental right; they are not even allowed to make the simplest care decision on their own. Clearly, the present regime of residential care in China has failed to ensure institutionalized elders' right to self-determination, autonomy, and, ultimately, dignity.

Conclusion and recommendations

China's commitment to taking care of its rapidly ageing population through the provision of sufficient long-term care services is incontrovertible and honourable. However, such commitment must build upon on a robust legal-regulatory framework of residential care, ensuring the quality of service rendered to institutionalized older persons and to protect their basic human rights. In order to resolve the dilemma of social justice and health equity for the aged, it is imperative to standardize regulatory mechanisms that govern residential care at a national level.

Such legislation needs to expand beyond vague delineations to provide clear definition of the duties, responsibilities, and operational standards of residential care homes, as well as to impart decisive standardization of the training, skill levels, and professional ethics required of all care workers for older persons. Furthermore, it is of the utmost importance to establish a comprehensive monitoring and auditing system to ensure that residential homes and their workers respect and uphold elders' right to appropriate care, self-determination, autonomy, and dignity.

Perhaps the most immediate solution can begin by developing and enacting a professional code of conduct to tighten current regulation of residential care homes, providing clear and robust guidelines for daily operation, care coordination, and management. First and foremost, residential care homes need to be categorized according to the types of care they provide with reference to the dependency levels of their residents. Second, the law should clearly stipulate the corresponding ratio requirements between professional and allied health workers and residents, while setting out the exact duties required from different levels of care staff. Third, regular training and supervision should be provided and made mandatory so as to ensure and enhance the quality of care provided. Fourth, the central government should set national standards for minimum quality of care and quality of life in residential care settings and a quality framework to enforce quality standards.

As suggested by Feng *et al.* (2014), although a nation-wide approach to monitoring the provision and quality of all residential care homes may be overly ambitious for a large and varied country like China, initial steps to establish a facility-level data collection system should be taken so as to foster evidence-based practice and evidence-informed policymaking. Demonstration projects in major cities using standardized health assessments and online reporting systems can be a start. To date, Senior Service Informatics Development Committee (SSIDC), which are managed by the China Association of Social Welfare, is taking the lead in developing a comprehensive data collection system to assist regular oversight of service provision, commissioned by the Ministry of Civil Affair. It was reported that Beijing, Jiangsu, and Anhui were selected to participate in the pilot study and 100 demonstration facilities from each province have completed data collection at the end of 2012. Although a nation-wide assessment and online reporting system is not ready yet, it is evident that the government has realized the importance of data and real time information in regulating and directing more person-centred care in residential care homes.

In essence, long-term care in China has expanded rapidly and purposefully within the past decade. Yet the challenge of governance of residential care requires further enhancement of services for older persons and further implementation of human rights laws, both of which would be impossible without an unshakeable commitment to human dignity. The success of care for the ageing population of the People's Republic of China now rests in the fundamental basis of social justice and health equity among all of its citizenry.

References

AGE Platform Europe. (2010). European Charter of the Rights and Responsibilities of Older People in Need of Long-term Care and Assistance. Retrieved from http://www.age-platform.eu/images/stories/22204_AGE_charte_europeenne_EN_v4.pdf

Chan, C.L.W., Ho, A.H.Y., Leung, P.P.Y., Chochinov, H.M., Neimeyer, R.A., Pang, S.M.C., & Tse, D.M.W. (2012). The Blessings and Curses of Filial Piety on Dignity at the End-of-Life: Lived Experience of Hong Kong Chinese Adult Children Caregivers. *Journal of Ethnic and Cultural Diversity in Social Work*, 21, 277–296.

Chan, K.Y., Wang, W., Wu, J.J., Liu, L., Theodoratou, E., Car, J., Middleton, L., Russ, T.C., Deary, I.J., Campbell, H., Wang, W. & Rudan, I. (2013). Epidemiology of Alzheimer's Disease and Other Forms of Dementia in China, 1990–2010: A Systematic Review and Analysis. *The Lancet*, 318 (9882), 2016–2023.

Chen, S. (1996). *Social Policy of the Economic State and Community Care in Chinese Culture: Aging, Family, Urban Change, and the Socialist Welfare Pluralism*. Brookfield, VT: Avebury.

Cheung, C.K., & Kwan, A.Y.H. (2009). The Erosion of Filial Piety by Modernisation in Chinese Cities. *Ageing and Society*, 29(2), 179–198.

Cheung, S.F. (2013). *Interpretation of the Rules for the Administration of Elderly Care Institutions*. Ministry of Civil Affairs. Retrieved from http://fss.mca.gov.cn/article/ylpx/pxkj/201307/20130700487896.shtml

Chinanews. (19 April 2013). *Residential Care Home Elderly Frozen to Death in the Woods, Responsibility Lies with Elder's Son for Hiding her Mental Health History* (in Chinese). Retrieved from http://www.chinanews.com/sh/2013/04-19/4747421.shtml

Chow, N.W.S. (2006). The Practice of Filial Piety and its Impact on Long-Term Care Policies for Elderly People in Asian Chinese Communities. *Asian Journal Of Genontology and Geriatrics*, 1(1), 31–35.

Chow, N.W.S., & Lum, T.Y.S. (2008). Trends in Family Attitudes and Values in Hong Kong. Report Submitted to the Central Policy Unit (CPU) of HKSAR Government. Retrieved from http://www.cpu.gov.hk/doc/tc/research_reports/20080822%20Trends%20in%20family%20attitudes%20and%20values%20in%20Hong%20Kong.pdf

Day, P. & Klein, R. (1987). The Regulation of Nursing Homes: A Comparative Perspective. *The Milbank Quarterly*, 65(3), 303–347.

Delisle, J. (2013). From Economic Development to What – and Why? China's Evolving Legal and Political Engagement with International Human Rights Norms. In G. Yu (ed.), *Rethinking Law and Development: The Chinese Experience*. New York: Routledge, pp. 107–145.

Ding, H. (2011). China's 'Socializing Social Welfare' Policy: A Study on Service Quality in Society-Run Homes for the Aged in Beijing. *China Journal of Social Work*, 4(2), 137–151.

Feng, X.L., Pang, M., & Beard, J. (2014). Health System Strengthening and Hypertension Awareness, Treatment and Control: Data from the China Health and Retirement Longitudinal Study. *Bulletin of the World Health Organization*, 92, 29–41.

Feng, Z., Zhan, H.J., Feng, X., Liu, C., Sun, M., & Mor, V. (2011). An Industry in the Making: The Emergence of Institutional Elder Care in Urban China. *Journal of the American Geriatrics Society*, 59(4), 738–744.

Feng, Z., Gung, X., Feng, X., Liu, C., Zhan, H.J., & Mor, V. (2014). Long-term Care in China: Reining in Market Forces through Regulatory Oversight. In V. Mor, T. Leone, & A. Maresso (eds), *Regulating Long-Term Care Quality: An International Comparison*, pp. 409–443.

Gu, S., & Liang, J. (2000). China: Population Aging and Old Age Support. In V.L. Bengtson, K. Kim, G.C. Myers, & K. Eun (eds), *Aging in East and West: Families, States, and the Elderly*. New York: Springer, pp. 59–93.

Guan, X., Zhan, H. J., & Liu, G. (2007). Institutional and Individual Autonomy: Investigating Predictors of Attitudes Toward Institutional Care in China. *International Journal on Aging and Human Development*, 64(1), 83–107.

Ho, A.H.Y., Chan, C.L.W., Leung, P.P.Y., Chochinov, H.M., Neimeyer, R.A., Pang, S.M.C., & Tse, D.M.W. (2013). Living and Dying with Dignity in Chinese Society: Perspectives of Older Palliative Care Patients in Hong Kong. *Age and Ageing*, 42(4), 455–461.

Ho, A.H.Y., Leung, P.P.Y., Tse, D.M.W., Pang, S.M.C., Chochinov, H.M., Neimeyer, R.A., & Chan, C.L.W. (2013). Dignity amidst Liminality: Suffering within Healing among Chinese Terminal Cancer Patients. *Death Studies*, 37(10), 953–970.

Ikels, C. (1993). Chinese Kinship and the State: Shaping of Policy for the Elderly. In G. Maddox & M.P. Lawton (eds), *Annual Review of Gerontology and Geriatrics*. New York: Springer, pp. 123–146.

Information Office of the State Council. (1991). *White Paper: Human Rights in China*. Beijing: Information Office of the State Council. Retrieved from http://www.china.org.cn/e-white/7/index.htm

Information Office of the State Council. (2000). *White Paper: 50 Years of Progress in China's Human Rights*. Beijing: Information Office of the State Council. Retrieved from http://www.gov.cn/english/official/2005-07/27/content_17730.htm

Information Office of the State Council. (2005). *White Paper: China's Progress in Human Rights in 2004*. Beijing: Information Office of the State Council. Retrieved from http://www.gov.cn/english/official/2005-07/28/content_18115.htm

Information Office of the State Council. (2006). *The White Paper: The Development of China's Undertakings for the Aged*. Beijing: Information Office of the State Council. Retrieved from http://www.china.org.cn/english/aged/192020.htm

Information Office of the State Council. (2013). *White Paper: Progress in China's Human Rights in 2012*. Beijing: Information Office of the State Council. Retrieved from http://news.xinhuanet.com/english/china/2013-05/14/c_132380706.htm

Kinsella, K., & He, W. (2009). *An Aging World: 2008*. US. Census Bureau, International Population Reports, P95/09–1. Washington, DC: US Government Printing Office.

Ministry of Civil Affairs. (1999). *Provisional Measures for the Management of Social Welfare Institutions*. (in Chinese). Beijing: Ministry of Civil Affairs. Retrieved from http://www.mca.gov.cn/article/zwgk/fvfg/zdshbz/200711/20071110003485.shtml

Ministry of Civil Affairs. (2001). *Basic Standard for Social Welfare Institutions for the Elderly* (MZ008–2001) (in Chinese). Beijing: Ministry of Civil Affairs. Retrived from http://fss.mca.gov.cn/article/ywbz/200712/20071210005095.shtml

Ministry of Civil Affairs. (2009). *Circular on conducting inspections on the implementation of 'Two gui fan, One biao zhun' in aged care institutions* (in Chinese). Beijing: Ministry of Civil Affairs. Retrieved from http://kjbz.mca.gov.cn/article/mzbzxg/201106/20110600159044.shtml

Ministry of Civil Affairs. (2013a). *China Civil Affairs' Statistical Yearbook* (Statistics of China Social Services) (in Chinese). Beijing: China Statistics Press.

Ministry of Civil Affairs. (2013b). *Notice on Implementation of the Rules for the Permission to Establish Elderly Service Institutions and the Rules for the Administration of Elderly Care Institutions* (in Chinese). Beijing: Ministry of Civil Affairs. Retrieved from http://fss.mca.gov.cn/article/ylpx/flfg/201307/20130700488052.shtml

Ministry of Civil Affairs. (2013c). *Plan for Standardizing Elderly Service Institutions (2013–2017)* (in Chinese). Beijing: Ministry of Civil Affairs. Retrieved from http://www.mca.gov.cn/article/mxht/mtgz/201312/20131200561691.shtml

Ministry of Civil Affairs. (2013d). *Rules for the Administration of Elderly Care Institutions*. (in Chinese). Beijing: Ministry of Civil Affairs. Retrieved from http://www.mca.gov.cn/article/zwgk/fvfg/shflhshsw/201306/20130600480076.shtml

Ministry of Civil Affairs. (2013e). *Rules for the Permission to Establish Elderly Service Institutions*. (in Chinese). Beijing: Ministry of Civil Affairs. Retrieved from http://www.mca.gov.cn/article/zwgk/fvfg/shflhshsw/201306/20130600480075.shtml

Ministry of Construction and Ministry of Civil Affairs (1999). *The Code for Design of Buildings for Elderly Persons* (JGJ 122–99) (in Chinese). Beijing: Ministry of Construction and Ministry of Civil Affairs. Retrived from http://www.yanglao.com.cn/article/6488.html

Ministry of Labour and Social Security. (2002). *The National Standards for Old-Age Care Workers* (in Chinese). Beijing: Ministry of Labour and Social Security. Retrieved from http://wenku.baidu.com/view/8bdb93d784254b35eefd34d9.html

National Human Rights Action Plan of China [NHRAP], 2009–2012.

National People's Congress. (2004). *Constitution of the People's Republic of China*. Beijing: National People's Congress. Retrieved from http://www.npc.gov.cn/englishnpc/Constitution/node_2825.htm

National People's Congress. (2009). *General Principles of Civil Law of the People's Republic of China*. Beijing: National People's Congress. Retrieved from http://www.lawinfochina.com/display.aspx?id=1165&lib=law

Qu, X. (2009). Major Theories on Human Rights in the 30 Years of Reform and Opening-Up. In X. Xu (ed.), *Human Rights Research* (Vol. 8). Jinan: Shandong People's Press, pp. 1–66.

Shang, X. (2001). Moving toward a Multi-Level and Multi-Pillar System: Changes in Institutional Care in Two Chinese Cities. *Journal of Social Policy*, 30(2), 259–281.

Sixth National Population Census Office of State Council. (2010). *Major Figures on the 2010 Population Census of China* (in Chinese). China Statistics Press.

Spector, W.D., Fleishman, J.A., Pezzin, L.E., & Spillman, B.C. (2001). *Characteristics of Long-Term Care Users* (D.o.H.C.S. Committee on Improving Quality in Long-Term Care, Trans.). Rockville, MD: The Institute of Medicine.

Standing Committee of the National People's Congress. (2009). *Tort Law of the People's Republic of China*. Beijing: Standing Committee of the National People's Congress. Retrieved from http://www.lawinfochina.com/display.aspx?lib=law&id=7846&CGid=

Standing Committee of the National People's Congress. (2012). *Law on Protection of the Rights and Interests of the Elderly*. Beijing: Standing Committee of the National People's Congress. Retrieved from http://www.lawinfochina.com/display.aspx?lib=law&id=1159&CGid=

State Council. (2010). *The National Development Mid- and Long-Term Framework on Human Capital 2010–2020* (in Chinese) Beijing: State Council. Retrieved from http://www.mca.gov.cn/article/zwgk/fvfg/zh/201110/20111000185430.shtml

State Council. (2011a). *The 12th Five-Year Developemnt Plan (2011–2015)* (in Chinese) Beijing: State Council. Retrived from http://www.cmab.gov.hk/doc/12th_5yrsplan_outline_full_text.pdf

State Council. (2011b). *Notice on the Issuance of the 12th Five-Year National Population Development Plan* (in Chinese). Retrieved from http://www.nhfpc.gov.cn/guihuaxxs/s3585u/201305/358859f35ff64c65a2ca9264d6e30af2.shtml

State Council. (2013). *State Council Opinions on Accelerating the Development of Elderly Services* (in Chinese). Beijing: State Council. Retrieved from http://www.gov.cn/zwgk/2013-09/13/content_2487704.htm

Sun, P. (2014). *Human Rights Protection System in China*. Berlin Heidelberg: Springer.

United Nations. (2013). *World Population Prospects: The 2012 Revision.* New York: United Nations, Department of Economic and Social Affairs. Retrieved from http://data.un.org/Data.aspx?d=PopDiv&f=variableID%3A44

Vocational Skill Assessment and Guidance Centre of Ministry of Civil Affairs. (2014). Seeking Opinions on Report of Vocational Assessment of Old-Age Care Worker 2013. *Information of Vocation Training and Assessment of Old-Age Care Worker*, 1. Retrieved from http://jnjd.mca.gov.cn/article/zyjd/ylhly/201401/20140100572623.shtml

Wong, Y.C., & Leung, J. (2012). Long-Term Care in China: Issues and Prospects. *Journal of Gerontological Social Work*, 55(7), 570–586.

Wu, B., Carter, M. W., Goins, R. T., & Cheng, C. (2005). Emerging Services for Community-based Long-term Care in Urban China: A Systematic Analysis of Shanghai's Community-based Agencies. *Journal of Aging and Social Policy*, 17(4), 37–60.

Wu, B., Mao, Z., & Xu, Q. (2008). Institutional Care for Elders in Rural China. *Journal of Aging and Policy*, 20, 218–239.

Wu, Y., & Dang, J. (2013). *China Report of the Development on Aging Cause.* Beijing: Social Sciences Academic Press.

Zhan, H.J., Luo, B., & Chen, Z. (2012). Institutional Elder Care in China. In S. Chen & J.L. Powell (eds), *Aging in China: Implications to Social Policy of a Changing Economic State.* New York: Springer, pp. 237–260.

Zhang, C. (2013). Chronic Diseases, Labour Suppply and Medical Expenditure at Older Age: Evidence from China. *Frontiers of Economics in China*, 8(2), 233–259.

5 The residential care of older people in England and the special relevance of dignity and human rights

Helen Meenan

Introduction

In recent times the British media has often highlighted the poor, negligent and some-times fatal care of older people. This raises questions about how we deliver care to older people and how that care is regulated and supervised. This chapter will delve beneath the headlines to ascertain if this initially negative image is justified and will try to present a more balanced picture. During the period of writing, one tell-ing document and a telling story were published in England. A report by Baroness Kingsmill CBE into the working conditions of workers in the care sector across the UK, describes exploitative work practices affecting the 'almost invisible' 1.8 million care workers in the UK. In it she describes how care workers are under-valued, under-paid and under-trained.[1] The English media gleefully highlighted the story of Bernard Jordan, aged 89, a navy veteran who ran away from his care home, to attend the D-Day anniversary celebrations in Normandy. Typically, the stories were titled 'The great escape' and claimed that Mr Jordan had been banned by his resi-dential care home from attending and related how he left the home with his medals hidden under his coat.[2] This story raises questions about a resident's relationship with his care home and the perceptions and realities of the roles on both sides.

The focus of this chapter is the residential care sector for older people in England, which is one of the four nations that comprise the UK, the others being Scotland, Wales and Northern Ireland. Facts and statistics will concern England alone, where possible. However, many statistics and trends are only available for England and Wales together and others are only available for the UK as a whole. This chapter will attempt to show that despite a recent painful period in the resi-dential care sector, there may now be hope for a brighter future. This hope has its

1 The Kingsmill Review: Taking Care: An independent report into working conditions in the Care Sector by Baroness Denise Kingsmill CBE, 2014, http://www.yourbritain.org.uk/uploads/editor/files/The_Kingsmill_Review_-_Taking_Care_-_Final_2.pdf.

2 While he believed that staff would be displeased if he revealed his plans, the home later clarified that it had had not banned him from going but merely failed to get him a place on the official trip, *The Daily Telegraph*, Saturday, 7 June 2014.

seeds in the considerable spotlight shone on this sector and efforts to reform social care and its inspection systems. Change is also underway in law and regulation but until now it seems that English registration requirements may not have been rigorous enough and enforcement mechanisms have not produced a strong enough deterrent effect for care home owners, managers and staff. Despite everything, there is undoubtedly a good deal that other countries can learn from the English experience and innovations.

Part I: Population ageing in England

There are 53.9 million people living in England and there are 11.1 million people aged over 65 in the UK as a whole,[3] with the majority of these living in England and Wales. The proportion of the UK population aged 65+ will rise from 17.7% currently to 23.5% in 2034.[4] By 2050, one in four people in the UK will be over 65 but the fastest growing segment of the population is the over 85s, which will double in size by 2050. In 2010 there were 1.4 million people over 85 in the UK and this number is expected to grow to 3.6 million or nearly 5% of the population by 2035.[5] There is also significant growth in the oldest old. One in five 20 year olds born in the UK today is predicted to not only reach but to surpass 100 years of age.[6] The number of centenarians in the UK population was estimated at 12,640 in 2010 and is projected to reach 100,000 by 2035.[7]

This chapter will show that between the late 1950s and the mid-2000s, people entering residential care have become older. In addition, dementia has been growing and the Alzheimer's Society estimates that there will be over 1 million people in the UK with dementia by 2021 and this is expected to rise to 1.7 million by 2051. Dementia has been a rising issue on the political agenda in the UK since the 1990s (Johnson, Rolph and Smith, 2012).[8] These changes will produce direct consequences for the volume of care and the type of care needed; the number of people aged 65 and over with care and support needs is estimated to rise by 87 per cent between 2001 and 2051 (Equality and Human Rights Commission, 2009).

3 *Mid-2013 Population Estimates* UK Office for National Statistics, 2014.
4 Age UK, Factsheet *Later Life in the United Kingdom*, January 2015, p. 3.a.
5 ONS Statistical Bulletin, Older People's Day 2011, 29 September 2011, http://www.ons.gov.uk/ons/dcp171778_235000.pdf.
6 *Living Beyond 100 A report on Centenarians*, November 2011, ILC-UK, Valentina Serra, Jessica Watson, David Sinclair and Dylan Kneale, http://www.ilcuk.org.uk/images/uploads/publication-pdfs/LivingBeyond100Full_1.pdf.
7 ONS Statistical Bulletin, Older People's Day, 2011 Statistical Bulletin, http://www.ons.gov.uk/ons/dcp171778_235000.pdf.
8 So much so that the British Government hosted a G8 Dementia Summit in 2013 with the Prime Minister declaring that dementia has emerged as, 'the key health challenge of this generation requiring a global response', Andrew Sparrow, theGuardian.com 11 December 2013.

When does old age start in England?

If the World Health Organization reports that most developed countries have accepted 65 years as the definition of an older person,[9] how true is this for England? The answer to this question depends very much on the context. The age at which someone could claim their state pension was originally set at 65 for a man and 60 for a woman in 1925 and is now in the process of being equalised at 65 for both sexes by 2018 and at age 67 between 2026 and 2028.[10] The state pension age is now subject to review every five years with the next review due in 2017.[11] It is true that the original ages of 65 and 60, respectively for claiming a state pension were outdated and did not reflect gains of 20 years to the average lifespan since the 1950s (UN Report of the Second World Assembly on Ageing, 2002).[12] However, these ages were also accepted and were assumed to mark the commencement of old age in other fields such as social science and medical research (Janet Roebuck, 1979). Even now with a small increase bringing the state pension age up to 67, it still cannot be said that it necessarily marks when old age commences today.

In the UK self-perceptions of age and old age are growing in importance and deviate markedly from the modern state pension age. In one recent survey, British people saw middle-age as either starting at 53 or disappearing due to longer life and better health.[13] Another poll has revealed that the majority of people over 40 believe that old age starts at 80, reinforcing the idea that self-perceptions of age are very important at this moment in time.[14] Today it appears that state pension age is not automatically assumed to be the age at which old age commences in England. However, the Care Quality Commission (CQC), which regulates all adult care in England, classifies adult services, including residential care homes, by age for adults aged 18 to 65 years and adults over 65 years. This may well reflect regional variations in life expectancy throughout England, for example people in the north of England live shorter lives than those in the south,[15] and the impact of various health conditions on some adults.

9   WHO Health Statistics and Information systems Definition of an older or elderly person, http://www.who.int/healthinfo/survey/ageingdefnolder/en.

10 State Pension age timetables, https://www.gov.uk/government/uploads/system/uploads/attachment_data/file/310231/spa-timetable.pdf.

11 BBC, 'State pension age to be reviewed every five years', 14 January 2013, http://www.bbc.co.uk/news/business-20993027.

12 Madrid 8–12 April 2002, p. 5.

13 benenden health, 'Study reveals changing attitudes to "middle age"', 28 August 2013, https://www.benenden.co.uk/media-centre/study-reveals-changing-attitudes-to-middle-age.

14 Huffington Post, 20 February 2014, 'Old Age Doesn't Start Until 80, Study Finds'.

15 Office for National Statistics, 'Life expectancy at birth and at age 65 for local areas in England and Wales, 2009–11', http://www.ons.gov.uk/ons/rel/subnational-health4/life-expectancy-at-birth-and-at-age-65-by-local-areas-in-england-and-wales/2009-11/index.html.

Is there a caring culture in the UK?

At first sight there does not appear to be a strong cultural or familial tradition of caring for older parents and relatives in the UK. This can be attributed to a number of factors: the very independent nature of many adults, historically smaller numbers of children in recent decades and a greater emphasis on nuclear rather than extended families than in many other countries. The UK is also a large country with most of the population dispersed in large cities and much mobility throughout the life course for study and work and therefore geographical distance often separates family members and friends. However, the reality may at least partly belie this first impression. There are 6.5 million people in the UK who care for a loved one who is older, disabled or seriously ill and every day 6,000 people become informal carers (Carers UKa) with the number of people with caring duties set to rise from one in eight adults to six in ten adults. In our lifetime the number of carers will rise to 9 million people (Carers UKa).

However, a recent study revealed that two-thirds of British people feel they could do more to take care of elderly relatives, a third believing they did not visit them enough and some only seeing elderly relatives a couple of times a year. The main reasons given were busy lives and living too far away.[16] This may go some way to explaining the 'epidemic' of loneliness affecting older people in the UK which has recently emerged as a major issue. A million older people in the UK have not spoken to anyone for a month and 5 million older people consider a pet or the television to be their main companion.[17] It may also be relevant that nearly half of all people aged 75 and over live alone in the UK today (Age UK, 2015).

The nature of residential care

It is estimated that there are 12,525 residential homes and 5,153 nursing homes in the UK, housing approximately 405,000 people aged 65 and over (Age UK, 2015). Residential care for older people broadly comprises two categories: nursing homes which are also known as care homes with nursing and provide 24-hour qualified nursing care and residential care homes which provide general care. The growth in the proportion of older people in the population and the oldest old is predicted to increase both the demand for residential care and the complexity of care needs in England.[18] Traditionally, three sectors have been the main providers of residential care for older people in England and the UK, the state through local authorities,

16 Cloudbuy, 'Carer's Week 2014: Busy Lives and Distance Make Caring Difficult', 10 June 2014, http://www.cloudbuy.com/news/carers-week-2014-busy-lives-distance-make-caring-difficult.html.

17 *The Times*, Thursday 19 June 2014 p. 4 and Age UK Later Life in the United Kingdom Factsheet, February 2015 at p. 22–23.b.

18 Royal College of Nursing, Policy Briefing 04/2010 Care Homes Under Pressure an England Report, http://www.rcn.org.uk/__data/assets/pdf_file/0006/314547/Policy_Report-Care_Homes_under_pressure_final_web.pdf at pp. 1, 3, 6 and 9.

the voluntary sector (non-profit and typically, for example, single religion, single gender or retirees from certain fields such as the cinema industry or the armed forces) and the private sector. Local authorities are no longer major providers of residential care but purchase much elder care provision from the private sector, which has become increasingly corporatised in recent years; the voluntary sector is interesting, although small it will be shown that it has been quite a stable source of residential care for older people (Johnson, Rolph and Smith, 2012).

The evolution of residential care in England

It may not be a stretch to say that a form of residential care has existed in England since the 10th century when the oldest recorded alms house was founded; alms houses were a refuge for the poor, including the old. The twelfth century saw early English hospitals accommodate older patients with specialist hospitals emerging to cater for 'the ailing aged pauper' (Midwinter, 2011). The late 1890s, when some aged paupers were accommodated in workhouses established under the Poor Law, is a reasonable staging post. Not least, because 4 per cent of people over 65 were resident in workhouses, which roughly equates with the percentage of over 65s in state supported residential care in the UK today.[19] Workhouses were generally grim institutions. However, then as now, public provision was only one source of residential care for older people together with private homes and alms houses (Lievesley, Crosby and Bowman, 2011).

Perhaps the richest source of recent historical research comes from a major study carried out in the 1950s by Peter Townsend, an eminent sociologist, who visited 173 residential care homes in England and Wales (Peter Townsend, 1962). This research is all the richer and more valuable for having been revisited by Johnson, Rolph and Randall in a book originally published in 2010, which gives us a healthy span of 50 years' reflection on the state of residential care for older people. Johnson and her team re-visited a small sample of homes from Townsend's study and made some valuable observations on continuity and change in this sector.

In the 1950s Townsend set himself the intriguing research question: 'Are long-stay institutions for old people necessary in our society and, if so, what form should they take?'[20] One of Townsend's most compelling findings was that 47% of the residents in former Public Assistance Institutions (PAIs), one form of public home for older people, were men who were living there because they had nowhere else to go. This contributed to his views that residential care for older people should be abandoned as the seriously unwell could stay in hospitals and nursing homes and the others could live in their own homes with some domiciliary support.[21] Another finding was the extreme disparities in size and quality between care homes. Some

19 *Ibid.*

20 Peter Townsend, *The Last Refuge: A Survey of Residential Institutions and Homes for the Aged in England and Wales* (London: Routledge and Kegan Paul, 1962) at p. 3.

21 As reported by Johnson, Rolph and Smith at p. 9; they also report that his views were regarded by some as anti-institutional, p. 10.

(the former PAIs) were located in large cities and accommodated more than 1,000 people often in dormitories.[22] Townsend found the majority of homes to be of poor quality; in general they were the local authority homes and the larger homes. By contrast some of the smaller homes provided a very high standard of care particularly in the voluntary sector, which Johnson, Rolph and Smith later found to be the most stable sector.[23] Of considerable interest is a further finding by Townsend that about half of the residents were not physically or mentally incapacitated, further feeding his belief that these residents did not necessarily need to live in aged care.[24]

Johnson, Rolph and Smith make several observations on how residential care has changed. Three are relevant here. The first was a shift in the provision of care from the public sector to the private and voluntary sectors and, the public sector now provides fewer care home places than either of them.[25] The second was the ageing of care home residents, the majority of residents are now over 85 compared with 42% of male residents and 54% of female residents who were over 80 in Townsend's survey.[26] The third is that generally care home residents are frailer today and this has implications for their independence and freedom compared with the 1950s when residents were positively encouraged to leave the home.[27] One of Johnson et al.'s most striking revelations was the near disappearance of shared bedrooms and of segregation by gender; today segregation is more likely to be according to functional ability.[28] The Johnson et al. study revealed a trend for specialisation in the surviving homes especially towards dementia care, but some homes that previously catered for one kind of community had relaxed their rules, for example to allow women to live there.[29] Johnson, Rolph and Smith also describe the corporatisation of care homes between 1988 and the late 1990s, when the major providers more than doubled their share of the for-profit care home market, reducing the number of owners in the care home sector.[30] Simultaneously many of the smaller homes and smaller nursing homes closed down.

Two particular issues that concerned Townsend were how to create a home from home and staff training. As regards the former, it seems that while people now have their own rooms and more privacy, the feeling of being part of a family which was common in many homes in the 1950s[31] is not necessarily the case today. Despite a number of architectural and other improvements, today's homes may feel a little institutional,[32] probably owing in part to the increased frailty of many residents. As regards training, Johnson reports Townsend's conclusion that

22 Johnson, Rolph and Smith supra at p. 7.
23 *Ibid.* at p. 9, p. 21 and p. 84.
24 *Ibid.* at p. 9.
25 *Ibid.* at p. 21.
26 *Ibid.* at pp. 20–21. They suggest that the ageing of the care home population has also changed the gender balance with far fewer male than female residents today at pp. 86–87.
27 *Ibid.* at pp. 91–93 and 155.
28 *Ibid.* at p. 113.
29 *Ibid.* at p. 83.
30 *Ibid.* at pp. 28–29.
31 *Ibid.* at p. 137.
32 *Ibid.* at pp. 125–126.

there was a 'woeful lack of training instruction' in the late 1950s in caring for elderly and frail people and that he recommended there should be at least one full-time qualified nurse for every four residents.[33] It is now clear that Townsend's recommendation was not taken up; the Royal College of Nursing has found that some care homes have as little as one registered nurse for every 35 patients in a day shift.[34] Nor was another one of Townsend's recommendations taken up, that of social science or social medicine qualifications for managers.[35]

Alternative models of care in England

Traditionally residential care for older people in England has connoted living in a residential care home, but a range of other options is available. Starting with home care, a user remains in her home and is visited by domiciliary carers who might assist with bathing, nutrition and so forth. Assisted living refers to a (smaller) rental or specially purchased property with communal services and leisure activities within the scheme. This may also be known as sheltered housing. Extra care or extra sheltered housing describes a user moving to a retirement village or community designed for older people, which also combines the independence of an appropriate dwelling with more advanced on-site care and communal services for when the older person can no longer live in their home. There are approximately 600,000 older people living in sheltered housing in the UK today.[36] Assisted living often facilitates the communal living of a diverse range of older people; it may also encourage independence for as long as possible.[37]

These models of care have the advantage of each person having their own front door, perhaps an unquantifiable psychological benefit. They generally facilitate couples living together for as long as possible and a certain degree of privacy, control and independence or certainly the important self-perception of these benefits. We shall see below that residential care homes and nursing homes are regulated by the CQC, as are the service users, but a key difference is that in extra care housing services, the care people receive is regulated by the CQC but the accommodation is not.[38] In the meantime, an upmarket magazine[39] recently featured

33 *Ibid.* at p. 103.
34 RCN Policy Unit, Policy Briefing 04/2010Care Homes Under Pressure – an England report, April 2010 at p. 10, http://www.rcn.org.uk/__data/assets/pdf_file/0006/314547/Policy_Report-Care_Homes_under_pressure_final_web.pdf.
35 Townsend *supra*, at p. 421.
36 Department for Communities and Local Government, 'Millions invested to create new wave of silver surfers', Wednesday, 13 January 2010, http://www.wired-gov.net/wg/wg-news-1.nsf/0/937 10FD3BF16CF40802576AA0042CA7B?OpenDocument.
37 Independent Age, Guide 30 Extra care housing 2012–13, at pp. 4 and 8, http://www.housingcare.org/downloads/kbase/2954.pdf.
38 From 1 April 2015, Regulation 1(1), Schedule 1, of the Health and Social Care Act 2008 (Regulated Activities) Regulations 2014, Statutory Instrument, No. 2936 2014, includes personal care by reason of old age, illness or disability in the activities regulated by the CQC, which replace Health and Social Care Act 2008 (Regulated Activities) Regulations.
39 *Tatler Magazine*, September 2014.

the top nursing and residential homes for older people in England, most of which are nearly double the cost of an average residential care home. Some of them still follow single religion, single gender or single former occupation recruitment. While they demonstrate a taste for expensive, high-end residential care for a small minority of older people[40] (in common with Israel, as described in this volume) the emphasis appears to be on style, tradition, leisure activities and a relaxed, happy and social environment. However, an intergenerational arts charity, *Magic Me*,[41] has been breathing new life into eight ordinary care homes in London by means of school children's visits, monthly cocktail parties and themed evenings.

Who pays for care?

The question of who should pay for long-term residential care was a major theme in the care of older people for a number of years (Sutherland, 1999; Wanless, 2006; Dilnot, 2011). In theory, care can be paid for in three ways. The state via local councils can pay for long-term care, people can pay for their own care (self-funders) and care can be paid for through a combination of state and private funding. If the care home costs more than the council will pay, a third party (typically a relative) is permitted to top up the care home fees on the older person's behalf. In practice, around 36% of long-term care is self-funded (CQC, 2012/13) and only 9.8% of places are funded by the local authority with some top up from a private source, such as a relative.[42]

The question of who pays for an older person's care has far-reaching human rights implications which will be discussed later in this chapter. For now, our starting point is that every older person in England is entitled to ask for a free assessment of their care needs, regardless of their financial circumstances (Age UK, 2013).[43] This is carried out by the local authority and if it decides that a person needs a place in a care home it will then carry out a financial assessment. At present, the National Health Service (NHS) is responsible for paying the full cost of care for residents who need to be in a home with nursing care for serious health reasons (NHS continuing healthcare) (Age UK, 2014). The NHS is also responsible for the costs of care provided by registered nurses in any kind of care home.[44]

Funding is undergoing change. As of April 2015 all councils in England will provide deferred payment agreements, so no one will have to sell their home to pay for their care during their lifetime, if their savings and investments (not including the value of their home or pension) are less than £23,250. In 2016, as a result of the phased implementation of the Care Act 2014, there will be a maximum limit of £72,000 on the amount of care costs a person will have to pay; any care

---

40 The report also included some long-standing solid voluntary homes.

41 http://www.magicme.co.uk.

42 CQC, The State of Health Care and Adult Social Care in England 2012/13 at pp. 24 and 10.

43 Age UK, Care Homes finding the right care home, 2013, http://www.ageuk.org.uk/Documents/EN-GB/Information-guides/AgeUKIG06_Care_homes_inf.pdf?dtrk=true.

44 *Ibid.* at p. 7.

costs incurred above that limit will be paid for by the state but this amount does not include the accommodation costs of a care home. From April 2016, people with around £118,000 worth or less, of property and savings, will start to receive financial help from the state with their care home costs (Department of Health, Guidance Care Act, 2015).

Reform of adult social care

The need for reform of adult social care was a prominent issue from the mid-2000s onwards. The trend is away from paternalism and towards choice, control, well-being, prevention and personalisation of care for adult users of social services including, older people (Equality and Human Rights Commission, 2009); Equality and Human Rights Commission, 2011).[45] Overall, the main trend which has emerged is to assist older people to live independently in their own homes for as long as possible and for local authorities to support them with at home services often procured from independent providers (Wanless, 2006). While the care of older people is only one element of the totality of adult social care in England, the Equality and Human Rights Commission (EHRC) went so far as to develop seven principles for action for the reform of social care, including that equality and human rights law and practice be recalibrated to respond to our ageing society.[46] The Care Act 2014 is an important milestone in the quest for reform of adult social care and will be discussed below.

Dignity in the care of older people: a more specific focus emerges

Throughout this time of reflection and change, dignity has grown in prominence in social care. Dignity is now a seemingly permanent central theme in reporting on, and any debate on, the care of older people in England. It also emerges as a unifying theme between the National Health Service (NHS) and campaigning organisations for older people. Collaborative work between bodies such as Age UK (the UK's leading campaigning organisation and charity for older people) and other bodies is a meaningful and very positive characteristic of the promotion of age, ageing and older people in the UK. One example of this collaborative approach is the report *Delivering Dignity* (Commission on Dignity in Care for Older People, 2012), published in 2012 by an independent Commission on Dignity in Care for

---

45 A key part of the current care landscape, is that demographic pressures are increasing at the same time that financial resources are being reduced and the number of older people in local authority supported residential and nursing homes, has grown by more than 20% between 2005/6 and 2012/13 (Care Quality Commission The state of health care and adult social care in England 2010/11 p. 84; Age UK Care in Crisis 2014 http://www.ageuk.org.uk/Documents/EN-GB/Campaigns/CIC/Care_in_Crisis_report_2014.pdf?epslanguage=en-GB?dtrk%3Dtrue).

46 Equality and Human Rights Commission, 'From safety net to springboard: A new approach to care and support for all based on equality and human rights' (2009) at pp. 56–57.

Older People (the Commission).[47] The Commission was established in response to investigations into serious failings in care in hospitals and care homes for older people, and aimed to establish the standard of care older people have a right to expect. It recommended a major cultural shift in how the system approaches dignity to ensure that care is person-centred and not task-centred and highlighted the need for enough staff to provide personalised care. Therefore, it dealt with *how* care should be delivered and explained person-centred care, as per the NHS Constitution,[48] as articulating what the whole care sector should be aiming to achieve:

> Person-centred care champions compassion and respect, and puts the individual at the heart of all decisions. The focus is on the relationship with the person behind the task, not on the task for its own sake. From the moment an older person first has contact with a hospital or care home, it is vital that they are seen as an individual and are not defined by their illness.[49]

It also suggests that 'everybody involved in the care of older people must feel personally responsible for championing dignified care'.

Delivering Dignity's strategies to support its aims include good training and including dignity skills in appraisals of staff performance, as well as establishing a College of Care for this very loosely trained workforce with low job status. However, in order to deliver dignified care and to challenge undignified care (a key thrust of the report), it strikes this writer that dignity also needs to be related to human rights. Then the possibilities of a broader human rights approach to delivering care can be explored and, together with dignity, can help a care-giver to find the dividing line between acceptable and unacceptable ways of delivering care. This report also reminds us that: 'Care homes must be more than places where the only goal is to keep residents clean, dressed and well fed. This means turning task-oriented care on its head.'[50]

In 2013, the CQC published a report into dignity and nutrition in care homes which involved unannounced inspections of 500 care homes, including 217 homes with nursing care.[51] The CQC found that one in six of the inspected care homes (87 homes) were still not encouraging people to eat and drink sufficient amounts, did not always give people a choice of food or support them in making that choice and

---

47 Comprised of the NHS Confederation, Local Government Association and Age UK.

48 NHS Constitution 2009 which provides, *inter alia*, the right for each person to be treated with dignity and respect, in accordance with their human rights, note the NHS Constitution for England, 26 March 2013.

49 Delivering Dignity, at p. 10.

50 *Ibid.* at p. 21.

51 Care Quality Commission, Time to listen: In care homes: Dignity and nutrition inspection programme, 2012 Care Quality Commission, March 2013. This followed its earlier report into dignity and nutrition on hospital wards for older people in 2011, and coincided with a further report on this subject in 2013, Care Quality Commission, Time to listen in NHS hospitals: Dignity and nutrition inspection programme 2012, March 2013, http://www.cqc.org.uk/sites/default/files/documents/time_to_listen_-_nhs_hospitals_main_report_tag.pdf.

failed to identify or provide support for people who were at risk of malnutrition. While the remaining results were quite encouraging, the CQC was further able to make links between standards that were not being met (as the Northern Ireland report below, had already done) and to establish differences between homes with nursing care and homes without nursing care and differences between homes that care for people with dementia and homes that do not.

It found that homes that failed to respect and involve people, were more likely to fail to meet people's nutritional needs. About half of the homes that did not meet people's nutritional needs also did not meet the standard on staffing and more than half of the homes not meeting people's nutritional needs also did not meet the standard on record-keeping. It also found that more homes that provide nursing care were failing to respect and involve people than homes without nursing care, whereas more homes without nursing care were failing to meet the staffing standard than homes with nursing care. Finally, homes that did not care for people with dementia performed better than homes that did on four out of the five standards and, very importantly, not all staff caring for people with dementia had the appropriate skills, knowledge and experience. The report concluded that the majority of homes were caring for people with dignity and respect and supporting them to make sure their nutritional needs were met but that many of the issues encountered by the CQC arose from cultures of care that put tasks before people. One of its key recommendations was that older people are treated with dignity and respect at all times. Two things can be said about the findings of this report. First, the level of care can be variable between the different kinds of care homes and second, the findings concerning people with dementia are troubling and may well highlight a particularly vulnerable group within residential care for older people in England. The results of this sample may suggest that those providing dementia care require particularly sound training, and robust supervision by regulatory authorities.

A plethora of organisations is involved in providing guidance on dignity and on the improvement of life in residential care in the UK. Four are mentioned here. The first is the Dignity in Care Network (DCN) which comprises individuals and organisations who try to put dignity and respect into care services in the UK and facilitates 50,000 individuals who are dignity champions. According to DCN, dignity champions believe that being treated with dignity is a basic human right and they try to act as role models and to educate and inform others in their workplace. They are part of the dignity in care campaign which started in 2006 and has the following aim:

> The campaign's core values are about having dignity in our hearts minds and actions, changing the culture of care services and placing a greater emphasis on improving the quality of care and the experience of citizens using services including NHS hospitals, community services, care homes and home support services.

The second is the My Home Life (MHL) project (Joseph Rowntree Foundation, Tom Owen, Juliette Meyer et al (Age UK 2012)), a three-year study of good practice in care homes for older people in the UK which, unlike a number of the reports detailed in this chapter, had a very positive outlook in that it did not comment on the absence of good practice. The focus of the study was how to promote voice, choice and control for older people and how to develop leadership in care homes and involved a leadership support programme for 250 care home managers. It is worth noting that the word dignity is seldom mentioned in this report, which takes an over-arching approach, although the concepts and application of voice, choice and control would arguably feed into the dignity of older people and the idea of supported, transformational leadership would feed into the dignity of the managers and staff. The heart of the MHL approach is relationship-centred care emphasising the quality of the relationships between older people, their families and care home staff.

Two of the most striking findings were that moving to a care home was a positive experience for some older people who had been isolated or frail and that negative stereotypes of care homes affected the confidence of managers and staff.[52] The third is the Six Senses research which fed into the MHL project and into the *Delivering Dignity* report above (Nolan et al., 2006). The Six Senses report included empirical research involving older people, their families and carers and was carried out by nursing experts with the aim of showing how an 'enriched environment' could be achieved for all in a care home. It advises care homes for older people to aim for the following six senses, which are ideally realised in an inclusive, relationship-centred environment, they are: a sense of security, a sense of belonging, a sense of continuity, a sense of purpose, a sense of achievement and a sense of significance. The Six Senses report also provided a definition of dignity from its literature review on dignity (Davies et al., 1999):

> Dignity, although difficult to define is essentially about feelings of personal worth and identity and is necessary for a good quality of life. Both dignity and quality of life are basically subjective phenomena requiring that practitioners understand the values and preferences of older people. In other words there is a need to 'know' the patient.[53]

This is a useful definition in that it relates specifically to older people in residential care. Finally, it is worth noting the existence of the Nursing and Care Quality Forum which aims to improve the quality of care across all care settings and to:

- deliver the *fundamental elements of good care* – compassion, dignity, respect and safety – first time, every time and to everyone;
- achieve their ambition of providing the *very highest quality of care* through supporting the adoption of best practice and promoting innovation.

---

52 And that the partner organisations in MHL should seek ways of achieving more balanced media coverage.

53 Davies *et al.*, 1999 at p. 25.

These individual groups and investigators represent a quest for better care within social care in the UK but we must ask ourselves: how can we pull all of these and other efforts together to achieve a more uniform approach across the care sector? How can these ideals be harmonised and translated into good care-giving?

The regulation of long-term care for older adults in England

Registration of long-term care institutions has been with us in some form since the Nursing Homes Registration Act 1927, when local authorities were responsible for inspecting nursing homes in their borough. Since that time certain gaps have often characterized the practice of registering and inspecting homes. For instance, Townsend found that publicly owned homes were not subject to registration or inspection procedures in the 1950s, some private and voluntary homes were exempt and others had not been inspected for up to five years.[54] Between 1927 and 2000, there were also different types of regulations and regulators for each type of home, community-based services were unregulated and publicly owned homes were inspected but not registered.[55] The Care Standards Act 2000 established an independent national regulator with powers to register, inspect and sanction every kind of care home and home care agency. In the early 2000s risk-based regulation was introduced to focus attention on organisations most at risk of failure, which continues today (Juliette Malley et al., 2014).

What kind of regulation

England has been classified as having an inspection-based regulatory system for residential care (Mor, Leone and Mareso, 2014)[56] where the enforcement of regulations is a 'classic policing function' in which providers who do not meet the requirements are identified and punished (Wiener, 2014). England's inspection system has also been described as being risk-based and its regulatory environment as 'dynamic' (Juliette Malley et al., 2014).[57] Despite current change, the guiding principle of the timing of inspections being risk-based continues to be a key feature, even after the current one-off inspection of every care home. It is worth noting that England's essential care standards have recently been replaced by new fundamental standards, under the Care Act 2014 for health in 2014 and for social care in 2015.[58] They may well have a sound impact in due course.

The functions of regulating, inspecting, monitoring and enforcement of care homes and nursing homes have been in the hands of a 'new' single national regulator, the CQC since 2009, which is responsible for over-seeing health and social

---

54 Johnson, Rolph and Randall *infra* at p. 165.
55 Juliette Malley *et al. infra* at p. 180.
56 At p. 448.
57 At p. 181.
58 Scheduled for 2015.

care. The CQC issues an annual report on the state of health and social care and provides a website where any member of the public can access information about the role of the CQC and about any registered care home. Importantly, this information also includes details from recent inspections. Adult social care in England is undergoing change and is in the process of implementing a new regulatory approach under the Care Act 2014, which provides *inter alia* for a new ratings system and taking on a financial monitoring role for some service providers. A new office of Chief Inspector of Adult Social Care was created in 2013 and, in 2014, 13 heads of adult social care inspections were appointed across England to assist her. At the time of writing, the Government has published plans to require all service providers regulated by the CQC to display their inspection rating in a visible place and on their websites,[59] the CQC has published information to providers on the use of covert or overt surveillance to monitor care.[60]

Inspections

A new inspection system was introduced for health services during 2014 and for social services (including care services for older people) in 2015. Previously, the CQC carried out scheduled inspections, which were unannounced, responsive inspections which were also unannounced and related to a lack of information about a service or particular concerns about care and, themed inspections which focused on particular standards and a sample of homes.[61] The new inspection system comprises announced and unannounced inspections and focused inspections and will usually examine quality and safety of care based on five key questions: is a service safe, effective, caring, responsive to people's needs and well-led? The CQC has spelt out what it means by each of these terms and 'caring' means that staff involve older people and treat them with compassion, kindness, dignity and respect (Care Quality Commission, 2014a). Inspectors will also talk to more staff during inspections and the new regime will reinforce the risk-based model by basing inspections on the rating of the service and they will not inspect each home annually. However, the CQC will now use Intelligent Monitoring to help it decide when, where and what to inspect, including listening better to people's experiences of care (CQC, 2013a; CQC, 2014b). One of the most significant changes, is the increased use of Experts by Experience on the CQC's inspection teams, that is people who have experience of receiving care and specialist advisers (CQC, 2013a). Another is a pledge to inspect during evenings and

59 Department of Health, Display of Performance Assessments Response to the Consultation – Placing a legal requirement on registered providers to display the rating published by the Care Quality Commission, January 2015, https://www.gov.uk/government/uploads/system/uploads/attachment_data/file/399862/SoTD_Response_acc.pdf.

60 CQC, Using surveillance Information for providers of health and social care on using surveillance to monitor services, December 2014, http://www.cqc.org.uk/sites/default/files/20141215_provider_surveillance_information.pdf.

61 J. Malley *et al.* at p. 189.

weekends when people can experience poorer care (CQC, 2014b). What is of particular interest, is the current initial assessment visit by the CQC of prospective care homes or nursing homes prior to registration and the carrying out of a fit person's interview before the home can open.[62] A home today can expect to be inspected within its first year of operation and should loosely expect to be inspected each year thereafter, however, this can be delayed by the CQC where there is no apparent cause for concern in favour of deploying resources to inspect homes that may have been brought to their attention for significant reasons or because they are struggling.[63]

The new inspection system will increase the number of unannounced inspections. In the period from Autumn 2014 to March 2016, the CQC is inspecting each of the 25,000 care homes, nursing homes and domiciliary care agencies, which will be awarded a new rating of outstanding, good, requires improvement or inadequate. The inspection of every care home in England is very welcome, essential and important at this stage. At the moment, it appears that inspections will return to a risk-based approach thereafter.[64] Perhaps one of the greatest sources of hope for a better future comes from the CQC's 2013–2016 strategy which promises a more robust test of fitness for those applying for registration. However, examining the new online registration form as this book goes to publication, reveals a blank space for the registered person to inserts any relevant skills and qualifications. The accompanying guidance is vague with no specific requirements or exemplars, stating:

> If you plan to manage the regulated activities in this application on a day-to-day basis and you will be in day-to-day charge of carrying on yourself the law requires that you have the *relevant qualifications, skills and experience* to do so. Where this is the case, you must describe them in this section. Please provide dates for qualifications and relevant experience.
>
> (emphasis added)[65]

Similar provisions apply for partnerships but they have the advantage of combining their skills and qualifications to achieve registration; there is a similar reference to *particular qualifications* (emphasis added) but no further elucidation for either type of applicant as to what they might be.[66] While this appears a little un-prescriptive, it reflects the practice of the CQC to judge each applicant on

---

62 Personal contact with the CQC on 24 March 2015.

63 *Ibid.*

64 However, in its efforts to deal with a number of serious scandals in hospitals and care homes, the CQC hired many extra inspectors in 2012, 134 of whom are alleged to have failed basic competency tests in a 'flawed' recruitment process (Laura Donnelly, One in 10 NHS watchdog staff should not have got the jobs Documents reveal one in 10 inspectors working for the Care Quality Commission failed competency tests but will not be fired, *Daily Telegraph*, 9 July 2014.

65 Accessed on 21 March 2015, http://www.cqc.org.uk/content/applying-new-provider-guidance#16.

66 *Ibid.*

a case-by-case basis.[67] In any event, directors and managers will be required to declare in their statement of purpose that they will answer for how they plan to deliver effective, safe, compassionate and high-quality care. The CQC sees this as an effective way of holding people to account for the quality of care provided by their organisation.[68] Another is the CQC's intention to create a training academy for its own staff[69] presuming this includes inspectors it should help to ensure reliable standards of competency going forward.

Enforcement powers

As of 1 April 2015, the CQC has a new enforcement policy[70] with a range of powers to achieve enforcement which broadly fall into two categories: requiring improvement (formerly known as compliance) and enforcement, which involve escalating levels of response. Requirement notices are for breach of regulations or poor ability to comply with regulations and, for example, the people using the service are not at immediate risk of harm and the provider has no history of poor performance. The CQC can require care managers to report to them with the action they propose taking. The CQC can also issue warning notices to require improvement, for example for failing to meet a condition of registration or about a continuing breach of a legal requirement.

A higher level of enforcement has the purpose of protecting people who use services from harm, or the risk of harm, by *forcing* improvement and involves civil enforcement powers. These encompass imposing, varying or removing conditions of registration, suspending registration, which they anticipate using rarely, cancelling registration which affects all the locations where the registered person carries on the regulated activity, and would normally follow considerable efforts to get registered owners to meet their legal requirements. The CQC also has urgent procedures at their disposal and can perform any of the civil enforcement powers on an urgent basis with immediate effect.[71] The CQC will only use urgent powers where they believe that without amending a condition or urgent suspension of registration a person will or may be exposed to harm and, unless they apply for the urgent cancellation of registration, a person will be exposed to serious risk to their life, health or well-being. Importantly, the enforcement policy sets out the 2014 Regulations, breach of which now constitute criminal offences, which include need for consent, safe care and treatment, safeguarding service users from abuse and improper treatment, meeting nutritional and hydration needs, duty of candour, requirement as to display of performance assessments, statement of purpose, notice of absence, notice of changes and notice of death of service user.[72]

---

67 Personal contact with CQC on 24 March 2015.
68 CQC 2013–2016 Strategy at p. 18.
69 *Ibid.* at p. 25.
70 CQC Enforcement Policy, February 2015, http://www.cqc.org.uk/content/enforcement-policy.
71 Providers may of course appeal against these decisions.
72 In these circumstances, the CQC can proceed to prosecution without serving a warning notice.

The highest level of enforcement aims to hold providers and individuals to account for failure and involves the criminal powers of simple cautions, penalty notices and prosecution.[73] The enforcement policy sets out lengthy criteria for consideration before prosecution, for example avoidable harm (whether of a physical or psychological nature) to a service user or a service user being exposed to a significant risk of such harm occurring. Payment of a fixed penalty in a penalty notice enables a registered person to avoid prosecution. The highest fixed penalty in the enforcement policy is £4,000 for a provider and £2,000 for a manager for each of the following: failure to comply with regulations about quality and safety, carrying on a regulated activity without being registered, failure to comply with conditions of registration and carrying on a regulated activity while registration is suspended.[74] These financial penalties are surprisingly modest especially when measured against the potential for harm that the breaches represent. However, at prosecution stage for those offences (plus an additional one of 'false descriptions of concerns'), the fines are now unlimited and there appears to be the possibility of a jail term of 12 months for carrying on an activity without being registered.[75]

The CQC inspectors now use an enforcement decision tree[76] to decide whether to use enforcement powers. The decision tree has four stages: stage 1, initial assessment; stage 2, legal and evidential review; stage 3, selection of the appropriate enforcement action – this involves consideration of 3A, seriousness of the concern (from low to extreme)[77] and 3B multiple or persistent breaches to be taken into account; stage 4, final review. The impact of the concerns in stage 3 will be taken into account and can be classed as minor, moderate or major. The policy states that the CQC will seek to take progressively stronger action in proportion to the scale of the impact on people using the service, as well as the number of people affected. Also taken into account, is whether the likelihood of the facts giving rise to concern will happen again is remote, possible or probable. A number of principles guide the new enforcement powers. One of these is *being on the side of people who use regulated services* which includes: 'We will not tolerate breaches that add up to inadequate care, whether they give rise to a risk of harm or not. Where there are failures in care that do not improve, we will be prepared to use our enforcement powers.' *Integrating enforcement into our regulatory model* is another principle and clearly states: 'Enforcement is a core part of CQC's operating model.' Proportionality guides the action that the CQC will take and it is also guided by the principles of consistency and transparency.

73 For individuals there is an added fit and proper person requirement.
74 At p. 34.
75 At p. 35.
76 CQC Enforcement decision tree, February 2015, http://www.cqc.org.uk/sites/default/files/20150209_enforcement_decision_tree_v1_final.pdf.
77 See p. 12 of CQC Enforcement decision tree.

Complaints

The CQC does not resolve individual complaints.[78] Care homes are required 'to establish and operate effectively an accessible system for identifying, receiving, recording, handling and responding to complaints'[79] and any complaint that is received must be investigated and necessary and proportionate action must be taken in response to any failure identified by the complaint or investigation.[80] In the first place service users must report any complaint to the manager of their care home. However, it can easily be envisaged that some older people could be put off complaining for fear of retaliation. If the service user remains unhappy with the outcome, she can report it to the Local Government Ombudsman (LGO), which is an independent body that can recommend a range of actions by the provider but cannot hold an individual worker to account. The LGO's decision cannot be appealed but it can be reviewed by the High Court where a legal flaw is alleged. Since 1 April 2013, the LGO's decisions are published without naming any individual except where discretion demands that a decision not be published. Importantly, the CQC will now examine how providers deal with concerns, complaints and whistle-blowing in every inspection.[81] Moreover, the CQC can now require any service provider to provide a summary of complaints under the complaints system, responses by them to the complaints and any further correspondence with the complainants and any other relevant information the CQC may request.[82]

The Care Act 2014

England's Minister for Care and Support has described the Care Act 2014 as the most significant reform of care and support in more than 60 years, which has created a single modern law that makes clear what kind of care people should expect.[83] The Act places a general duty on a local authority to promote an individual's well-being, which has nine dimensions including personal dignity, protection from abuse and neglect, relationships and control by the individual over day-to-day life. A local authority must also have regard to eight matters when exercising its functions, which include starting with the assumption that the individual is best-placed to judge their own well-being.[84] The Act places a prevention duty on local authorities to provide or arrange for services, facilities or resources which will prevent or

---

78 CQC What we do and how we do it, p. 6, http://www.cqc.org.uk/sites/default/files/documents/20131108%206657_CQC_Aboutus_A5_Web%20version.pdf.

79 Regulation 16(2) of the Health and Social Care Act 2008 (Regulated Activities) Regulations 2014.

80 Reg. 16(1).

81 CQC 2014c at p. 13.

82 Reg. 16(3) of the Health and Social Care Act 2008 (Regulated Activities) Regulations 2014.

83 'Care and Support Minister Norman Lamb talks about the biggest reforms to the social care system in more than 60 years', https://www.gov.uk/government/speeches/care-bill-becomes-care-act-2014.

84 And the individual's views, feelings, wishes and beliefs and the importance of the individual participating as fully as possible in decisions and being provided with information and support to enable her to participate.

delay the development of, or reduce the need for, care and support.[85] It also places a duty on them to identify adults in their area with needs for care and support which are not being met.[86] An interesting innovation is a duty to prevent a carer's need for care and support and a duty to meet a carer's (here typically referring to a domiciliary setting and would often be a relative) need for care and support and their right to receive services.[87]

Local authorities now have a duty to establish an adult safeguarding board (SAB) to protect adults in their area, where an adult has needs for care and support, is experiencing, or is at risk of, abuse and neglect and because of those needs is unable to protect herself from abuse or neglect, or the risk of it.[88] The Act places a temporary duty on the local authority to meet care and support needs of adults and their carers where the registered person cannot do so because of business failure.[89] This is very relevant in England, in light of the failure of the Southern Cross Group of care homes below and the need for continuity for residents in the event of similar cases in future. The Act allows the CQC to assess the financial sustainability of a care provider and may require the provider to produce a plan to mitigate risk and arrange for, or require a person with professional expertise to carry out, a review of the business.[90]

The Act abolishes a local authority's power to remove a person in need of care from her home in England,[91] which had clear potential to breach human rights.[92] In addition to the appointment of three different chief inspectors for each area the CQC supervises, the Care Act requires them to have regard to the importance of safeguarding and promoting its independence from the Secretary of State, when exercising their functions on its behalf. It empowers the CQC to conduct reviews, assess performance and publish reports on the areas under its purview and outlines offences relating to the supplying of information that is false or misleading.[93] Penalties for that offence are a fine or imprisonment for not more than two years, or both. A court may also make a remedial order requiring the provider to remedy the situation or a publicity order requiring the provider to publicise facts including details of the offence and the conviction. Finally, the Act makes clear that where a provider provides care and support, either in a service user's own home, residential care home or residential care home with nursing, and the care is arranged or paid for by a local authority, the service provider is deemed to be exercising a function

---

85 S. 2(1) of the Care Act 2014.
86 S. 2(2)(b) of the Care Act 2014.
87 Ss. 2(2)(c), 10, 13(1) and 20 of the Care Act 2014.
88 Ss. 43 and 42(1) of the Care Act 2014.
89 S. 48 of the Care Act 2014.
90 S. 55 of the Care Act 2014. Note where the CQC believes that a care provider is likely to be unable to carry on the business due to business failure, it must notify the local authority (s. 56).
91 S. 46 of the Care Act 2014.
92 See for instance, Department of Health, Review of Health and care powers of entry at p. 4, https://www.gov.uk/government/uploads/system/uploads/attachment_data/file/395759/PoE_Report.pdf.
93 S. 92 of the Care Act 2014.

of a public nature.[94] The history and special importance of this development for older people receiving care will be highlighted in Part II of this chapter, which deals with human rights.

Legal change

The Health and Social Care Act 2008 (Regulated Activities) Regulations 2014[95] ('the 2014 Regulations') are an essential part of the implementation of the Care Act 2014. They contain the new duties and prohibitions for registered providers and registered persons in a section entitled Fundamental Standards. Dignity and respect are also given far greater prominence than before and point towards a more enlightened approach to providing care, which may help to shift the focus away from a series of tasks which poor or pressurised carers were often culpable of and squarely onto the older person. Under the Regulations, person-centred care requires that the care and treatment of service users must be appropriate, meet their needs and reflect their preferences.[96] The Regulations maintain the previous obligation to carry out an assessment of the user but it is an assessment *inter alia* of their needs and preferences for care and treatment and designing care or treatment with a view to ensuring service users' welfare. They also maintain a requirement to provide for the making of reasonable adjustments (to enable the service user to receive their care and treatment);[97] this is very important for older people, many of whose needs change over time.

The fundamental standard on dignity and respect makes clear what a registered person must do to comply with this requirement namely, promote the privacy, autonomy, independence and involvement in the community of the service user and, have due regard to any of the protected characteristics of the service user[98] (this refers to age, disability, gender reassignment, marriage and civil partnership, race, religion or belief, sex and sexual orientation). Care and treatment must not be provided in a way that *inter alia* includes unlawful discrimination or restraint that is unlawful, unnecessary or is not proportionate to the risk posed if the service user was not subject to control or restraint.[99] There is a new requirement to *mitigate* the risks of any unsafe care or treatment[100] and a requirement for staffing supervision.[101]

Clear personal and professional criteria are set out for all service providers. Where the service provider is an individual or partnership, they must be of good character, by reason of their health (after reasonable adjustments are made) be

---

94 S. 73 of the Care Act 2014.
95 The Health and Social Care Act 2008 (Regulated Activities) Regulations 2014.
96 Reg. 9(1)(a)-(c) of the Health and Social Care Act 2008 (Regulated Activities) Regulations 2014.
97 *Ibid.* at reg. 9(3)(h).
98 *Ibid.* at reg. 10.
99 *Ibid.* at reg. 13.
100 *Ibid.* at reg. 12(2)(b).
101 *Ibid.* at reg. 18.

able to properly perform tasks that are intrinsic to carrying on the activity or, in the case of a partnership, to their role in carrying on the regulated activity, and have the necessary qualifications, skills and experience (or through a combination of them for partners). Similar requirements apply to registered managers.[102] All of these people must additionally supply detailed information and evidence.[103] Where the service provider is a body other than a partnership, it must give the CQC details of the person employed as director, manager or secretary of the body and who is responsible for supervising the management of the carrying on of the regulated activity (the nominated person).

Fit and proper persons and duty of candour[104]

The Regulations also require that 'fit and proper persons' are employed. This means they must be of good character, have the necessary skills, competence, qualifications and experience which are necessary for the work and be able by reason of their health (after reasonable adjustments are made) to carry out the tasks intrinsic to their work.[105] Very importantly, in light of the scandals below, they provide that sufficient numbers of suitably qualified, competent, skilled and experienced staff be deployed[106] to meet the requirements of Part 3 of the Regulations which includes: fundamental standards, safe care and treatment, assessment of risks, mitigation of risk, safe management of medicines, safeguarding service users from abuse and improper treatment, meeting nutritional and hydration needs, among others. It is worth noting that CQC registration regulations already required service providers to notify the CQC of any event that might prevent them from carrying on the regulated activity safely, including 'an insufficient number of suitably qualified, skilled and experienced persons being employed'.[107] It can be concluded from our sample of scandals below that scant attention was paid to this provision by a small minority of homes in the past. There is also the distinct possibility that those service providers were unaware of this and other important requirements, which would be disappointing as the CQC has a history of providing guidance on registration and other areas to assist compliance.

Of the new provisions, one of the most eye-catching is the new duty of candour.[108] It came into force for NHS service providers in 2014 and for social care

---

102 *Ibid.* at reg. 4.

103 *Ibid.* at Sch. 3.

104 These requirements have been extended to all registered providers from April 2015, not just health providers, see http://www.legislation.gov.uk/uksi/2015/64/pdfs/uksiem_20150064_en.pdf.

105 Reg. 19 of the Health and Social Care Act 2008 (Regulated Activities) Regulations 2014.

106 *Ibid.* reg. 18.

107 Reg. 18 of the Care Quality Commission (Registration) Regulations 2009.

108 *Ibid.* reg. 20. Note, a duty of candour already existed in the NHS Standard contract for organisations providing services (Department of Health, Introducing the Statutory Duty of Candour, see *A consultation on proposals to introduce a new CQC registration regulation*, March 2014, p. 11.

service providers in April 2015. This duty requires providers to be open and transparent with relevant persons in relation to services provided to service users. Where things go wrong, the provider must contact the relevant person about a notifiable safety incident, advise them of any recommended enquiries, issue an apology and keep a record of a written account. A notifiable safety incident means any unintended or unexpected incident during the provision of a service which, could or has resulted in the death of a service user or severe harm, moderate harm or prolonged psychological harm of the service user. Prolonged psychological harm refers to a period of at least 28 days.

Residential care: performance in recent years

In the interests of balance, and before looking at the scandals, it is useful to take a step back and see how residential care for older people is and has been performing overall. This exercise will reveal that clearly the majority of homes are meeting the standards when inspected. If, however, what appears to be a small enough percentage were translated into a number of care homes or, better still, a number of residents and patients, it would help to give a more human face to the reality of failing homes. A report of the English Parliament's Joint Committee on Human Rights[109] (JtCHR Report 2007) into abuse and neglect suffered by older people in care homes is a useful starting point. It details how more than a fifth of care homes failed minimum standards of privacy and dignity, but this represented a marked improvement from 59% of care homes meeting these standards in 2003.[110] A number of trends emerge from the body of reports since that time; the first is that the numbers of compliant homes have continued to improve since a low base in 2003. However, it will be shown that we are left with a fairly persistent figure of at least 10% of non-compliant homes. Another trend is for some fluctuation in the areas where homes are found to be performing poorest. More recently, the emergence of staffing issues, the absence of a manager and poor record-keeping are critical factors affecting care. The issue of wide-spread variation in quality of service has been identified lately. Finally, nursing homes continue to lag behind residential care homes quite consistently.

The CQC has published five State of Care reports since it became the first independent regulator of health and social care in 2009, until the time of writing. In 2010 it published its first report under the then new system of registration and regulation,[111] its second report in 2010/2011 stated that it concentrated resources

---

109 HL Paper 156-I HC 378-I House of Lords House of Commons Joint Committee on Human Rights, The Human Rights of Older People in Healthcare Eighteenth Report of Session 2006–07.

110 Apart from privacy and dignity, areas of concern included malnutrition and dehydration, abuse and rough treatment, neglect, carelessness and poor hygiene, bullying, patronising and infantilising attitudes towards older people, fear among older people of making complaints and eviction from care homes.

111 http://www.cqc.org.uk/sites/default/files/documents/state_of_care_2010_11.pdf.

where there are concerns about care, which remains the case today.[112] The State of Health Care and Adult Social Care 2011/12[113] entered a more detailed and descriptive phase. It highlighted the need to ensure that people are treated with dignity and respect, and are not defined in terms of the 'illness' they have or the 'task' they represent, as one of the most important, if not the most important, feature of high quality care service. Inspectors found that when problems arose, the most common issue was a lack of person-centred planning. Another common problem was the lack of a good manager at the service or the absence of one altogether. Only 89% of the inspected residential care homes and only 80% of the nursing homes inspected met the standard for ensuring that people are given the food and drink they need and help to eat and drink. This translates into 233 residential care homes and 273 nursing homes that did not meet this standard out of the pool of homes inspected. It is therefore not surprising that the English media seizes on such findings with front page headlines such as: '600 die of thirst in care homes', and other headlines such as, 'One in seven care homes is failing to give elderly enough food' and, the more recent 'Dehydration kills 2 people every week in care homes'.[114]

In the 2011/12 State of Health Care and Adult Social Care report the management of medicines was the standard with the poorest performance across adult social care; only 74% of residential care homes and 67% of nursing homes met this standard respectively.[115] The report identified a range of staffing problems across adult social care. Ensuring there are enough staff to provide a good service was a significant issue in care homes and a number of providers were unable to support their staff with proper training, supervision and appraisals. The report also highlighted that there were no statutory reporting requirements in this sector. The poorest performance was in records and record keeping, where 78% of residential care homes and 70% of nursing homes met the standard. The report adds that, as with other sectors, problems with this standard are often early signs of ability to perform in other areas.[116]

The State of Health Care and Adult Social Care in England 2012/13[117] announced the following changes: a new Chief Inspector of Hospitals and a new Chief Inspector of Adult Social Care and a new focus for inspections on five

112 http://www.cqc.org.uk/sites/default/files/documents/state_of_care_2010_11.pdf. But note the current one-off inspection of all care homes and care home agencies which will end in 2016.

113 http://www.cqc.org.uk/sites/default/files/documents/cqc__soc_201112_final_tag.pdf.

114 *Daily Mail*, Monday, 31 January 2011 front page, *Daily Mail*, Monday, 17 October 2011, p. 10 and *Daily Mail*, Monday, 2 December 2013, p. 20. Note, this newspaper has run a dignity for the elderly campaign since 2002, http://www.dailymail.co.uk/news/article-1313495/Daily-Mail-honoured-Dignity-Elderly-campaign.html.

115 Poor performance was also reported in relation to the standard ensuring the care and welfare of people who use services, with only 82% of residential care homes and 72% of nursing homes complying. Given that the number of inspected homes for this standard was 7,617 and 3,544 respectively, this was very worrying.

116 P. CQC, *The state of health care and adult social care in England An overview of key themes in care in 2011/12* at p. 97.

117 http://www.cqc.org.uk/sites/default/files/documents/cqc_soc_report_2013_lores2.pdf.

questions and on encouraging care services to improve.[118] The CQC promised that the new system would be more rigorous than the existing generic model and promised to 'have zero tolerance for services where people are failed on the most fundamental aspects of care'.[119] Importantly, it also wished to highlight the hospitals, care homes and care services where people receive good or outstanding care. Despite improvements in each type of care, in around 10% of cases people received poor quality care.[120] This report shows that despite progress nursing homes still lag behind other care services for quality and safety of care. One in five nursing home inspections revealed safety concerns and staffing issues; the figure for residential care homes was one in eight.[121] When the CQC analysed the notifications of deaths it found a link with high staff turnover rates, which suggests to it that too many staff changes may result in gaps in care.[122] It found that the failures it discovered were not trivial and gave the example of people being given the wrong kind of medicine and poor record-keeping of who needs which medicine.[123]

There was also a lack of consistency in the care given by individual providers who may have given good care in some areas but poorer care in others and it found a variation in the quality of care across the country and in all sectors.[124] The CQC noted a continuation in the trend for a decline in the number of residential care homes and an increase in the number of nursing home beds and a trend for people living longer in their own homes. As regards the suitability and quantity of staffing, the biggest improvement was in nursing homes, but across social care the relevant standards were met in only 87% of inspections. Staffing remained a recurrent theme in all respects, as was the lack of a good manager or the absence of a manager in 10% of inspections; the mere change in registered manager following action by the CQC was often all it took for the quality of care and experience of residents to be dramatically improved.[125]

The State of Care 2013/14, the CQC's most recent report at the time of writing, states that in addition to many examples of good and outstanding care:

> There are big differences in the quality of care that people experience from different providers, in different places and sometimes at different times of the day or day of the week.[126]

This clear description denotes a problem with the fundamentals of care and a volatility in care-giving that is concerning. The professional structure in which

---

118 Are services safe, effective, caring, responsive to people's needs and well-led?
119 CQC, *The state of health care and adult social care in England 2012/13* at p. 3.
120 *Ibid.* at p. 22.
121 *Ibid.* and p. 27, respectively.
122 *Ibid.*
123 *Ibid.* at p. 4 and p. 27.
124 *Ibid.* at p. 18. The CQC issued 40% more warning notices to providers than in the previous year, arguably this can be interpreted as a sign of improved detection and enforcement, *ibid.* at p. 23.
125 *Ibid.* at p. 35.
126 CQC, State of health care and adult social care in England, 2013/2014 at p. 11, http://www. cqc.org.uk/sites/default/files/state-of-care-201314-full-report-1.1.pdf.

care is given clearly still lacks elements that would ensure a more even and reliable experience for residents. Perhaps the above statement also reflects the fact that the new system is starting to unearth a far more insightful understanding of what is actually happening in care homes. Two findings are particularly interesting, people living in nursing homes continued to receive poorer care than people living in care homes without nursing and smaller residential care homes were more likely to perform better than larger ones.[127] The CQC highlighted its concern for the shortage of nurses in care homes and the need to encourage more nurses to work in them. It found that care homes without a registered manager were more than twice as likely to be non-compliant than care homes with a registered manager.[128]

The year 2015 commenced with the first three adult social care services achieving the highest care rating under the new system. One of these, the Prince of Wales House, was the first care home to be rated Outstanding under the latest inspection system. This home, with a capacity for 49 older people, including those with dementia, was a homely place and in the words of the inspector, 'there was a sense of a big family and a real buzz . . . It was evident that when people move in here, life doesn't stop'.[129] The registered manager had introduced a 'whole team approach' whereby all staff share responsibility for people's well-being, safety and security and she believed that the commitment to the residents came from the home's owners who pass on an incredible ethic to every member of staff.[130] Importantly, there was an emphasis on each resident as an individual and caring about their priorities. The home had also installed a small bar, which demonstrates that it is not just exclusive, high-end care homes that can attempt a lighter, more social atmosphere.

The way forward

The most recent State of Care report clearly highlights staff recruitment and training as a major issue for the future.[131] The CQC's strategy for 2013–2016 gets to the heart of matters stating:

> We recognise that quality care cannot be achieved by inspection and regulation alone. The main responsibility for achieving quality care lies with professionals, clinical staff, providers and those who arrange and fund local services.[132]

---

127 *Ibid.* at p. 32.
128 *Ibid.* at p. 42.
129 Press Release CQC, 7 January 2015, 'Every person who comes through our doors is an individual', http://www.cqc.org.uk/content/every-person-who-comes-through-our-doors-individual.
130 *Ibid.*
131 State of Care 2013–2014 Infographic, http://www.cqc.org.uk/sites/default/files/state-of-care-2013–14-infographic_0.pdf. The State of Care Report 2013-2014 is available at, http://www.cqc.org.uk/sites/default/files/state-of-care-201314-full-report-1.1.pdf.
132 CQC, *Raising standards, putting people first: Our strategy for 2013–2016*, Foreword, p. 1. http://www.cqc.org.uk/sites/default/files/documents/20130503_cqc_strategy_2013_final_cm_tagged.pdf.

A slight extension of this idea of the sharing of responsibility, among *all* the people involved in caring for an older person in a care home could be a very important sign-post in England.

Specific themed reports into different facets of adult social care are likely to continue and dementia has continued to emerge as a focus with a major review of the care for people with dementia published by the CQC in 2014, which states:

> Overall we found more good care than poor in the care homes and hospitals we visited, but the quality of care for people with dementia varies greatly and *it is likely that they will experience poor care at some point along their care pathway.* Clear guidance has been available for years, but improvements in care are still needed and overdue.
>
> (emphasis added)[133]

More specifically, the CQC found aspects of poor or variable care across 90% of care homes and hospitals they visited.[134] Following this report the CQC will establish a new national specialist adviser for dementia care and it will train its inspectors in what good dementia care looks like so as to feed into the consistence and robustness of its judgements.[135]

The scandals

A good place to start the sorry saga of care home failings is with the Orchid View home. This home was owned by Southern Cross, a company which owned around 750 care homes, representing 9% of the total market, before it closed down in 2011. An English coroner ruled that neglect arising from institutionalised abuse at Orchid View directly contributed to the deaths of five residents.[136] Despite high fees of £3,000 a month, the coroner found that the home was completely mis-managed and understaffed. The deaths included the overdose of one resident with the blood thinning drug Warfarin and the destruction of that patient's medi-cal notes by the home. In all, the coroner found that 19 residents had received sub-optimal care and she criticised the CQC for having given the home a 'good' rating in 2010. Apart from serious neglect, leading to death, the home was found to be unclean and residents unkempt.[137] This home came to the attention of the

---

133 CQC, *Cracks in the Pathway*, October 2014, Summary p. 6, http://www.cqc.org.uk/sites/default/files/20141009_cracks_in_the_pathway_summary_final_1.pdf.

134 *Ibid.* at p. 8.

135 *Ibid.* at p. 13.

136 'Britain's cruelest care home: "Institutional abuse" contributed to deaths of five pensioners', Cahal Milmo, *The Independent*, Saturday 19 October 2013, http://www.independent.co.uk/news/uk/home-news/britains-cruellest-care-home-institutional-abuse-contributed-to-deaths-of-five-pensioners-8889770.html.

137 18 October 2013, Orchid View inquest: Home riddled by 'institutional abuse', http://www.bbc.co.uk/news/uk-england-sussex-24579496.

authorities when a care worker contacted the police after a nurse informed her of 28 drug errors in one night shift.

Concerns were first raised by 11 whistle-blowers about the Old Deanery Care Home in 2012, which led to it being given a warning notice by the CQC. In 2013 the home was inspected and passed by the CQC. However, at the time of the inspection, reporters from the BBC's *Panorama* programme were working under-cover and found a woman with dementia being slapped by a care worker and being mocked and taunted by other care workers.[138] Other residents called out for assistance but their call bells had been unplugged. The company which owned the home summarily dismissed the worker who slapped the resident and immediately suspended eight others. Commenting on this home, the BBC's health correspondent Nick Triggle remarked that the problem with care homes is that it is much easier to hide abuse than it is in hospitals, which are essentially open environments.[139]

An official enquiry into Parkside House in Northamptonshire found that five people aged between 83 and 100 had died from causes consistent with severe neglect.[140] It was not until one woman was admitted to hospital in 2009 with severe pressure sores, dehydrated and unresponsive that the neglect was uncovered. Sadly, she died the next day.[141] The CQC cancelled the home's registration and it is noteworthy that the home had been rated 'adequate' by the CQC's predecessor in 2008. Unfortunately, the enquiry also found that there were clear signs that standards had been slipping at the home after that. At Oban House nursing home, a granddaughter hid a camera for three days which recorded her 98-year-old grandmother calling out 321 times for help to visit the toilet before a care worker finally came and treated her roughly.[142] The film was passed on to the BBC's *Panorama* programme. Two employees were later convicted of common assault on this woman.[143]

One of the most striking cases concerns a senior care worker in Ashwood Care Centre, a care home also owned by Southern Cross. The care worker was jailed for three years for administering unprescribed drugs to six dementia patients while on night shifts during 2010. The drugs induced sleep and necessitated mobile patients

138 Emily Dugan, 'Elderly care home abuse: Shocking footage shows elderly residents being taunted and assaulted at Essex care home', *The Independent*, Wednesday 30 April 2014, http://www.independent.co.uk/news/uk/home-news/shocking-footage-shows-elderly-residents-being-taunted-and-abused-at-essex-care-home-9303888.html.

139 'Care homes: The known and the unknown', April 2014, http://www.bbc.co.uk/news/health-27225318.

140 Independent author: Graham Sloper, Independent Chair Serious case review: Marie Seaton, Serious Case Review, Executive Summary, Parkside House, June 2010, http://www.northamptonshire.gov.uk/en/councilservices/social-care/plans/safeguarding/Documents/PDF%20Documents/Final%20Parkside%20v4%20executive%20summary%20for%20publication.pdf.

141 'Five nurses struck off over Parkside House neglect', *Northampton Chronicle & Echo*, 13 December 2013.

142 She was also told to use her incontinence pad.

143 Emily Dugan, 'Elderly care home abuse: Shocking footage shows elderly residents being taunted and assaulted at Essex care home', *The Independent*, Wednesday 30 April 2014, http://www.independent.co.uk/news/uk/home-news/shocking-footage-shows-elderly-residents-being-taunted-and-abused-at-essex-care-home-9303888.html.

being brought to bed in wheelchairs. Part of the prosecution's case was that the care worker was seen putting two chairs together to go asleep and a colleague reported her suspicions to the police.[144] In a final example which shows the disconnect between care and culture on the one hand and effective oversight on the other, Ash Court Care Home received a rating of 'excellent' from the CQC but secret film later showed an Alzheimer's patient being repeatedly abused by a member of staff.[145]

The impact of neglect, abuse and poor care on the sufferers and their families, viewers of English television and readers of English newspapers is not insubstantial and it is frightening. These examples and others may well deflect attention from good care practised in other homes, or even practised by other staff in the same care homes, but they are shocking and raise the question whether certain sectors are unsuited to being run by very large companies or a very corporate business model. While some of the homes that Townsend visited in the 1950s accommodated 1,000 people, ownership of many homes by large corporations did not exist until the 1990s. Even though this sample is small and represents the media highlights, some further observations can be attempted here. Under-staffing and failure to cope with complex patient needs can contribute to neglect. But they must not be allowed to excuse it.

With a minority of carers the problem starts with their recruitment; they are quite possibly not suited to working on a one-to-one basis with people, let alone vulnerable adults. A small proportion of people may be drawn to work for the elderly because they have few tangible skills or qualifications and perhaps cannot easily obtain other types of work. The job requirements have traditionally been quite loose (now potentially improving) and the field has no over-arching professional body in this country. In addition, employment conditions in this sector are erratic. The public budget on adult social care was cut by 8% between 2010/11 and 2012/13 at a time when the number of elderly and disabled people needing care had grown.[146] Some 220,000 people working in care receive less than the minimum wage and local authorities often cut costs by reducing fees to service providers who then pass on the reduction to care workers.[147] Moreover, one-third of care workers are on zero hours contracts.[148]

---

144 'Southern Cross care home worker drugged six dementia patients "so she could get a good night's sleep"', Leon Watson, Mail online, 21 August 2012, http://www.dailymail.co.uk/news/article-2191453/Southern-Cross-care-home-worker-drugged-dementia-patients-good-nights-sleep.html#ixzz3Q8RnDGvl.

145 By Jane Worroll, 22 April 2012, 'I used a spy camera to catch a care home thug beating up my mother': How a daughter's suspicions lead to her uncovering harrowing abuse, http://www.dailymail.co.uk/news/article-2133673/BBC-One-Panorama-Undercover—Elderly-Care-Ash-Court-residents-daughter-uncovers-harrowing-abuse.html#ixzz3Q8Uy9Cvs.

146 The UK Parliament's Public Affairs Committee's Report 2012/13 into Adult Social Care, (Public Accounts Committee – Sixth Report Adult Social Care in England HC 518 Ordered to be printed on 2 July 2014).

147 *Ibid*. Note, the poor working conditions of care workers was the subject of the more recent Kingsmill Review *supra*.

148 *Ibid*.

The Regulated Activities Regulations 2014 above require important information such as a full employment history, together with a satisfactory written explanation of any gaps in employment.[149] They also require satisfactory verification as to the reason why any previous employment concerning children or vulnerable adults ended.[150] The incoming Care Certificate, discussed below, will be a welcome first step to fill some of the training and qualification gaps but it is not a national qualification. In the meantime, it is clear from the examples above that poor basic care and cleanliness often go hand in hand with more serious neglect as often does poor record-keeping. It is also clear that no one person should administer drugs alone in a care setting. Not only should careful, accurate records be kept of the administration of medicines but these should be counter-signed by another member of staff. The English public has a role to play. It is increasingly well informed about how to choose a care home with a growing number of websites devoted to this issue, and an experienced care home worker has recently published a book on what to look for in a good care home.[151] Care staff have a role to play. During 2012/13 the CQC re-established its whistle-blowing hotline which resulted in a ten-fold increase in the number of calls with concerns;[152] this procedure is aimed at care workers and service providers are encouraged to have a whistle-blowing policy.[153]

Fundamentally, a more robust system is required to detect and act on failings in the early stages and the current period of one-off inspections of *all* care homes in England is to be welcomed. Above all an older person's experience in a care home cannot depend on luck. Prior to the 2013–2016 strategy and following it, a risk-based principle will continue to govern the timing of inspections. In the view of this writer, something more may be required. If, as the CQC asserts today, care homes have a pre-registration assessment visit before they are registered, and typically are inspected within the first year of registration, something more may be needed to nip problems in the bud. Certainly existing homes that re-open under new management should be treated as new homes and be pre-assessed and inspected in the first year of operation, some of the homes mentioned above re-opened with some of the same staff. This (if not already done) would help to reassure the public about any legacy issues.

This writer welcomes the many recent changes in this field but questions whether some of them have gone far enough. It is imperative that owners, operators and managers know the legal requirements for setting up a care home and

---

149 Sch. 3 of the Health and Social Care Act 2008 (Regulated Activities) Regulations 2014.
150 *Ibid.* at reg. 7.
151 Adeline Dalley, *Behind those care home doors How to avoid care 'professionals' with their eyes wide shut* (The Choir Press, United Kingdom, 2014).
152 UK Parliament Report 2012/13 *supra*. See also, *Raising a concern with CQC a quick guide for health and social care staff about whistleblowing*, http://www.cqc.org.uk/sites/default/files/documents/20120117_whistleblowing_quick_guide_final_update.pdf.
153 http://www.cqc.org.uk/sites/default/files/documents/20131107_100495_v5_00_whistle blowing_guidance_for_providers_registered_with_cqc.pdf.

their ongoing legal obligations thereafter. In the English context, it is also imperative that this knowledge is tested satisfactorily as a pre-condition for registration
of a care home. The CQC's plans for an amended Statement of Purpose in the
registration process to include a declaration by directors and managers that they
will answer for how they plan to deliver services, although a start, do not go far
enough.[154] As far as this writer understands it, the declaration will not establish
that providers have a suitable and objectively verifiable knowledge of the applicable legal requirements and their ongoing duties to uphold the fundamental standards, *before* they are allowed to deliver care to their very first resident. There are
self-evident doubts about the knowledge base of some people opening and running care homes as well as their employees who deliver care.

Constructive developments for care staff: a brighter future?

Sadly, the problems in the care sector are very similar to those experienced in
some areas of the NHS, but something good has come from them. The most
well-known was a system failure at the Mid-Staffordshire NHS Foundation Hospital where an independent inquiry under Robert Francis QC found that around
500 patients had died needlessly between 2005 and 2008. Common problems
included call bells being unanswered and food and drink being left out of reach
of patients. One of the notable issues identified in the first Francis Report as
contributing to poor care was historic under-staffing. Partly in response to the
failures at this NHS hospital, Camilla Cavendish was asked to carry out a review
into health care assistants and support workers in the NHS and social care and
recommended a Care Certificate for them.[155] This certificate has been devised
by Health Education England and Skills for Health together with Skills for Care
(SFC), an employer-led organisation which works with adult social care employers
to develop the skills, knowledge and values of 1.5 million employees. The Care
Certificate is intended to cover the first stage of working life in the care sector. For
a full-time worker it should take 12 weeks to achieve in the workplace.[156]

The Care Certificate will be based on a workbook setting out evidence of practice, but quality assurance-like training and assessment is the responsibility of the
employer and it is not intended that it will be a national qualification. However,
it will be evidence towards further qualifications and apprenticeships in health
and social care. It replaces earlier induction standards and national minimum
training standards and while it is not currently mandatory as such, there is a clear
expectation that new staff will achieve it. The CQC will also expect to see Care

---

154 CQC, *Raising standards, putting people first Our Strategy for 2013–2016*, p. 18.
155 Skills for Care, *The Care Certificate*, http://nwl.hee.nhs.uk/files/2014/07/Care-Certificate-briefing-and-Qs-and-As-PDF.pdf.
156 Skills for Care, *Question and Answers on the Implementation of the Care Certificate for Health and Social Care Professionals*, http://www.skillsforcare.org.uk/Document-library/Standards/Care-Certificate/Question-and-Answers-Social%20Care%20Professionals.pdf.

Certificates as evidence of the new fundamental standards on staffing and that fit and proper persons are employed. There are 15 standards assessed in the Care Certificate which include how to work in a person-centred way, awareness of mental health, dementia and learning disabilities, privacy and dignity and safeguarding adults. The certificate is intended to be portable but any new employer is expected to ensure that an employee has the relevant competences. From March 2015, social care employers are required to record Care Certificate completion in the National Minimum Data Set for Social Care[157] and the Care Certificate was introduced properly in April 2015. The possibility of joining an apprenticeship programme[158] is still available for the next and higher stages of a career in social care and there is also a possibility of achieving a diploma.

Part II: Human rights and residential care for older people

England has an unwritten Constitution which is not contained in any single document. The English legal system is also characterised by the role of parliamentary sovereignty, whereby acts of Parliament are supreme. This means that England's accession to a supra-national organisation or an international treaty requires not only that the treaty be signed and ratified but that it is enacted in English law by Parliament. Most of England's human rights today that would be relevant for the care of older people derive from the European Convention on Human Rights and Fundamental Freedoms (ECHR) by virtue of the UK's membership of the Council of Europe. England's relationship with the Council of Europe and its court, the European Court of Human Rights is complicated. There often appears to be a great deal of mistrust of these bodies by British politicians and the British media in particular.[159] Media coverage would tend to suggest that it is only terrorists and asylum seekers who benefit from human rights under the ECHR in this country. Whereas one of the groups which potentially has the most to gain from human rights and a human rights approach based on the ECHR is older people.[160]

The Human Rights Act

In accordance with parliamentary sovereignty, the UK adopted the Human Rights Act (HRA) in 1998 to implement most of the ECHR into national law. The biggest change arising from the HRA is that people in the UK can bring a claim to assert their human rights against the state in their local courts, rather than first

---

157 *Ibid.*
158 http://www.skillsforcare.org.uk/Qualifications-and-Apprenticeships/Apprenticeships/Apprenticeships.aspx.
159 This article attempts to challenge some of the popular myths, Afua Hirsch, *Five myths about the European court of human rights*, Guardian online, Monday 7 February 2011, http://www.theguardian.com/commentisfree/2011/feb/07/european-court-human-rights-prisoners.
160 Even though this Convention contains no rights specific to older people.

exhausting all national remedies before the case being appealed to the European Court of Human Rights. The added advantage is that human rights remedies can potentially be achieved far more quickly, which is of the utmost importance for older people. Like the ECHR, the HRA is only addressed to the state and public bodies. This fact has unexpectedly brought the care home sector to the forefront of legal and public attention in recent years. One of the main cases to do so was *YL v Birmingham City Council*,[161] which concerned a typical human rights issue. Mrs YL, an older care home resident with Alzheimer's disease, attempted to fight eviction from her care home on the basis that any transfer to another home would be detrimental to her health and the increased distance would make it difficult for her husband and family to visit her. Mrs YL invoked Article 8 ECHR, the right to respect for private and family life. However, Mrs YL was a publicly funded care home resident who had been placed in a private care home by her local council. She claimed that the home was performing 'functions of a public nature' under the HRA. A majority in the House of Lords disagreed and held that such homes were not subject to the HRA. This judgment left Mrs YL without a remedy under the HRA and brought into question the implications of public authorities purchasing care home places in the private sector.

The very public disapproval of this judgment led to a change in the law and the adoption of section 145 of the Health and Social Care Act 2008, which essentially ensured that human rights protection would follow a public patient into a private care home. While this development arguably closes a specific loophole, it also raises other human rights issues. If a public resident in a private care home enjoys human rights protection, what about her fellow resident who pays for herself at the same home? As the law currently stands, the self-funding resident of a private care home in the UK is not protected by the HRA. However, there have been some attempts to mitigate this. Baroness Hale who delivered one of the sympathetic dissenting judgments in the *YL* case, discussed the plight of other residents who would not have a remedy against the home under the HRA and expressed the view that:

> There may be other residents in the home for whom the public have not assumed responsibility. They may not have a remedy against the home under the Human Rights Act, although there may well be circumstances in which they would. But they will undoubtedly benefit from the human rights values which must already infuse the home's practices . . .[162]

In an ideal world Baroness Hale's views would be true for homes with staff trained in human rights and following a human rights approach. When homes, with or without these pillars, fail their residents the ultimate human rights sanction of a remedy under the HRA is unavailable to self-funding residents and this

---

161 [2007] UKHL 27, [2008] 1 AC 95.
162 *Ibid.* at para. 68.

reveals a very stark contrast in a mixed care home. Where does all of this leave older people who are assessed as needing publicly funded care by their local council, which then demands a top-up fee from a third party, typically a relative? Given that the lion's share of the care home fee is typically paid by the council, the Care Act 2014 confirms that such an older person would benefit from human rights protection.

If the shortcomings of a human rights culture are obvious for self-funding older people in a mixed care home, can it be argued that older people in residential care, are such a vulnerable group that all of them should enjoy the full range of human rights protection, even self-funders in entirely private care homes? In 2012 the Human Rights Commission of Northern Ireland published a report into nursing home care for older people in Northern Ireland ('the Northern Ireland report').[163] In its conclusions, the Northern Ireland report recommended universal human rights protection for older people in residential care when it stated:

> Taking into account, the extreme vulnerability of nursing home residents, the Commission therefore recommends that:
>
> . . . Legislation is enacted to extend the definition of 'public function' in Article 6(3)(b) of the *Human Rights Act 1998* to include the provision of accommodation together with nursing or personal care for *all* residents in care homes.[164]

The Care Act 2014 was drafted *inter alia* to help make the assessment and allocation of care fairer and also dealt with this issue. For the first time a clause, Clause 48 was drafted which would have extended the protection of the HRA to all users of social care which are regulated by the CQC. However, this clause was dropped during the Bill's passage through Parliament on the basis that the HRA was never intended to regulate purely private relationships (such as those between a self-funder and a private care home).[165] Instead a revised clause provided that people receiving publicly arranged or publicly funded social care will enjoy the protection of the HRA and their provider will be taken as exercising a function of a public nature. In May 2014 the Care Bill became law as the Care Act 2014 and does not extend the protection of the HRA any further than that of publicly funded or publicly arranged placements.

The original legal loophole exposed in *YL* and other cases has been closed but they raised a disparity in the same care setting which is troubling given the nature of abuse and neglect seen above in some UK care homes. The argument that a private resident has an entirely private relationship with her care home is partly

---

163 Northern Ireland Human Rights Commission, *In Defence of Dignity The Human Rights of Older People in Nursing Homes*, March 2012, http://www.nihrc.org/documents/research-and-investigations/older-people/in-defence-of-dignity-investigation-report-March-2012.pdf.

164 At p. 70.

165 Patrick Wintour, *U-turn over human rights protection for home care*, Guardian Online, Thursday 24 February 2014, http://www.theguardian.com/society/2014/apr/24/uturn-human-rights-home-care.

negated by the fact that apart from extra care housing (where it is just the care services and not the accommodation which is inspected), all private care homes in England are subject to inspection and regulation by the CQC. For this reason, and also by virtue of the intimate and life-supporting nature of even basic care around nutrition, feeding and cleanliness, the relationship is entirely different from that of a guest and a hotel. Publicly funded residents have an important remedy under the HRA for breach of their human rights which is all the more important as the CQC does not investigate complaints from individuals. Age UK also reminds us that local authority statutory complaints and NHS complaints procedures are only available to people whose care is arranged by their local authority; self-funders can complain to the Local Government Ombudsman (LGO) like anyone else.[166] Thus, publicly funded residents have a wider choice of avenues of complaint compared to private self-funders whose redress may well be any stipulated in the contract with their care home followed possibly by the LGO. The grey areas discussed here are brought into stark reality when we realise that all residents are affected by the approach and practices of the home where they are placed and public residents are not immune to them. For example, Northamptonshire County Council had placed five residents in Parkside House, two of whom were among a total of five old people who died from severe neglect, as shown above.

What is the added value of human rights for older people?

The HRA makes it unlawful for a public authority to act in a way which is incompatible with an ECHR right.[167] This also applies to employees of public authorities, including when delivering a service to the public.[168] However, taking an action against a body performing a function of a public nature when things go wrong has its place, but it is reactive and depends on knowledge, time and access to advocacy. The voluntary application of a human rights approach is proactive and could help to improve institutional culture across the board for all residents in care homes, not just publicly funded ones. The adoption of a human rights approach is not a new idea in the UK.[169] In 2009, the Human Rights Commission of England and Wales (now the Equality and Human Rights' Commission) published a report of an inquiry to examine how far a human rights culture was embedded in the services of public authorities with some positive results.[170] More recently, the

---

166 Age UK, Factsheet 59 July 2014, *How to resolve problems and make a complaint about social care.*
167 S. 6 of the Human Rights Act 1998.
168 Ministry of Justice, *Making sense of human rights, A short introduction* (2006), p. 10, https://www.justice. gov.uk/downloads/human-rights/human-rights-making-sense-human-rights.pdf.
169 For example, the UK Parliament's Joint Committee on Human Rights Eighteenth Report in 2007 recommended a strategy to make the HRA integral to policy-making and social care across the Department of Health and that the then inspectorate for health, social care and mental health, adopt a human rights framework for all its work. Crucially, it also advocated better staff training in human rights principles and their inclusion in health professionals' qualifications.
170 The Inquiry found that a number of health trusts and other public bodies had successfully adopted a human rights approach which went beyond the level of compliance and recommended that human rights should be mainstreamed into the work of those who provide public services including, decision-making processes, policies and procedures.

Northern Ireland report of 2012 above found a low level of awareness of human rights even among managers and legally responsible people and that:

> while staff receive training on a range of issues relevant to human rights standards, human rights standards are not at the heart of training.[171]

Most staff training in care homes appears to be short and individual to that home or the company which runs it. The issues raised in this chapter point to a need for a (preferably) national training scheme so that staff are prepared for the work and have portable, transferable, identifiable and measurable skills. The Skills for Care, Care Certificate is a step in the right direction but only covers the first stage in a caring career. Is it enough? Putting human rights at the heart of all training for care giving to older people would give a distinct approach to the sector and would help to refresh it from within at a time when public confidence and staff morale are being rebuilt and ahead of a greater number of older people requiring residential care at ever older ages.

It is worth noting that the CQC has adopted the principle of promoting equality and diversity and human rights. It has developed a human rights approach to regulation and asserts that this approach is embedded in its new inspections. Apart from applying the FREDA (fairness, respect, equality, dignity and autonomy) principles, right to life and rights of staff to its five key questions in inspections, it also aims to encourage the improvement of service providers and its own continuous improvement as its new inspection model develops.[172]

Training older people and their representatives in human rights: an idea whose time has come?

Between 2008 and 2011, Age UK in conjunction with the British Institute of Human Rights (BIHR), an independent human rights charity, ran a project to train disadvantaged older people and volunteers how to use human rights in their daily lives. The project raised awareness of the usefulness of human rights and empowered a number of older people to use human rights arguments with service providers. Since then the BIHR has produced guides on how to use human rights in health and care and in voluntary and community organisations.[173] The former advocates person-centred care as one of the benefits of human rights and the latter shows how community organisations can use human rights to hold decision-makers to account. The BIHR has also produced a guide for older people and a guide for carers, which importantly embraces the human rights of the carer and the person who is cared for.[174]

---

171 *Supra* at p. 71.
172 CQC, *Human rights approach for our regulation of health and social care services*, September 2014, http:// www.cqc.org.uk/sites/default/files/20150416_our_human_rights_approach.pdf.
173 *The Difference It Makes Putting Human Rights into the Heart of Health and Care 2013* and note *Making Rights Happen*.
174 *A Guide for Older People* (2nd edn) BIHR, 2010 and *Your Human Rights A Pocket Guide for Carers* (BIHR 2012), respectively.

An excellent example of the power of human rights arguments is the case of Mr Driscoll, who was unable to walk, and Mrs Driscoll, who was blind, but who together had complemented each other's capabilities.[175] This couple was separated for months when Mr Driscoll was deemed eligible for a care home place but his wife was not. The Driscolls, with the support of a number of organisations and the British press, successfully relied on their right to respect for private and family life to persuade the local authority to place them together in residential care. The Age UK/BIHR pilot also demonstrates that human rights can be used effectively as a tool to achieve a desired outcome through persuasion. The problem is that public and professional awareness of this approach is patchy. It now needs to be pulled together for this sector.

Food for thought

This chapter and book do not allow space to explore all and every human rights avenue. It is not the last word but the following case is hugely thought-provoking and may be relevant for older people in residential care and other settings. In *Z and Others v United Kingdom*[176] the ECtHR found a violation of Article 3: 'No one shall be subjected to torture or to inhuman or degrading treatment or punishment.' This distressing case concerned four children who alleged that 'the local authority had failed to take adequate protective measures in respect of the severe neglect and abuse which they were known to be suffering due to their ill-treatment by their parents and that they had no access to a court or effective remedy in respect of this. They relied on Articles 3, 6, 8 and 13 of the Convention'. The abuse of these children by their parents took place over a four-year period and resulted in psychiatric and physical injury. The Court decided that State Parties are:

> obliged under Article 1 of the Convention to secure to everyone within their jurisdiction the rights and freedoms defined in the Convention, taken in conjunction with Article 3, requires States to take measures designed to ensure that individuals within their jurisdiction are not subjected to torture or inhuman or degrading treatment, *including such ill-treatment administered by private individuals . . . These measures should provide effective protection, in particular, of children and other vulnerable persons and include reasonable steps to prevent ill-treatment of which the authorities had or ought to have had knowledge* (see, *mutatis mutandis, Osman v. the United Kingdom*, judgment of 28 October 1998, *Reports* 1998-VIII).

> (emphasis added)

---

175 'Marriage of 65 years gives no guarantee of sharing a care home, finds Alison Steed', *The Telegraph*, 1 February 2006. *The Human Rights Act Changing Lives* (2nd edn) BIHR at p. 14.

176 Case of *Z and others v. United Kingdom*, (Application no. 29392/95), para. 3, http://hudoc.echr.coe.int/sites/eng/pages/search.aspx#{"fulltext":["Application no. 29392/95"],"itemid":["001-59455"]}.

Older people in residential care, particularly those with dementia and those who are very frail would almost certainly qualify as 'vulnerable persons'. This case may suggest a potentially interesting legal avenue where a local authority or other state body ought to intervene even where the ill-treatment is at the hands of private individuals. Certainly, the role of the CQC is brought into very sharp focus as it has oversight of *all* care homes in England. One particular disadvantage for older people in residential care may well be that they lack the small possibility of their issues being picked up by the public if they are behind the closed doors of a care home.[177] There is also a real issue of how to establish that the authorities ought to have knowledge of ill-treatment? Some of the care home scandals outlined above, where homes achieved a rating of 'good' or higher only shortly afterwards to cause neglect and cause or hasten the death of their residents, may lead to a little head-scratching. It is not just the CQC that has potential under the *Z case* argument. If all nurses who work in care homes are paid for by the NHS might there be a special obligation on nurses to intervene? These are issues for another day.

Summary and conclusion

The residential care of older people in England has experienced considerable detailed regulation (this writer would venture the term 'hyper-regulation') and has had a national body to supervise it even before the period of scandal. It also exists in a constantly changing and fast-moving policy environment. Moreover, it receives a good deal of attention from numerous worthwhile bodies and the media and has undergone a number of 'new' inspection systems, even since 2000. Despite all of this activity, something went badly wrong for a period of time when even some homes that had passed inspections horrifically neglected some older residents, occasionally resulting in their death. In a country with a risk-based inspection system and certainly, until now, little deterrent effect for inappropriate home or staff behaviour, it can be concluded that the system was not robust enough to protect all older people in residential care. There is a sense that something basic was at fault, highlighting the need for better oversight by the CQC of all care homes and nursing homes to supplement its risk-based approach, the need for proper training and (national) accreditation of all care-givers in care homes and appropriate pay and conditions for them, the need for a national register of all people working as care-givers in care home settings *inter alia* to help increase a deterrent effect on behaviour, the need for proper training for care-givers, managers and home owners which must include a knowledge of the applicable law and their ongoing legal duties and a knowledge of human rights and their specific application to the residential care for older people. This would help to guide care workers as to their own behaviour and alert them to unacceptable behaviour among their colleagues.

---

177 In the *Z* case, even the police reported the children's appalling living conditions to social services.

Under the latest inspection regime, all social care settings in England should be rated by March 2016. This will be a fresh start for this sector. But will it be enough? What happens then? In light of the recent past, a risk-based inspection system has a question mark over it in this country. However, the new more rigorous approach to inspections may help to gradually heal some of the problems from within, by providing a more accurate picture of the real quality of care. This is all the more important as the majority of care homes in England are changing, their residents are entering them at older ages and many are more likely to be frailer at the beginning of their life in a home than in the past. It seems therefore that this sector may be moving closer to Townsend's idea that fit older people should not reside in care homes.

The growing trend for older people to live at home for as long as possible, and enter care at older ages, shows clearly what direction we are moving in. Whether the environment and the regulations have changed enough to cope largely remains to be seen given the newness of many regulations. That we must remain vigilant and that there are ongoing and legacy problems with this sector is evidenced by CQC inspection results from February 2015 which found Merok Park Home 'inadequate' in all categories. A neighbour of the home heard the residents crying and screaming to get out and some residents had been starved.[178] When the home's owners, a multi-millionaire couple, were invited to comment by the press, they replied 'We are not interested'.[179] We have sadly come full circle. Question marks remain over the ease of registering as care home owners, lack of suitability, lack of requisite knowledge by service providers among others and a lack of deterrence. The Minister of State for Care and Support has said in a review of hospital abuse, 'where serious abuse happens, there should be serious consequences for those responsible . . . When failure occurs, repercussions should be felt at all levels of an organisation'.[180] It is very doubtful that enough perpetrators have been brought to justice for the abuse and neglect of older people in residential care, to deter the lazy, careless and nasty few.

But this sector is transitioning under new regulations. The recent legislation's strengths include the fundamental standards that must now infuse adult care in England and clear instructions regarding staffing, but its weakness remains the apparent tenderness (and lack of a requirement of clear and specific professional knowledge of the applicable law) with which it and the CQC treat prospective owners and managers of care homes. However, the newness of some regulations means that their processes may need to time to develop. Of undoubted value, is

---

178 Among many damning findings the home was dirty, under-staffed, did not have a registered manager for four months and the provider did not have oversight of the home.

179 'Torment of grandmother in crisis care home: 89-year-old given just weeks to live pleads "I'm starving" as she begs for food on camera', http://www.dailymail.co.uk/news/article-2917388/Torment-grandmother-crisis-care-home-89-year-old-given-just-weeks-live-pleads-m-starving-begs-food-camera.html#ixzz3RpgbzXXX.

180 Department of Health, 'Transforming care: A national response to Winterbourne View Hospital' *Department of Health Review: Final Report* at p. 5.

the new role of head of social care in England. This survey has also revealed that apart from expensive or exclusive single community homes, being in a residential care home remains a largely institutional experience. This will hopefully change. Frail residents too deserve not only a safe but also a relaxed and happy atmosphere with suitable stimulation even if 'fun' is out of their reach.

It has been shown that a number of public reports have highlighted the need for a complete culture change in homes for older people and among their staff. Various approaches were advanced, most of which have their roots in a human rights approach and training based on dignity, human rights principles and values. There is no shortage of signposts to show the way forward. Above all various bodies have shone a spotlight on issues of staffing, be they insufficient numbers of staff, untrained, lowly paid or unsuitable staff and the importance of *how* care is delivered. It seems that there have been disconnections between some homeowners and their staff and between some staff and residents. It is surprising that nursing homes still lag behind residential care homes quite consistently over the past five years in achieving the standards measured by the CQC, especially as at least some of their staff are nurses who are properly trained, accredited and supervised. This needs further scrutiny to ascertain why this should be so.

What we have learned above all is this sector is too sensitive for usual cost-cutting approaches to running a business. The hiring of too few staff, local authorities paying less to private care homes per place and residential care homes passing on that reduction to their staff have all been factors in the ultimate quality of service provided. Against all of this, the care of older people in residential care, hospitals and by domiciliary care has been a very prominent issue in England. In the opinion of this writer, most of society here cares and cares deeply about this issue. If we can bridge the gap between regulation and experience, which arguably human rights awareness and proper recruitment and training of staff can help to achieve, England will hopefully become a more secure and lovely place to grow old in, whether at home or in a residential care setting. And residential care will truly be a 'last refuge'[181] rather than a last resort.

Bibliography

Age UK, *Delivering Dignity* (2012), http://www.ageuk.org.uk/Global/Delivering%20Dignity%20Report.pdf?dtrk=true

Age UK (2012), Joseph Rowntree Foundation, Tom Owen, Juliette Meyer with Michelle Cornell, Penny Dudman, Zara Ferreira, Sally Hamilton, John Moore and Jane Wallis (contributing authors), *My Home Life: Promoting Quality of Life in Care Homes*, http://www.jrf.org.uk/sites/files/jrf/care-home-quality-of-life-full.pdf

Age UK (2013), *Care Homes: Finding the Right Care Home*, http://www.ageuk.org.uk/Documents/EN-GB/Information-guides/AgeUKIG06_Care_homes_inf.pdf?dtrk=true

Age UK (2014), Factsheet 29 'Finding Care Home Accommodation', April 2014.

---

181 As coined by Peter Townsend.

Age UK (2015), 'Later Life in the United Kingdom', http://www.ageuk.org.uk/Documents/EN-GB/Factsheets/Later_Life_UK_factsheet.pdf?dtrk=true

Care Quality Commission (2010), The State of Health Care and Adult Social Care in England, 2010/11, http://www.cqc.org.uk/sites/default/files/documents/state_of_care_2010_11.pdf

Care Quality Commission (2011), The State of Health Care and Adult Social Care in England, 2011/12, http://www.cqc.org.uk/sites/default/files/documents/cqc__soc_201112_final_tag.pdf

Care Quality Commission (2012), The State of Health Care and Adult Social Care in England, 2012/13, http://www.cqc.org.uk/sites/default/files/documents/cqc_soc_report_2013_lores2.pdf

Care Quality Commission (2013), *Time to Listen: In Care Homes: Dignity and Nutrition Inspection Programme 2012*, http://www.cqc.org.uk/sites/default/files/documents/time_to_listen_-_care_homes_main_report_tag.pdf

Care Quality Commission (2013a), *A Fresh Start for the Regulation and Inspection of Adult Social Care: Working Together to Change How We Inspect and Regulate Adult Social Care Services*, http://www.cqc.org.uk/sites/default/files/documents/20131013_cqc_afreshstart_2013_final.pdf

Care Quality Commission (2013b), *Raising Standards, Putting People First: Our Strategy for 2013–2016*, http://www.cqc.org.uk/sites/default/files/documents/20130503_cqc_strategy_2013_final_cm_tagged.pdf

Care Quality Commission (2014), The State of Health Care and Adult Social Care in England, 2013/14, http://www.cqc.org.uk/sites/default/files/state-of-care-201314-full-report-1.1.pdf

Care Quality Commission (2014a), *How CQC Regulates Residential Adult Social Care Services: A Guide for Providers* http://www.cqc.org.uk/sites/default/files/20150325_asc_residential_services_provider_handbook_march_15_update_01.pdf

Care Quality Commission (2014b), *Our New Approach to Regulating and Inspecting Services: A Guide for Providers* http://www.cqc.org.uk/content/how-we-inspect-and-regulate-guide-providers

Care Quality Commission (2014c) *How CQC Regulates Residential Adult Social Care Services Provider Handbook* October 2014, http://www.cqc.org.uk/sites/default/files/20150325_asc_residential_services_provider_handbook_march_15_update_01.pdf

Carers UK (Carers UKa), *Why We're Here*, http://www.carersuk.org/about-us/why-we-re-here

Commission on Dignity in Care for Older People (2012), *Delivering Dignity*, http://www.ageuk.org.uk/Global/Delivering%20Dignity%20Report.pdf?dtrk=true

Dalley A (2014), *Behind those care home doors* (The Choir Press, UK).

Davies S, Nolan MR, Brown J and Wilson F (1999), *Dignity on the Ward: Promoting Excellence in Care* (Help the Aged, London).

Dilnot Andrew (2011), *Fairer Care Funding The Report of the Commission on Funding of Care and Support*, July 2011, http://webarchive.nationalarchives.gov.uk/20130221130239/http://dilnotcommission.dh.gov.uk/files/2011/07/Fairer-Care-Funding-Report.pdf

Department of Health, Guidance Care Act (2015), factsheets 5 & 6 (last updated 4 February 2015) https://www.gov.uk/government/uploads/system/uploads/attachment_data/file/366085/Factsheet_5_-_Charging.pdf https://www.gov.uk/government/uploads/system/uploads/attachment_data/file/400816/Factsheet_-_Funding_Reform.pdf

Equality and Human Rights Commission (2009), *From safety net to springboard A new approach to care and support for all based on equality and human rights* http://www.equalityhumanrights.com/publication/safety-net-springboard

Equality and Human Rights Commission (2011), *Personalisation in the reform of social care: key messages* http://www.equalityhumanrights.com/sites/default/files/documents/care_and_support/personalisation_in_the_reform_of_social_care_-_key_messages.pdf

House of Lords House of Commons Joint Committee on Human Rights HL Paper 156-I HC 378-I *The Human Rights of Older People in Healthcare* Eighteenth Report of Session 2006–07, http://www.publications.parliament.uk/pa/jt200607/jtselect/jtrights/156/156i.pdf

Johnson J, Rolph S and Smith R (2012), *Residential Care Transformed Revisiting 'The Last Refuge'* (Palgrave Macmillan).

Leone T, Mareso A and Mor V (2014), 'Regulating quality of long-term care – what have we learned?' in Vincent Mor, Tiziana Leone and Anna Maresso, eds, *Regulating Long-Term Care Quality: An International Comparison* (Cambridge University Press), pp. 447–476.

Lievesley N, Crosby G and Bowman C (2011), *The Changing Role of Care Homes*, BUPA and Centre for Policy on Ageing, http://www.cpa.org.uk/information/reviews/changingroleofcarehomes.pdf

Malley J, Holder J, Dodgson R, and Booth S (2014), 'Regulating the quality and safety of long-term care in England', in Vincent Mor, Tiziana Leone, Anna Maresso, eds, *Regulating Long-Term Care Quality An International Comparison* (Cambridge University Press), pp. 180–210.

Midwinter E, (2011), 'A historical perspective: The precursors of residential care', in Lievesley and Crosby and Bowman, pp. 9–11.

Mor V, Leone T and Maresso A, eds (2014), *Regulating Long-Term Care Quality An International Comparison* (Cambridge University Press).

NHS Constitution 2009.

NHS Constitution 2013, https://www.gov.uk/government/uploads/system/uploads/attachment_data/file/170656/NHS_Constitution.pdf

Nolan, M, Brown J, Davies S, Nolan J and Keady J (2006), *The Senses Framework: Improving care for older people through a relationship-centred approach* (University of Sheffield).

Northern Ireland Human Rights Commission (2012), *In Defence of Dignity The Human Rights of Older People in Nursing Homes*, March 2012, http://www.nihrc.org/documents/research-and-investigations/older-people/in-defence-of-dignity-investigation-report-March-2012.pdf

Roebuck J (1979), 'When Does "Old Age" Begin?: The Evolution of the English Definition', *Journal of Social History* 12(3) 416–428.

Sutherland, Sir Stewart (1999), *With Respect to Old Age: Long Term Care – Rights and Responsibilities A Report by The Royal Commission on Long Term Care* (The Stationery Office), http://webarchive.nationalarchives.gov.uk/20140131031506/http:/www.archive.official-documents.co.uk/document/cm41/4192/4192.htm

Townsend P (1962), *The Last Refuge: A Survey of Residential Institutions and Homes for the Aged in England and Wales* (London: Routledge and Kegan Paul).

UN (2002), *Report of the Second World Assembly on Ageing*, Madrid 8–12 April 2002 http://daccess-dds-ny.un.org/doc/UNDOC/GEN/N02/397/51/PDF/N0239751.pdf?OpenElement

Wanless D (2006), *Social Care Review, Securing Good Care for Older People Taking a Long Term View* (Kings Fund).

Wiener (2014), Foreword, In Vincent Mor, Tiziana Leone and Anna Maresso, eds, *Regulating Long-Term Care Quality An international Comparison* (Cambridge University Press).

6 In search of rights in a paternalistic environment

The Israeli experience of regulating residential care for older persons

Israel Doron

Part 1: Background of Israeli society and its ageing population

Established in 1948, the State of Israel is a young and evolving democracy with an exceptional mix of modern and traditional values. As described by Lowenstein and Doron (2013), Israel is a modern 'Western' country with relatively high standards of living, education, technology and health. At the same time however, Israel also has a strong traditional and family-oriented culture that mixes the Jewish majority's traditions and religious values with those of the country's Muslim, Christian and Druze minorities (groups that constitute about 20% of Israel's population). Even within its Jewish majority, the Israeli society is a multicultural mix of secular, traditional and orthodox groups, which in themselves represent diversity in origins and socio-economic backgrounds (Brodsky, Shnoor, & Be'er, 2013). Finally, recent social trends, such as modernization, urbanization and a shift to a more neo-liberal political culture, have to some extent eroded familial and communal commitments to elder care. For example, in some Arab communities, where traditionally care for older persons was provided by family members within multi-generational shared households, new institutional and residential care settings have been established for the first time (Azaiza, Lowenstein, & Brodsky, 1999).

Israel is not only a young country it is also a relatively young society. It was formally established in 1948, after around three decades of British Mandate rule. Due to the historical context of its establishment, i.e. the Holocaust and waves of young Jewish immigrants from both Eastern Europe and Arab countries, Israel started its history as a very young society: less than 3% of its population was over 65. However, very quickly Israel has experienced a relatively quick process of ageing: the growth rate of the older population was double the rate of the general population. For example, while the general population in Israel grew (in absolute numbers) 4.3 times since 1955 up to 2010, the older persons population grew 8.9 times at the same period of time (from 85,200 up to 763,400) (Brodsky, Shnoor, & Be'er, 2013).

As of today (2015), the total population of Israel is nearly 8 million people, and the older population aged 65 and older consists of about 10% of its population (around 800,000 persons). It is expected that within the next two decades the proportion of older people will increase to about 13% of the population and will exceed one million persons. From a 'speed of ageing' perspective, Israel is going to be one of the fastest ageing countries within the developed world in the next two decades.

The relatively vast ageing of Israel's society is primarily the result of increased life expectancy. In 1965 life expectancy was 70.5 years for males and 73.2 years for females. By 2010 it has risen by more than 10% and reached 79.7 years for men and 83.4 for women. Ageing is also related to the composition and ageing of cohorts from previous immigration waves. These waves, especially from the former Soviet Union during the 1990s, have brought a high percentage of older people (16%).

The ageing of Israeli society brings with it the various health and policy challenges that commonly accompany it. Close to 24% of the older population report difficulties in performing activities of daily living (ADL, measured with the Katz scale). The percentage is higher among non-Jews (nearing 45%) (Brodsky, Shnoor, & Be'er, 2013). However, the vast majority of the older population in Israel continues to live in the community and 'age in place': only 4.1% of the Israel older population is living in institutions and residential care settings, as the vast majority continues to live, despite disability, in the community (Brodsky, Shnoor, & Be'er, 2013). It is this relatively small – yet important – group of older persons, which live outside their homes and communities that will be the focus of this chapter.

Part 2: Israel's residential care services

In general, residential care settings for older persons in Israel consists of the following three 'types':

a   Assisted Living Facilities (mostly for independent persons).
b   Homes/Sheltered Homes for the Aged (mostly for frail persons).
c   Nursing Homes/Hospitals for Geriatric Patients (mostly for dependent and cognitively incompetent persons).

We will hereby describe each of the different 'types' separately:

Assisted living facilities

In general, assisted living was almost 'unknown' in Israel until the early 1980s. As will be described later on, the historical residential care settings were based on homes-for-the-aged and/or nursing homes or hospitals that were formed in the early years of Jewish settlement in Palestine. However, as described by Doron and Lightman (Doron & Lightman, 2003; Lightman & Doron, 2005) in the early 1980s, government planners in Israel increasingly saw assisted-living as a free market alternative to the supply of institutional care by the state; and private entrepreneurs recognized assisted-living as a potential source of profit. The

Table 6.1 Key Figures on Assisted Living in Israel

Year	Total Numbers		Rate per 1,000 elderly
	Facilities	Beds	
1985	52	4,876	14
1990	70	6,170	15
2004	165	21,315	33
2009	181	22,866	34

All data take from Brodsky, Shnoor, & Be'er, 2013

combination of these elements brought about a wave of entrepreneurial activity (Shtarkshall 1987).

This intense activity completely changed the assisted-living landscape in Israel over two decades. In 1981 there were only 4,438 assisted-living units (13.1 per 1,000 citizens aged 65 or more years), but between 1985 and 1989 the number of programmes rose by 40%, and by 2000 had increased by approximately 300%. Over the period, the number of living units rose to 17,963, or 31 units per 1,000 Jews aged 65 or more years. The private for-profit sector displayed particularly dramatic growth. It accounted for less than 1% of provision in the early 1980s, but grew by 2001 to control more than 29% of all assisted-living units. Public involvement has significantly expanded as well, and government-owned housing groups such as *Amidar, Shikmona, Parzot* and *Halamish* created many and diverse assisted-living schemes throughout the country.

As seen in Table 6.1, in 2009 there were approximately 181 assisted-living programmes in Israel, and they housed just under 23,000 people aged 65 or more years. There is great variation in the level and the quality of both accommodation and care. The residents of assisted-living schemes are older (77 years) and have more women (74%) than people aged 65 or more years in the country as a whole (73 years and 55% women). In 1990, 75% of the assisted-living populace was over 75 years of age, compared to 43% of older people in the community; while those living alone formed 76% of assisted-living residents, compared to 40% of older people living in the community (Bar & Factor, 1993). More recent studies and data display similar trends and findings (King & Shtarkshall, 1997).

With a few minor exceptions (mostly serving recent older immigrants), assisted-living in Israel has never been funded by the social welfare system. Hence, the responsibility and burden of cost of living in an assisted-living facility is placed on older people or their family members. As elsewhere, the actual cost of living in an assisted-living setting in Israel varies considerably (Metlife, 2002): payment usually involves a substantial entry fee, a fixed monthly maintenance fee and fees for various services consumed. In 2002, the deposit ranged from US$ 40k to US$ 250k in the more exclusive projects: the operator deducted 2–3% of the deposit each year (Sheffer, 2002). As a result of these high prices, assisted-living remains beyond the reach of the poor and non-Jewish older population, most of whom have just two options: continued residence in their homes with limited community-based services, or a move to a fully funded government institution.

Sheltered homes/homes for the aged and nursing homes

Historically, and as described in length by Lowenstein and Iecovich (1995), the beginning of residential care for older persons in Israel started in the late nineteenth century: these new residential care settings were initiated by local communities, and were funded by wealthy Jews in the diaspora, who supported the establishment of homes for poor and lone older persons. These homes were usually established next to a synagogue or an existing community/public activity and resembled similar homes for the aged that were established in the Jewish communities in Eastern Europe.

The first home for the aged was built in the old city of Jerusalem in 1878, and started as a 'tea house for the elderly'. The house was intended for poor older persons without family and without the ability to care for themselves. Soon after, and up to the establishment of the State of Israel, other similar homes were established for different Jewish sub-groups, usually based on their country of origin. All these homes were characterized as being the outcome of local, not-for-profit organizations, funded by donations and philanthropy, aimed at needy, lonely and poor elderly.

The establishment of the State of Israel reshaped the landscape of residential care and the field of homes for the aged. Several key actors played a role in shaping the development of residential care in Israel. The first key actor was a body known as '*MALBEN*': this body was established by means of an agreement between the government of Israel and the American Jewish Joint Distribution Committee (known as 'the Joint'), for the purpose of establishing social services and new care settings for the new country that was just established and had almost no funds of its own. The Joint provided funds and *MALBEN* used them to either purchase existing facilities that were used for other purposes (e.g. past British military bases) and to 'transform' them into not-for-profit homes for the aged; or to fund the construction of new residential care settings around the country. All these settings were publicly operated, either directly by the government by *MALBEN*, and funded mostly by private donations or government support. During the 1970s, under an agreement between the Joint and the Israeli government, *MALBEN* was transformed into a new body, known as *ESHEL*, which took over the responsibility to develop institutional care settings for older persons in Israel.

The second key actor in the field was '*MISHAN*', a body established by the Jewish/Israeli Labor Union for the purpose of providing care of its ageing members. Unlike *MALBEN*, the funding here was based on the membership fees of the Labor Union, and this was viewed as part of a broader social commitment of Israel's Labor Union to care for its members in all fields of life and in all ages. Here, the residents were not necessarily poor or needy, but rather aimed at older persons who had difficulties in living in the community on their own for various socio-medical reasons. However, the basis of operation was not-for-profit, and was managed by representatives of the Labor Union.

The third key actor in the field was the New Immigrants Organization. As the Jews immigrated to Israel from different countries, it was common for the different groups to establish their own self-help organizations. These membership organizations were based on voluntary contributions and support of their members, which were all from the same country of origin. For example, new immigrants from Holland, Bulgaria or Germany – all established their own organizations, each in turn provided its own residential care settings for its older members. These settings maintained the cultural and ethnic tradition of the country of origin, and accepted only members from its organization.

The last key factor in the development of residential care for older persons in Israel was the private sector. As seen above, in the early years of the Jewish society in Palestine, and later on in the early years of the state of Israel, the private sector played a very minor – if not insignificant – role in developing residential care settings for older persons in Israel. For-profit residential care settings were few, and some had a bad reputation for low quality of care. This low quality of care was the outcome of poor physical conditions (old and mal-maintained housing), unprofessional and low-paid staff, and lack of professional training and knowledge by the operators.

However, due to many changes to Israeli society, including not only the ageing of its society and the growing need for a much larger number of residential care facilities, but also a shift in its political orientation into a less socialist and a more capitalist society, caused the private sector to become a much more significant player in this field. Since the 1980s, there were many new care settings for older persons built by the private sector, and for profit. In general, especially at the first years of this trend, the quality of care and quality of services provided in these settings improved dramatically, and with the rise in the general living standards of Israeli society, the competition in the field raised the level of care, especially in the more expensive care settings.

The increased involvement of the private sector was also the outcome of yet another important trend. Many of the residents of the homes for the aged in the not-for-profit settings, started their lives in these settings while being still independent or frail. However, as the years passed by, many of them became fully dependent, and sometimes became subject to multiple illnesses or mental decline due to dementia. Many of the not-for-profit settings did not have the knowledge or the capabilities to provide the necessary care for these new needs, while the government did not provide solutions of its own. Hence, the private sector filled in this gap.

The significant growth of the private sector brought with it however not only positive changes, but also new challenges as well as negative effects. One negative side effect was the decrease in quality of care over time in some of the institutions, erosion in the quality of working force in private settings, and, in some extreme cases, abuse and neglect of older residents, side effects which reflected the attempts of the private sector in more recent years to increase its profits. In one famous case, a nursing home provided much smaller portions of food to its residents in order to reduce costs, which caused some residents to suffer malnutrition. This reality was also reflected in findings of a recent study in Israel, which found that about 70% of the participants (510 nursing home staff members) reported to have witnessed at least one case of abuse or neglect in their institution within the last 12 months (Ben-Natan, Lowenstein, & Eisikovitz, 2009).

Moreover, in the first decade of the new millennium, nursing homes were placed under new financial pressures as government contracts reduced the fees paid for publicly funded beds. The question of the legality of these governmental cuts reached the Israeli courts, which ruled that it was illegal for the Ministry of Health to reduce the payments for nursing homes without taking into account the real costs these institutions had to carry while fulfilling government standards of care (A.C. 2724/2007, *Ateret Avot Nursing Home et al., v. The Ministry of Health et al.*). The outcome was that the Ministry of Health had to raise the fees paid to nursing homes. However, more and more private for-profit nursing homes do not accept any more publicly funded patients, and prefer to accept only private clients, which are charged much higher rates than those paid by the government.

The overall picture

The overall picture of Israel's residential care (not including assisted living) is as follows:

Table 6.2 Key Figures in Israeli Residential Care

	Total	Under the Ministry of Welfare		Under the Ministry of Health	
Population		*Independent*	*Frail*	*Fully dependent*	*Mentally impaired*
%	100	7%	24%	56%	13%
Numbers	29,379	610	8,509	16,403	3,857
Rate per 1,000 elderly	39 (3.9%)	12		27	
Type of Provider					
Government	1,644 (6%)	589		742	313
Private – Not For Profit	10,350 (35%)	3,724		5,586	1,040
Private – For Profit	17,385 (59%)	4,806		10,075	2,504

All data take from Brodsky, Shnoor, & Be'er, 2013

As can be seen from Table 6.2 above, the 'institutionalization rate' in Israel is around 4%, which is higher than other Mediterranean countries (e.g. Greece, Italy or Spain, which are around 2%), but lower than North American countries (e.g. USA or Canada, which are around 5% or higher) (Brodsky, Shnoor, & Be'er, 2013). Three very clear historical trends can be seen in the Israeli experience of developing residential care settings for older persons.

First, is the trend of *privatization:* residential care started in Israel before the establishment of the state by local and non-organized initiatives, based on charity and donations, aimed at poor and lonely Jews. Once the state of Israeli was established, for many years it continued to base its residential care services on not-for-profit organizations, funded either by Jewish donations or by membership support. It was only in the late 1970s that due to growing needs and change of political climate in Israeli society that the private sector significantly became a provider of residential care services for older persons. As can be seen in Table 6.2 above, as of today, the majority of residential care settings in Israel are operated by private, for-profit, organizations. This trend brought with it a mix of positive changes – rise in number of beds, competition for better services and consumer choice – but in some cases it also had negative effects – reduction in the quality of care, quality of the work force, and in some extreme cases even abuse and neglect.

Second, the changes in residents' profile: *the changed mix of residents from 'independent and frail' to 'fully dependent and mentally incompetent' and cultural change in minority groups:* in the early years, residential care was aimed mostly at independent or frail older persons who simply could not care for themselves. However, as the years passed by, the population mix changed significantly. In part this was the outcome of the ageing of the older population itself, giving rise to an older-old population with greater disability rates and higher co-morbidity and dementia. In part this was also due to the increased development of community-based services and 'ageing in place' ideologies in Israel, which supported older persons to continue to live in the community and delay or even prevent their move to residential care settings. The outcome today is, as seen in Table 6.2, that the majority of older persons in residential care settings are fully dependent.

Another change that was seen in recent years in Israel but is not shown in Table 6.2 above is the rise of institutionalization within the non-Jewish Arab minority. Traditionally, due to a combination of cultural, financial and structural factors, residential care was a non-existent and unacceptable service for older persons within the Arab population in Israel. Older Arabs were taken care of by family members, and usually within a multi-generational housing. However, as part of the modernization, urbanization and 'Westernization' processes that this minority group has experienced, new residential facilities have been built in Arab cities and villages in the last two decades. Moreover, studies have shown that there was indeed a growing need – as well as will – to place older Arabs in residential care settings (Azaiza, Lowenstein, & Brodsky, 1999).

Finally, the third significant trend is *the development of a for-profit assisted living facility 'industry' aimed at middle and upper classes:* the trend provided a new residential solution which promised a protected and supported environment, along with rich and diverse in-house social services, for independent older persons. Unlike the older persons in nursing homes and homes for the aged, who were considered as persons who are unable to care for themselves, the residents of assisted living were considered as those who were rich and able to care for their rights on their own.

As will be seen, this historical background as well as the recent trends had a significant impact on the legal regulatory framework on residential care in Israel, and on the human rights of older persons in these care settings. It should be noted that other socio-economic trends that occurred outside the residential care realm, such as the growing phenomenon of low-cost home-care migrant workers, indirectly also affected residential care in Israel, but these trends are beyond the scope of this chapter (see e.g. Iecovich & Doron, 2012).

Part 3: Israel's human rights protection system and older person's rights

General background on the country's human rights protection system

As described by Doron (2007), historically, and due to the British legal foundation that served as the basis of its legal system, for many years Israel did not have a formal constitution. Human rights were mostly recognized and protected by the precedents and court-made-law (common-law) of Israel's Supreme Court of Justice. Historically then, in the absence of a formal constitution or a statutory bill of rights, Israel's Supreme Court established itself as 'the protector of human rights' in Israel. However, despite their significance, these precedents could not replace the need for a constitutional framework for the protection of human rights.

This legal reality changed dramatically in 1992, after the enactment of two new 'Basic Laws': the Basic Law of Human Dignity and Freedom; and the Basic Law of Freedom of Occupation. These two new Basic Laws, which covered only parts of the full spectrum of human rights commonly found in modern bills of rights, were interpreted by the Israeli Supreme Court of Justice to be the trigger of what is now known as Israel's 'Constitutional Revolution'.

The outcome of the constitutional revolution is that today, in Israel, it is well established that both the legislature and the government cannot infringe fundamental human rights (although the scope of these fundamental rights is still limited). If and to the extent that human rights can be limited by acts of government or legislation, they must stand up to a constitutional threshold of proportionality and reasonability. Overall then, while Israel still lacks a full formal constitution or a full scale bill of rights, its basic human rights are protected within a constitutional framework as part of the highest binding legal norm. It is clear that within this framework, older persons in Israel in general, and those in residential care specifically, can enjoy the constitutional protection of their human rights – to the extent they exist for the general population.

Elder rights in Israel

For many years older persons, as such, were mostly 'invisible' to the legal system in Israel (Doron, 2007). There were no specific laws dedicated solely to the rights of older persons. 'Age' or 'old age' did not appear in many key statutes and in common articles mandating equality and anti-discrimination. For example, the original statutes prohibiting discrimination in employment, ensuring rights of patients, or protecting against libel, did not include 'age' as a protected social group.

As described by Doron (2007), until the end of the 1990s, the field of elder law was not recognized as such in Israeli law. It is true that there existed a variety of legal arrangements dealing with the rights of the old, but there was no awareness of the existence of a special branch of law concerning the rights of the old. This was expressed in several contexts. There were virtually no academic articles or books on the subject. There were no non-governmental organizations dealing with the promotion of the rights of the old. There were no courses in the faculties of law in which the subject was taught. There was no private bar or law firms that openly declared themselves as 'elder law attorneys'. And, there were virtually no scholars who focused their research on the subject.

This was also true at the level of national and local politics. Until the early 1990s, activities of organizations or other bodies concentrating on the rights of the old were extremely restricted. Legislative activity concerning the rights of the old at the parliamentary level (the *Knesset*) was also very limited (Doron, 2007). And, finally, the Israeli Bar Association, the professional union of all Israeli lawyers, had not set up a committee, or taken any special action, to deal with elder rights, and there was very little awareness of the economic and commercial potential of old people as a category of clients.

From the beginning of the 1990s, there began a significant change in this state of affairs – a change which is still in progress. First, at the academic level, articles and research projects on the subject of elder law, some of which will be discussed below, began to be published. Second, several non-governmental organizations were founded for the promotion of the rights of the old (e.g. the Association of Law in the Service of the Elderly). Third, a number of law faculties created academic courses for undergraduate and graduate students on the subject of old age and the law. And, fourth, several books were published which, for the first time, included a broad overview of the field of Israeli elder law in the legal library (Doron, 2007a; 2013).

Part 4: The legal regulation of residential care and the human rights of older persons

Before presenting the legal regulatory framework of residential care of older persons in Israel, a short background should be provided on the broader right to health in Israel. There are two key pieces of legislation in Israel regarding the right to health: the first is the National Health Insurance Act of 1994; the second is the Patient's Rights Act of 1996.

The National Health Insurance Act of 1994 defines the positive right to health in Israel. As described by Doron (2007), at the beginning of 1995 the right to health in Israel underwent a dramatic change when the National Health Insurance Act was enacted. For the first time in Israeli history, an overall universal health care insurance system granted all the residents of the state the right to enjoy a basket of health care services, provided by public health funds, as a matter of positive legal right. The law is financed mainly by the insured persons who pay regular fees for health care insurance and participate in various services (Gross, Rosen, & Shirom, 1999). The law establishes the mandatory provision of health services included in the 'basket' at a reasonable standard, at a reasonable time, and at a reasonable distance from the insured person's place of residence as a legal right. The law also sets a national ombudsman that is authorized to receive and handle complaints against Health Funds. By virtue of this law, all older people, like the rest of the Israeli population, are entitled to receive health services and choose the HMO (Health Management Organizations) through which they will receive these services.

However, and this is a key point in the human rights of older persons, residential care and institutional long-term care are not covered under the Israel National Health Insurance Act and are not included in the national 'basket' of health services. This means that each type of residential care setting has its own unique and different legal regulatory scheme – which will be detailed below. Moreover, there is no positive legal entitlement to receive residential care. To the extent that older persons may enjoy residential care funded by the state, it is subject to personal economic needs testing, and filial responsibility laws (which mandate family members' participation in covering the costs of residential care).

The Patient's Rights Act of 1996 defines the 'negative' rights to health in Israel. It provides and protects key liberties and basic human rights of patients within care relationships. These basic rights include the right to equality, to dignity, to quality of care, to choose one's care provider, to privacy, to secrecy, to information, to access to medical records, and not to be treated without providing informed consent. Among others, the law mandates every medical institution to nominate a person responsible for providing information on the rights of patients; for receiving and handling complaints of rights' violations; and for rights' education.

Both Acts described above are relevant and applicable as general pieces of legislation for all older persons in residential care. So, while keeping in mind that there is no positive right to residential care or institutional long-term care under Israel's National Health Insurance Act, but there are various liberty and patient rights for all residents in care facilities, we will hereby describe the different legal regulatory schemes for the different types of residential care for older persons in Israel.

Legal regulation of assisted living facilities

For many years there was a legal debate around the need for a regulatory framework for this residential setting (Doron & Lightman, 2003; Lightman & Doron, 2005). However, disagreements and lack of clarity with regard to the legal authority to make regulation left this field *de facto* without legal regulation. It was only after strong lobbying by the residents of assisted living facilities as well as rising concerns about the financial stability of some facilities and the security of significant sums of money that residents had deposited in the hand of these facilities.

This all changed in 2010, once a totally new law was passed, which became the Assisted Living Act, 2012. Assisted living is defined under this law as any cluster or a group of apartments, designated for older persons (60+), in either one or several nearby buildings, that offer and provide paid services beyond maintenance, cleaning or security. The core regulatory schemes for assisted living include the following elements:

a   all assisted living in Israel must hold a valid licence which is given by the Ministry of Welfare;

b   a licence to build and operate an assisted living facility will be granted only to those facilities who stand up to the minimal standards set up by the legislation and its future regulation (regulation which has yet to be formed);

c   before a resident enters an ALF, the ALF must provide at a reasonable time in advance, a detailed written disclosure document, which contains all material and relevant information regarding the terms and conditions of the living agreement in the ALF, the services, the costs, and his and her rights and the duties of the residents;

d   down payments made to the ALF as a deposit (above a certain amount) must receive a comparable guarantee (e.g. bank guarantee or an insurance policy);

e   there is a list of mandatory services which the ALF must provide (e.g. maintenance, cleaning, nurse provided health services), along with non-mandatory services;

f   a new supervision mechanism is established in the form of a National ALF Supervisor, with legal authority to inspect and to enforce the terms of the law.

The ALF Act includes a specific chapter on 'The Rights of the Residents' (Chapter D). These rights include: the right to manage one's life according to one's wishes and preferences (Art. 31), the right to contract with personal care service providers (Art. 32), to have a care-giver live in his or her living unit (Art. 33), to appoint a representative to make decisions on his/her behalf (Art. 34), to establish a board-of-residents, which represents the residents before the ALF management and before supervisory authorities (Art. 35).

Due to the fact that this law is relatively new, and the regulations of the law have not been formed yet, there is no body of case law or of actual practice, and the supervisory mechanism has not been established yet. It is still to be seen how this law will affect the lives and rights of older residents in ALF in Israel. However, due to the fact that the majority of ALFs in Israel are targeting the upper social class, already the actual standard of services provided are of high quality.

Legal regulation of sheltered homes for the independent and frail older population

Unlike the regulation of ALF, which is quite new, the legal regulation of homes for the aged has been established since the early days of the state. During the 1950s and 1960s, Israel started to formalize many of its social services. This was usually done under broad 'umbrella' legislation, with provided general powers and broad discretions to the social services, leaving much of key regulatory schemes to be provided under regulations and administrative guidelines.

This was the case with regard to the legal regulation of the homes for the aged. The broad legislative framework was the Supervision of Sheltered Houses Act of 1962 (SSHA). This act covered many different kinds of institutions: for persons with disabilities; for children; for persons with intellectual disability; for drug addicts and more. Independent and frail older adults were also 'bundled' within this act, as 'old people' were socially constructed in an ageist manner, viewing old age as an illness or pathologic inherent incapable of managing one's own life. The act itself is short, and requires all institutions to hold a licence, while providing broad authority to the Minister of Welfare to make regulations for each kind of institution.

The SSHA 1965 is thus a 'framework legislation', and the law itself is devoid of substantial content, it lacks any reference to human rights in general, or human rights of older persons specifically. The law bestows on the Minister of Welfare very broad authority to regulate the field through subordinances, decrees and guidelines. The practical result is that the rights of sheltered home residents are not decided by the legislature in a public process, but rather by unelected bureaucrats with the advice of experts whose views do not necessarily reflect the needs and priorities of older people. This type of regulation, in Israel at least, tends to be over-protective and paternalistic (Doron, 1997).

Throughout the years, various key sets of regulations were made for institutions for independent and frail older population: regulations regarding the supervision and inspection of sheltered homes; regulations regarding the manpower, staff and professionals working in sheltered homes (including job description; minimal professional requirements; and minimal staffing standards); and finally, regulations regarding the services and standards of the sheltered home itself.

As analyzed by Doron (1997), the 'spirit' and substantive content of these regulations represent a paternalistic approach. The older residents of the homes are construed as helpless persons, with very limited voice, and with a need for help and protection provided by professionals, who are responsible for their care – similar to the care provided to children or persons with disabilities. The very minimalistic bill of rights provided to the older residents under the regulations recalls a list of rights of inmates in prisons or total institutions, e.g. the right to receive mail, the right have a telephone, or the right to receive visitors. While the regulations allow for the establishment of a representative board of residents, and do mandate that assistance will be provided for any resident who wishes to file a complaint for violation of his or her rights, these are marginal to the overall regulatory framework.

It should be noted that the supervision of the homes for the aged in Israel is under the authority of the Ministry of Welfare and Social Services. This ministry has an inspection and supervision unit, which throughout the years has developed a unique mechanism for quality measurement and improvement (the Tracer Approach: Fleishman, 1997). However, despite this mechanism, some care facilities fail to provide the minimum standards, and some facilities operate illegally, without licence and outside the scope of the law. Moreover, it is interesting to note the little attention given within the regulations and the supervision process to the qualification and gerontology-specific professionalization of the staff working in homes for the aged (e.g. no requirement of specific training in the field of ageing). As noted by Doron (2007a), the lack of attention and emphasis to the gerontological knowledge within the regulatory framework of the residential-care labor force is yet another key legal weakness in this field.

Legal regulation of nursing homes for the fully dependent and cognitively impaired

Conceptually, residential care for fully dependent and mentally impaired older persons is provided by settings which are legally considered to be 'hospitals'. The outcome of this legal construction is that long-term care of older people in nursing homes is heavily regulated in Israel through the general healthcare legislative framework. The basis of the legal regulation of all medical institutions in Israel is the Public Health Act 1936 (and its regulations) that covers all hospitals, including geriatric hospitals and nursing homes for people with severe disabilities and mentally frail older people (Doron, 1997).

Once again, and similar to the SSHA, the Public Health Act is a framework legislation, which authorizes the Minister of Health to make regulations and guidelines for the regulation of the different elements of the healthcare services and professions. In practice, throughout the years, the Ministry of Health and its General Manager have framed a very long and detailed licence-based regulatory scheme that sets standards and minimum requirements for all nursing homes in Israel.

However, the very broad, extensive and detailed set of guidelines regarding the regulation of nursing homes has a very limited reference to the human rights of older patients. The main reference to these rights is made under a guideline for patient rights, which simply echoes the rights provided under the 1996 Patient Rights Act described above. No further specification or unique set of rights is provided for older patients under the regulatory scheme of nursing homes.

It should be noted that the supervision and inspection of nursing homes in Israel is under the authority of the Ministry of Health. This Ministry has an interdisciplinary unit which is responsible for timely inspections of all nursing homes. This inspections not only examine whether the nursing homes stand up for the minimal required legal standards, but also provide an overall 'grade' of the quality of the nursing home as an outcome of this assessment.

Finally, it should be noted that as far as regulations concern the care staff, while there is a legal requirement for a core of trained professionals (e.g. certified nurses, social workers or geriatricians), the majority of the actual care staff are non-professional workers. Under current regulations these care workers do not need to meet any minimal educational or professional requirement. The outcome is that this segment of the working force is low paid, holds low care skills, and in many cases includes non-Jewish, or new immigrants. Naturally, this reality influences the quality of care received by the older residents of these institutions.

The overall regulatory picture

A summary of all the different legal regulatory schemes is provided in Table 6.3:

Table 6.3 Summary of Specific Regulatory Framework

	Assisted Living Facilities	Homes for the Aged	Nursing Homes	Acute Care/ General hospitals
General HR Framework	Israel's Basic Law on Human Dignity and Liberty 1992; The Patient Rights Act 1996; The National Health Care Act 1994;			
Statutory Frame Work	The Assisted Living Act, 2012	The Supervision of Sheltered Homes Act, 1962	The Public Health Act, 1936	The National Health Insurance Act, 1994
Ministry in Charge	Ministry of Welfare	Ministry of Welfare	Ministry of Health	Ministry of Health
Funding	1. Private – the older person	1. Private – the older person 2. Private – the older persons 3. Private – the older persons' adult children and son/daughter-in-law 4. Public – the ministry of welfare	1. Private – the older person 2. Private – the older persons 3. Private – the older persons' adult children 4. Public – the ministry of health	1. Public – the patient's Health Fund
Service Providers	Private – for profit	Mix of for and not for profit providers	Mostly private, for profit	Public – not for profit

Part 5: Key case law and key strategic litigation in the field

As described above, for many years rights of older persons were not part of the main-stream human rights activities of NGOs or the legal profession in Israel. This was also reflected in the field of case law regarding the human rights of older persons in residential care settings. In general, very few key strategic or constitutional cases were brought before Israel's Supreme Court regarding the rights of older persons in residential care settings. Yet, two cases stand out: one, regarding the relationship between the right to residential care and the right to health under Israel's National Health Insurance Act; the other regarding the rights of older residents under contracts of residential care. We will describe the key elements of both decisions.

The Shaham case (2003)

The facts of the *Shaham* case were as follows: Mr Shaham's father, a man in his eighties, was hospitalized in 2002. During his hospitalization, the physicians concluded that he needed institutional long-term care. Mr Shaham had two other brothers, one was living out of Israel, and one was a pensioner. The Shaham family applied to the Ministry of Health to receive funding for the institutional long-term care of their father. The Ministry of Health approved the institutionalization of Mr Shaham's father, but ruled that in order to cover the costs, not only would his father's pension be taken (which covered less than 50% of the cost), but due to his relatively high income, Mr Shaham will have to pay about 50% of the cost.

Mr Shaham filed an application to the Israeli Supreme Court arguing that mandating him to pay for his father's institutional long-term care was unconstitutional as it breached his father's right to dignity and liberty under Israel's Basic Law on Human Dignity and Liberty. Moreover, according to Mr Shaham, this mandate is illegal in view of Israel's National Health Insurance Act, and Israel's filial responsibility law. In a nutshell, Mr Shaham argued that the rationale of Israel's National Health Insurance Act was to provide universal coverage of health care services – including institutional long-term care – as a social entitlement, and not as part of a needs-based or filial responsibility policy.

The Supreme Court of Israel rejected Mr Shaham's arguments on two grounds. First, the court ruled that under Israel's National Health Insurance Law, institutional long-term care was not part of the basic basket of services which are provided on a universal basis. Hence, the Ministry of Health policy to base its financial support for these services on filial responsibility principles was legal under the law.

More importantly, the Supreme Court ruled also, that while the right to institutional long-term care is an important part of the right to health, it is not an absolute right. Due to financial constraint, the state has the legitimate right to shape its legal policy in order to target its funds for those who are most in need. Hence, in the Supreme Court's opinion, a policy to base state funding for institutional long-term care based on personal and familial economic need is justified in order to use scarce public resources in a reasonable manner.

The estate of the late Hinda Milgrom case (1997)

The facts of this case were as follows: On 16 August 1983, Mrs Milgrom signed a contract with the *Mishan*, a company that owns and manages residential and nursing homes for older persons in Israel. Mrs Milgrom moved into *Mishan* home for the aged and lived there for approximately nine years during which she paid all her monthly bills in an orderly fashion. At the end of 1992, her health deteriorated and Mrs Milgrom required hospitalization. Following discharge and due to her poor health, Mrs Milgrom was moved to *Mishan*'s nursing home, where she remained for a period of four months until her death. At the time of Mrs Milgrom's transfer to the nursing home, she and her family members were requested to sign a new contract with *Mishan*. However, they refused. The ensuing legal conflict focused on the sum for which the deceased was billed for the last several months of her residence at the nursing home. *Mishan* was quoting a rate that was five times the rate paid at the retirement home. The basis for this high sum was Article 9C of the initial agreement, signed by Mrs Milgrom. Article 9C stated that the decision to transfer a *Mishan*'s retirement home resident to *Mishan's* nursing home will be determined by a medical opinion provided on behalf of *Mishan*. Furthermore, within this general context:

> ... the requesting party [the resident and his/her family] will be expected to pay *Mishan* for residence in the Nursing Home according to the accepted rates established periodically for hospitalizing *Mishan's* residents in the Nursing Home.

The claim made by the Mrs Milgrom's family was that Article 9C constituted a 'depriving-condition' according to Israel's Standard Contracts Act, and therefore it must be declared void.[1]

The Supreme Court of Israel ruled on several issues pertinent to residential care contracts. First, the court ruled that the purpose of a residential care contract is to establish a long-term relationship that remains in force despite circumstantial changes. This relationship accomplishes important social goals, among them providing residence and securing various needs and services essential to the older resident, while providing stability and security. A second ruling of the Supreme Court was to acknowledge the fact that the residential care facility is in fact the permanent and only home of the older resident for the rest of his/her life. Therefore, the language of the contract should be interpreted as extending the relationship between the two sides to such a time as when the resident requires hospitalization in the Nursing Home. The Supreme Court's third ruling stated clearly that consideration should be given to the fact that the relationship between the residential care providers and the resident creates a dependency of the latter on the former, in that residents often liquidate their home and assets to pay the entrance fee and create the funds necessary for ensuring future payments. In relinquishing a former home, residents become dependent on the residential care providers, their new home, to which they will become accustomed after several years. Finally, the Supreme Court also emphasized the importance of the principles of good faith, fairness, and reasonableness, which underlie the interpretation of residential care contracts:

> It is neither reasonable nor fair to assume that the establishment where the resident spent many years and which was considered a home, should estrange itself from the resident, effectively casting him/her away at old age. This does not conform to the principle of good faith.

Following these findings and rulings, the Supreme Court concluded that Article 9C constitutes a 'depriving-condition' according to the Standard Contracts Act, because it granted *Mishan* the power to unilaterally dictate future rates, a power that is not only absolute but also arbitrary. Therefore the article was declared void and the managers of the deceased's estate were ordered to pay *Mishan* for the time spent at the Nursing Home at the same rate as that paid for residence in the Retirement Home.

---

1 According to Israel's Standard-Contracts Act, the courts have the legal authority to declare specific conditions within a 'standard-contract' as void, if they are found to be 'depriving'. See V. Lusthaus & T. Spanic, *Standard Contracts* (Jerusalem: Nevo, 1994) [in Hebrew].

Throughout the years, the *Milgrom* ruling became the key precedent in Israel regarding the legal construction of contracts in residential care settings. The underlying values of fairness, good faith, and the rights of transparency and full disclosure have since become the standards for construction of legal rights of older persons in residential care in Israel.

Conclusion: Key issues in the human rights of older persons in residential care in Israel

Lack of a positive human right to residential long-term care

As described by Doron (2004), the main problem of the institutional solution, in relation to positive economic and social rights, is that in Israel residential care has never been considered part of the legal right to health; nor has it ever been provided for old people as part of the general system of health or welfare services. The state has provided prolonged institutional care for old people only on the basis of assessment of individual needs, and only then within the stringent budgetary limits of the ministries concerned. Moreover, by applying the principle of family responsibility, as defined in the Family Law Statute (Alimony), 1959, when the old people themselves are unable to afford the cost of institutional living the state has shifted the burden onto the shoulders of their family whenever it is able to pay the price.

The result is that the burden of residential long-term care falls mainly on the old people themselves or on their families (unless they are exempted as the result of a very strict means test). The economic burden is not equal as between different families, since those with higher incomes pay a relatively smaller proportion of their income for the same service. That part of the cost which is nonetheless financed out of the state budget does not cover all the clients' needs, in view of budgetary limitations, and so even those who are deemed eligible for a place in an institution often have to wait for a long time until a budgetary allocation is available, or, having no alternative, are forced to choose an unauthorized old age home, which is less expensive. Finally, the statutory division between the different authorities dealing with prolonged institutional care, and the division between them and the general national health service leads to bureaucratic complications and administrative failures which reduce the ability of old people to achieve their rights.

The absence of human rights ideology in regulating residential care

Beyond the fact that Israel lacks a positive economic right to residential care in old age, the overall regulatory scheme of residential care, in almost all three types of settings in Israel (maybe with the exclusion of the relatively new Assisted Living Act), is based on a paternalistic regulatory framework: it views older persons as a group that should be 'protected' by 'professionals' who know better, and at the same time gives very little place for the voice, preference, and right to self-determination in a residential context.

Many of the new concepts and values that have received broad attention in recent years, such as patient-centered ideology, choice-based policies and active ageing, are almost non-existent in the Israeli regulatory framework. In general, existing regulations can be characterized as being ageist: they are built upon a social construction of old age based on negative stereotypes and biases of old age. The mere fact of being 'old' allows the regulator to intervene in the lives of older persons in residential care under the excuse of the need for protection and care while ignoring the basic liberty and autonomy of the older individual.

The outcome of this legal situation is that the vast majority of older persons who either choose to, or are placed in residential care settings lack the ability to continue to enjoy the protection of fundamental rights of autonomy, liberty and dignity. This does not mean that they are necessarily subject to abuse or neglect, or that they are not well taken care of in the sense of providing all the necessary and minimal requirements of good care. It means that for many, their ability to maintain their personal preferences, their ability to make choices regarding their modes of care; their ability to voice their values and be an active participant regarding the care decisions made on their behalf – are not part of the existing regulatory framework in Israel. For example: they are not able to choose what they eat; when they will wake up, what social activities they will engage in; or which medical treatment they will receive.

An example of this paternalistic approach can be seen in the broad usage of legal guardianship over older persons in residential care in Israel. Both the regulatory and the 'cultural' frameworks described above, have led to a reality in Israel, in which many older persons who move to residential care settings are placed under plenary guardianship. The legal outcome, both formally and in practice, is stripping the older person from his or her legal status as an autonomous person. Actual decisions are made by the formal guardian and in many cases the voices and preferences of the older residents who are under guardianship are not heard or not considered (Doron, 2004a).

Therefore, embedding a human rights approach to Israel's residential care regulatory framework can potentially transform reality in three different ways. First, it can change the 'organizational culture' of managers, professionals, and workers in residential care settings, from that of a 'total institution' culture into a 'patient choice centered' organization. Second, it can change the ways in which older residents view themselves and control their lives within residential care, giving them voice, choice, and ability to influence their daily lives and decisions made regarding their care. Finally, it can change the way by which the supervisory process is conducted, giving more weight and place for quality care standards that measure and assess issues around residents' human rights such as: choice, voice, autonomy and participation – issues which are negligible in existing supervisory processes.

References

A.C. 2724/2007. (Tel Aviv Court of Administrative Affairs; Judge Michal Agmon-Gonen). *Ateret Avot Nursing Home et al., v. The Ministry of Health et al.* [Judgment: 23.5.2011).

Azaiza, F., Lowenstein, A., & Brodsky, J. (2001). Institutionalization for the Elderly is a Novel Phenomenon among the Arab Population in Israel. *Journal of Gerontological Social Work, 31(3–4)*, 65–85.

Bar, S., & Factor, H. (1993). A National Census of the Tenants of the Institutions for Continuing Care and Assisted Living Programs 1990. *Gerontology, 65*, 16–32 (in Hebrew).

Ben-Natan, M., Lowenstein, A., & Eisikovits, Z. (2009). Psycho-Social Factors Affecting Elders' Maltreatment in Long-Term Care Facilities. *Gerontology, 36(2–3)*, 81–107 (in Hebrew).

Brodsky, J., Shnoor, Y., and Be'er, S. (2013). *The Elderly in Israel: Statistical Abstract 2013.* Jerusalem: Eshel (in Hebrew).

Doron, I. (1997). Governing Law for Nursing Homes and Old Age Homes in Israel: A Look toward the Year 2000. *Surveys and Research in Gerontology, 104*, 22–26 (in Hebrew).

Doron, I. (2004). Social Rights for the Elderly. In Y. Rabin & Y. Shany (eds), *Economic, Social and Cultural Rights in Israel* (pp. 893–940). Tel-Aviv: The Ramat Hasharon Law College (in Hebrew).

Doron, I. (2004a). Ageing in the Shadow of Law: Elder Guardianship in Israel. *Journal of Ageing and Social Policy, 16(4)*, 59–77.

Doron, I. (2007). Elder Law in Israel: The Development of a New Field of Law. *Journal of International Aging, Law and Policy, 2*, 33–66.

Doron, I. (2007a). *Law, Justice and Old Age.* Jerusalem: Eshel (in Hebrew).

Doron, I. (2013). *Old Age in Courts of Justice: Older Persons and Ageism in Israel's Supreme Court of Justice.* Tel-Aviv: Resling (in Hebrew).

Doron, I. & Lightman, E. (2003). Market Control or Government Regulation? Assisted Living in Israel. *Ageing & Society 25(6)*, 779–795.

Fleishman, R. (1997). Regulation, Assessment, Follow-up and Continuous Improvement of Care – the RAF Method. *Gerontology, 77*, 55–73 (in Hebrew).

Gross, R., Rosen, B., & Shirom, A. (1999). The Israeli Health Care System after the National Health Insurance Law. *Social Security, 54*, 11–24 (in Hebrew).

King, Y. & Shtarkshall, M. (1997). *Public-Governmental Assisted Living: Characteristics and Needs of the Tenants and the Characteristics of Existing and Desirable Functioning Organizations.* Jerusalem: Eshel (in Hebrew).

Iecovich, E., and Doron, I. (2012). Migrant Workers in Eldercare in Israel: Social and Legal Aspects. *European Journal of Social Work, 15(1)*, 29–44.

Lightman, E., and Doron, I. (2005). Ageing in Place in Israel and Ontario. *Global Ageing, 3(3)*, 22–38.

Lowenstein, A., & Doron, I. (2013). Israel. In A. Phelan (ed.), *International Perspectives on Elder Abuse* (pp. 97–121). New York: Routledge.

Lowenstein, A. and Iecovich, E. (1995). *The Elderly, the Family, and the Institutional Settings.* Tel Aviv: Ramot (in Hebrew).

Metlife Assisted Living Market Survey 2002, http://www.metlife.com/Applications/Corporate/WPS/CDA/PageGenerator.

Sheffer, S. (2002). A Field with its Future in its Wake. *Ha'aretz Real Estate.* 26 May 2002, p. 11 (in Hebrew).

Shtarkshall, M. (1987). *Sheltered Housing for the Elderly in Israel: Developments Over the Past Five Years and Present Status.* Jerusalem: Eshel (in Hebrew).

The Arie Shaham v. Ministry of Health (2003). Supreme Court Case 4613/03.

The Estate of Mrs. Hilda Milgrom et al. v. Mishan Center et al. (1997). BRI, 1185/97 Piskei-Din. 52(4) 145.

7 Human rights and residential care for older people in Japan

Takashi Amano, Naoki Ikegami, Tomoaki Ishibashi

Introduction

Scandals exposed by the media often reveal the reality and make people aware of hidden social issues. However, although violation of human rights in residential care has been exposed over several decades in Japan, they have not led to strong regulations. This chapter will begin by presenting the background on the Japanese ageing society in general and formal residential care services for older people in particular. Next, the existing legal systems for protecting the human rights of older people in residential care will be described. The third section will provide information on the legal and regulatory framework. The fourth section will summarize problems in the Japanese systems and discuss the reasons why they have not been resolved. Finally, it would conclude with recommendations for other countries and for Japan.

General background

The age of 65 and over is when a person is regarded as "old" in Japan (MHLW, 2008a). The country has the highest proportion of older people in the world (OECD, 2014). The Japanese government estimates that there are approximately 31.9 million people who are age 65 years and older in October 2013, composing 25.1% of the total. The number of older people has consistently increased for more than 50 years and is expected to continue rising until 2042 (Cabinet Office Government of Japan, 2014).

Japan is regarded as an elder-friendly society because of its Confucian tradition (Formanek, 2008). There is a national holiday called the "Respect for the aged day (*keirō no hi*)" which celebrates and honors older people. Traditionally, Japanese households were composed of three generations: parents, the eldest son and his wife, and their children. In these households, it was the responsibility of the daughter-in-law to take care of the parents. In 2001, 32.5% of all households with people who need care were still in these "third generation households (*sansedai setai*)" and 42.4% of the primary caregivers were either the spouse of the child (22.5%) or the child (19.5%) (MHLW, 2001b). However, in 2013, the proportion of the "third generation households" had declined to 18.4% and that of the child's spouse as the primary caregiver to 11.2% (MHLW, 2013a). The implementation of the public long-term care insurance (LTCI) in 2000 has accelerated these changes. Yet, despite these changes, the caring of parents is still perceived as a family responsibility: 439,300 people gave up or changed their jobs in order to take care of their family members from 2007 to 2012 (Ministry of Internal Affairs and Communications, 2012).

There are many types of "residential care" for older people in Japan. We decided to include the types that provide care services to support activities of daily living (ADL), and excluded those that provide only meals. They have been grouped into four broad categories listed below. The numbers of users, and as ratios to the population 65 and over, of each type are shown in Table 7.1.

1) The welfare facilities for older people which were established by the Welfare Act for Elders [*rōjin fukushi hō*]. Their residents are the indigent without family or relatives who require only light care.

2) The LTCI facilities (traditional type) are for those with a moderate to high need of 24-hour support in ADL. In this category are the Special Homes for Aged, which were in the welfare sector, and the Health Facilities for Elders (HFE) and the Medical Long-term Care Sanatoriums [*kaigo ryoyōkata iryō shisetsu*] which were in the health sector, before being transferred to LTCI in 2000. The Convalescent HFE was established in 2006 to receive the Medical Long-term Care Sanatoriums which were planned to be phased out by the end of fiscal year 2011 (since extended to 2016). However, since their

Table 7.1 Number in residential services and as percentage of population 65

		Number	Percentage of population 65+*
Welfare facilities	Homes for the Aged	54,353	0.17%
	Care Houses	69,594	0.22%
LTCI facilities (traditional type)	Special Homes for the Aged	531,671	1.67%
	Health Facilities for the Elderly	346,696	1.09%
	Medical Long-term Care Sanatoriums	65,132	0.20%
LTCI facilities (new type)	Group Homes	181,702	0.57%
	Specified Facilities	193,433	0.61%
Health Insurance financed facilities	Patients hospitalized more than 90 days	22,300	0.7%
Total		1,464,881	4.60%

*2012 data for health insurance financed facilities and 2013 data for all other facilities and total. General population figures are for the corresponding year of each.

From Cabinet Office Government of Japan (2013 and 2014) and MHLW (2014a, b, and 2015a)

estimated number is less than 5% of the HFE, and the government statistics does not list them separately, we have listed them together with HFE in Table 7.1.

3) The LTCI facilities (new type) are composed of Group Homes for those with Alzheimer's and Specified Facilities which may be owned by for-profit organizations and are free to set their own charges for hotel services.

4) The health insurance financed long-stay patients. Hospitals provide a significant part of LTC in Japan. The number of patients hospitalized in non-psychiatric beds for more than 90 days (MHLW, 2014a) is listed in Table 7.1.

Historical development of welfare facilities for older people

The first public institutional care for older people was developed by the enactment of the Poor Relief Law [*kyugo hō*] in 1929, which was the first Japanese modern welfare law (Tanaka, 1993). Before the law, Asylums for the Aged [*yōrōin*] were established mainly by local benefactors, non-profit organizations, or religious organizations without subsidization from government. The law founded a legal basis for stipulation of asylums by local and central government (Hieda, 2012). However, the proportion of the frail older people who received residential care remained very low even after the enactment (Momose, 1997). After World War II (WWII), Japan had many children without parents, and people who were indigent or had disability. In 1950, the Public Assistance Act [*seikatsu hogo hō*] was enacted to help these people. Before this act, institutions were for all adults. This law differentiated institutions for older people from those for non-elderly adults and renamed those for older people as Institutions for the Aged [*yōrō shishetsu*]. The eligibility was still strictly limited to those who were indigent and had no family or relatives.

The first expansion of the above restriction was the enactment of the Welfare Act for Elders in 1963, which was spear-headed by Shintarō Seto, Director of the Institutional Division within the Social Affairs Bureau of the Ministry of Health and Welfare (MHW). He wanted to lay the ground work for a new government initiative in ageing because post-war poverty issues had been largely resolved by that time (Campbell, 1992). One tangible outcome, though on a very small scale, was the establishment of institutions for frail older people. They were not officially referred to as "nursing homes" because care was not under the direction of nurses, but under the rubric of welfare organizations. The literal English translation is Special Homes for the Aged [*tokubetsu yōgo rōjin hōmu*], and named as such so as to distinguish them from the Homes for the Aged [*yōgo rōjin hōmu*], which was renamed from the pre-existing Institutions for the Aged. The latter had been restricted to the indigent but the new type was not: it was for all older people who had more serious physical and mental disabilities. These two types of homes still exist and are defined as the welfare facilities for older people in the Welfare Act for Elders.

Another type of welfare facility for older people developed when the Welfare Act for Elders was enacted. This was the Low-cost Homes for the Elderly [*keihi rōjin hōmu*] for those who had low income but not so indigent as to be eligible for the Homes for the Aged. Older people have to contract with the facility in order to use this service. There were two types of Low-cost Homes for the Elderly: Type A and Type B. Food is provided in Type A but not in Type B. In both, residents are expected to be independent in ADL. Later, the government expanded the function of the Low-cost Homes for the Elderly and created the Type C called "Care Houses [*kea hausu*]". In Type C, the facility provides food, bathing, and consultation services (MHW, 1989b). Thus, there currently are three types of Low-cost Homes for the Elderly but only Care Houses are listed in Table 7.1. Note that Types A and B have not been allowed to be established since 2008.

Parenthetically, the Welfare Act for Elders also created the Fee-based Homes for the Elderly [*yuryō rōjin hōmu*]. However, among them, those that provide ADL support are now categorized as "Specified Facilities" in the LTCI, while those that do not would not be included in our definition of "residential care". Therefore, we have not included them in Table 7.1.[1]

Historical development of LTCI facilities (traditional type) and health insurance financed facilities

In 1973, the government made health care free (no copayment) to all older people 70 and over, and to those with disabilities 65 and over. This was when economic growth was at its peak and the expansion of the welfare state was being promoted by progressive prefectural governors. Since there was no limitation on the length of hospital stay, this policy unintentionally opened the door to hospital admissions for "social reasons". Patients whose families were unable or unwilling to take care of older people came to be admitted and remained in hospital until they died. Thus, many hospitals were transformed into *de facto* nursing homes. The proportion of the general population aged 65 and over who were hospital inpatients on the day of the annual survey doubled from 2% in 1975 to 4% in 1990, and came to constitute two-thirds of all older people who were institutionalized (MHW, 1975a, b; 1992a, b). The government attempted to remedy this situation by establishing Health Facilities for the Elderly (HFE) [*rōjin hoken shisetsu*] in 1986. The HFE was intended to function as an intermediate care facility between the hospital and the community and, as such, the length of stay of their residents was officially limited to three months. Another attempt made by the government was to improve the environment of the hospital beds for older people. In 1992, the government set high payment for "Long-term Care (LTC) Units [*ryōyō kata byōshō gun*]" which meet requirements of standards such as the size of the room per bed and having a dining room.

LTC services expanded rapidly after the implementation of the "Gold Plan" (officially, Ten Year Plan to Develop Health and Welfare Services for Elders) in 1989. It was part of the ruling Liberal Democratic Party's strategy to win back

1 Specified Facilities are composed of Housing with Services for Elders, Homes for Aged, Care Houses, and Fee-based Homes for the Elderly. 76% were Fee-based Homes for the Elderly in 2011 (MHLW, 2014d).

votes after nearly losing the election that followed the introduction of the VAT (value added tax) earlier in that year. Although the main focus of this plan was to expand community services, expansion of institutional care was also planned. The goal was to establish 240,000 beds of the Special Homes for the Aged, 280,000 beds of the HFE, and Care Houses for 100,000 people (MHW, 1989a). The expansion of LTC services under the Gold Plan proved so popular it was subsequently revised with higher targets in the five year "New Gold Plan" of 1994. The New Gold Plan's goals were generally met (Ministry of Health, Labour and Welfare: MHLW, 2001a). Although services did expand, they continued to be provided only by local governments or by special welfare organizations. As such, regulatory mechanisms covering the new types of service providers did not develop, and the services tended to remain focused on those with low income. Parenthetically, the expansion of health services such as HFE and visiting nurse agencies was also planned, but, unlike the tax-financed social services, health insurance did not cover the funding of their capital expenditures.

A major policy initiative after the "Gold Plan" was the implementation of the public LTC insurance (LTCI) [*kaigo hoken*] in 2000, which made LTC services an entitlement, regardless of income level or availability of family support, to all those 65 and over, and to those 40–64 with disabilities resulting from age-related diseases such as strokes or Parkinson's (Ikegami, 2007; Campbell et al., 2010). Public awareness of the rapidly ageing society, the growing inadequacy of informal care, problems of "social admissions" to hospitals, increasing pressure on general revenues, and problems with the bureaucratic administration of social services by municipal governments all contributed to the implementation of this new program. Half of the expenditures are financed by social insurance premiums levied on all those 40 and over, and half by general taxes, with an additional 10% copayment and the partial levying of "hotel costs" for bed and board. Although the LTCI is administered by municipal governments, it is a social insurance program based on the principle of individual entitlement with guaranteed benefits and free choice of providers. The standards and the LTCI fee schedule are nationally uniform, except for adjustments made in the reimbursed amount reflecting local living costs, and minor differences in how the prefectural governments disclose the audit reports of providers.

The maximum amount of benefits for purchasing LTC services is set for each of the seven levels of eligibility. Being eligible or not, and the level of eligibility, are determined by an assessment of the applicant's physical and mental status using a 74-item check list. The assessment is based on universal standards without any provisions for people with special needs, such as being blind. The amount for the highest benefit level is $3,600 per month, the lowest $500. Benefits are limited to services which must be purchased from certified providers. Cash allowances were excluded because feminists groups opposed them on the ground that it would not alleviate their care burden and might conversely increase the social pressure for them to provide care rather than to pursue career opportunities (Campbell, 2002). The fact that the tradition of live-in maids had practically died out and the virtual absence of immigrant labor may also have decreased the public demand for cash benefits.

The providers must be designated [*shitei*] by the LTCI in order to provide services under LTCI. They can be grouped into the following: the first are those that would have been in the social service sector (Special Homes for the Aged) prior to the implementation of LTCI; the second are those that would have been in the health care sector (Medical Long-term Care Sanatoriums (transferred from LTC Units) and HFE); the third are the new for-profit and non-profit organizations which were allowed entry into home and community-based care (HCBC) market, but not into the institutional care market, following the implementation of the LTCI.

In addition, the health insurance financed long-term care in hospitals has continued. When the LTCI was implemented, only half of the hospital convalescent beds were transferred. The rest remained and, in fact, increased after the government suddenly announced in 2005, that as part of a general policy to contain public expenditures, all Medical Long-term Care Sanatoriums would be abolished by the end of fiscal year 2011. To facilitate the transfer of Medical Long-term Care Sanatorium beds, a new type of institution, the "Convalescent HFE [*kaigo ryoyōkata rōjin hoken shisetsu*]", which has staffing and physical standards half way between Medical Long-term Care Sanatoriums and the HFE, was introduced. However, the National Association of Chronic Care Hospitals (2010), which includes both health insurance and LTCI financed LTC hospitals, has vigorously opposed the closure of Medical Long-term Care Sanatoriums beds. Very few of the Medical Long-term Care Sanatoriums have converted to this new type (MHLW, 2010d), while many have opted to be financed by health insurance. As part of the LTCI revision legislation passed in 2011, Medical Long-term Care Sanatoriums have been extended for another six years (MHLW, 2011b).

Historical development of LTCI facilities (new type)

The LTCI turned out to be very popular. Expenditure doubled from 2000 to 2010 to reach the current level of 1.4% of the GDP (MHLW, 2011a; OECD, 2011). It has crowded out services privately purchased so that virtually all LTC services are provided within the LTCI. Despite these increases, waiting lists for admission to nursing homes have continued to lengthen and now exceeds over one year (Nomura Research Institute, 2010). LTCI facilities are more popular than HCBC because they provide 24-hour coverage at relatively low out-of-pocket costs ($700 per month inclusive rate for a standard four bed room, with the amount reduced if the resident is low income). To meet this excess demand, two new types of institutions which are officially categorized as HCBC and therefore permissible for the entry of new for-profit and non-profit organizations have increased tremendously. The "Specified Facilities [*tokutei shisetsu*]" (similar to the Special Homes for Aged but with better amenities) and the "Group Homes" (single rooms with a common living area in units of less than ten for those with mild to moderate dementia). The reason why these facilities have increased so much is that, in contrast to the formal "institutions", they do not rely on subsidies for their construction costs and are able to set their own price for bed and board. In addition to these quasi-institutions, the number of "Housing with Services for Elders [*sa-bisu tuki kōreisha jutaku*]" in which services provided under the LTCI are paid on the same basis as in HCBC, has also increased. Some of them may have a home-helper agency, visiting nurse station and a physician's office on the ground floor of the same building. This type has been actively promoted by the government especially after the reform of the LTCI Act in 2006. The expression of "maintain dignity [*songen no hoji*]" was also stipulated in the purpose of the LTCI Act as part of the reform. The government declared that "flexible services should be provided according to characteristics of the community where older people have lived for long time" in order to "maintain dignity" of them (MHLW, 2006a).

General background on Japan's human-rights protection system and older person's rights

The Constitution of Japan is the basis of Japan's human rights protection systems. The draft of the current Constitution was developed under the occupation of the United States after WWII. One of the three important ideas in structuring post-WWII Japanese society was the commitment to human rights. Others were "Pacifism" and "Popular sovereignty" (Neary, 2002). Reflecting these goals, the constitution states that the "fundamental human rights" are "eternal and inviolate rights" that are "guaranteed to the people" (The Constitution of Japan Article 11; Ministry of Justice: MOJ, 2015d). The third Chapter of the Constitution lists those fundamental human rights of civil liberties and social rights that are guaranteed to the people. The civil liberties include the right for the following: freedom for political, economic, and social activities, to claim on the government, to criminal justice, to maintain the minimum standards of wholesome and cultured life, to an education corresponding to ability, to work, for workers to organize, bargain, and act collectively.

International movements have also shaped Japan's human rights protection systems. The inception of Japan's international human rights commitment was the ratification of the International Covenant on Civil and Political Rights (ICCPR) and International Covenant on Economic, Social and Cultural Rights (ICESCR) in 1979. After which Japan has continued to participate in many treaties related to human rights such as the Convention on the Elimination of All Forms of Discrimination against Women and Convention on the Rights of Persons with Disabilities. In addition, Japan has amended and enacted some of its laws after the ratification of these treaties as the Constitution of Japan stated: "The treaties concluded by Japan and established laws of nations shall be faithfully observed" (The Constitution of Japan Article 98 Section 2: MOJ, 2015e). For example, Japan enacted the Act on Securing, Etc. of Equal Opportunity and Treatment between Men and Women in Employment [*danjo koyōkikai kintō hō*]' (MOJ, 2015a) after the ratification of the Convention on the Elimination of All Forms of Discrimination against Women in 1986.

Elder-rights specific human right protection systems

Targeted human rights protection legislation for older people did not develop until recently. There are three major legal measures to protect elder human rights: prohibition of physical restraints is standard for LTCI facilities and welfare facilities, guardianship for adults, and the Act on the Prevention of Elder Abuse.

Prohibition of physical restraints

In the late 1980s, the media started to cover the problems in care for those "socially hospitalized" older people. Reports of media revealed many older people receiving poor and inappropriate care with heavy use of physical restraints (Okuma, 1988; The Asahi Shimbun, 1995). In response, some hospitals declared that they would abolish physical restraints in hospitals (The Asahi Shimbun, 1998).

The prohibition of physical restraints in facilities for older people became one of the concerns in the enactment of the LTCI in 2000. This regulation prohibits facilities to apply "physical restraints and other acts which restrict residents' activities" unless "the resident's life or health has been materially threatened". However, the restraint could be applied if there is documentation showing that the decision to apply restraints was made after having been discussed by the care team, the objective and the period are clearly stated, and explanations as to why restraints are necessary have been provided to the resident and/or family. Abolishment of physical restraints was made one of the conditions to be certified as a LTCI institution. The Welfare Act for Elders was also amended so that the restrictions would be the same. However, the regulations do not clarify what actual actions are to be considered as "physical restraints" and other "acts which restrict residents' activities". To clarify this and to facilitate the execution of prohibition in the field, the MHLW organized a committee for "Zero Physical Restraint Movement" immediately after the implementation of LTCI Act (MHLW, 2001c). The committee then issued the *Guidebook for Zero Physical Restraint Movement*. This Guidebook clearly states that physical restraints are physically, mentally, and socially harmful for older people and should be considered as a violation of human rights. It defines the actual actions of physical restraints. Table 7.2 shows the physical restraint procedures prohibited in this guidebook. The guidebook also states that physical restraints can be applied when the facility can prove that the following three conditions

Table 7.2 Physical restraint procedures prohibited in facilities

1 Tying a person to a wheelchair/bed to prevent wandering
2 Tying a person to a bed for fall prevention
3 Using siderails to keep a person in bed
4 Tying limbs to prevent a person from pulling out IV/feeding tubes
5 Applying mittens to prevent a person from pulling out IV/feeding tubes or tearing skin
6 Restricting a person with belts or tray tables to prevent sliding or rising from a (wheel) chair
7 Using a chair to prevent a person from being able to stand up
8 Using overalls over clothing to impede removal of clothes/diapers
9 Tying a person to a bed to prevent them from causing trouble to others
10 Giving an overdose of psychotropic drugs to reduce excitement
11 Locking a person in a room

From Kurata and Ojima (2014) modified by the authors

are met: being imminent (the resident's or other residents' lives are threatened by the resident's behavior), not substitutable (no other option is available for stopping the behavior), and temporary (the application of the restraint is only temporary).

However, when this regulation was introduced, there were no defined sanctions or punishments for violations. It was only in 2006 that a new standard was set by the MHLW (MHLW, 2006c). In the new standard, reimbursement from LTCI would be reduced if the facility applied physical restraints to residents without having documentation. Although this was an advance, the extent to which it has had any actual effects remains doubtful because investigation is limited to documentation. Observations of the residents are not conducted during audits.

System of guardianship for adults

Before the LTCI Act, LTC services for older people were provided through "welfare placement system [*sochi seido*]" by the government. Under this system, the government decided what to provide for whom. Service recipients were not allowed to choose providers. In contrast, the LTCI Act gave recipients rights to choose services by making them available based on an individual contract between the older people and the service provider. To resolve this issue for those with cognitive impairment, a major legislative reform was made in 1999 before the implementation of the LTCI that initiated a new system of guardianship for adults with impaired ability in decision making. The main feature of this system was that adult guardians can be appointed (by an individual or a court order) for people with impaired ability in decision making to take legal actions on behalf of the impaired older people. Legal actions may include managing property and contracting the use of health care services.

This Japanese system of adult guardianship has several problems from the viewpoint of protecting human rights of older people in residential care. First, the guardianship is focused more on property management and less on care services. The guardian's main role is 'domestic' property management (Arai, 2008). Second, the number of guardians involved in contracts of care still remains small. In fact, 69% of the reasons of applications for guardianship were property management in 2014 (Supreme Court of Japan, 2015). Third, the guardian does not act as an advocate of the resident. Guardians' rights are strictly limited to legal acts such as documentation for contracts. Although they 'shall respect the intention of the adult ward, and consider his/her mental and physical condition and living circumstances' (MOJ, 2015c), it does not mean that they are allowed to consent to healthcare received by the adult ward (Kinzai Institution for Financial Affairs, 1998). Therefore, residents of longterm care facilities with impaired ability of decision making may receive inappropriate and/or unwilling healthcare even if they have legal guardians under this system.

Act on the Prevention of elder abuse

Elder abuse caught social attention in the same period of time as physical restraints in hospitals emerged as a social problem. The book *Elder Abuse* [*Rōjin Gyakutai*] was published in 1987 (Kaneko, 1987). It was the first Japanese book to described elder abuse in Japan (Yamada, 2004). The MHW gave a grant for the first research project on elder abuse in which a survey was conducted in 1994. After this research was published, the general public started to recognize elder abuse as a social problem (Yamada, 2004). However, media coverages, research projects, and public attention did not immediately lead to any specific legal systems for preventing elder abuse even when the LTCI Act was enacted in 2000.

Nonetheless, the implementation of the LTCI Act brought more attention to elder abuse. Because home visiting services were expanded by the LTCI Act, many more formal caregivers served older people. These providers began reporting more elder abuse by family caregivers. The first nationwide research on elder abuse was conducted in 2003 (Association for Health Economics Research and Social Insurance and Welfare, 2004). Primary respondents of this investigation were care managers who were responsible for drawing their clients' care plans. Results from this research were published in 2004 and focused attention on the need for a legal system preventing elder abuse (Yamada, 2008). In response, the Act on the Prevention of Elder Abuse, Support for Caregivers of Elderly Persons and Other Related Matters [*kōreisha gyakutai no bōshi, kōreisha no yōgosha ni taisuru shien tō ni kansuru hōritsu*] was enacted in 2006.

One of the key features of this act is that it clearly defines elder abuse for the first time in Japanese law. According to the act, elder abuse comprises acts inflicted by an informal caregiver or a "care facility staff member [*yōkaigo shisetsu ju-jisha tō*]" to people age 65 or older and fall under any of the items listed in Table 7.3.

Table 7.3 List of abusive acts

Physical abuse	Inflicting an assault upon an elderly person that will cause or is likely to cause external harm to his/her body
Neglecting	Substantially failing to take care of an elderly person, including severely depriving the elderly person of food or leaving him/her unattended for a long period of time in a manner that would likely cause his/her health condition to deteriorate
Psychological abuse	Directing to an elderly person any words or deeds which would likely be significantly traumatic to him/her, including significantly abusive language or a significantly negative attitude toward him/her
Sexual abuse	Committing an indecent act against an elderly person, or making an elderly person engage in such an act
Economic abuse	The unjust disposal of an elderly person's property by a caregiver or relative, or any other unjust acquisition of a property benefit from an elderly person

From Ministry of Justice (2015b) and Dementia Care Research and Training Center Sendai (2009)

The second feature is that its focus is on early detection of and response to elder abuse (Dementia Care Research and Training Center Sendai, 2009). To achieve the purpose, this act stipulates the citizen's responsibility of reporting elder abuse in Article 7.1.

Article 7.1

In cases where any person has discovered an elderly person who is likely to have been subjected to elder abuse by a caregiver, and if such elderly person's life or health has been materially threatened, such person shall promptly report this to the relevant municipality.

Because "any person" includes people working at care facilities, the act also declares that "a confidentiality obligation shall not be construed to preclude any reporting" of elder abuse. In addition, the responsibility and authority of the municipality are also defined. When the municipality is informed of a report, it "shall promptly implement measures to confirm the safety of such elderly person and any other measures to identify the facts so notified or reported, and shall consult with parties that collaborate with such municipality pursuant to the provisions of elder abuse response partners regarding how to respond to such elder abuse". When the mayor of a municipality finds that "elder abuse by a caregiver may have posed a material threat to the life or health of an elderly person", he/she may instruct officials appointed by the LTCI act or other officials to perform an on-site inspection in the older person's domicile or residence. The mayor also may seek assistance from the chief of police with jurisdiction over the location of the domicile or residence of the relevant older person when he/she deems it necessary for the execution of the inspection.

The third feature is that it stipulates the responsibility of municipalities and care facilities for supporting caregivers and "care facility staff members". As expressed in the title, this act aims at "preventing" elder abuse and "supporting" caregivers. This idea stems from the underlying theory of elder abuse, that is, caregivers factors (such as care burden and lack of knowledge) are major risk factors for elder abuse. Reflecting the theory, Article 14.1 prescribes the responsibility of a municipality as it "shall, for the purpose of alleviating the burden on a caregiver, implement necessary measures, such as providing consultations, guidance and advice for the caregiver". In addition, Article 20 prescribes care facilities shall provide trainings for care facility staff members and "shall arrange a system for handling complaints raised by elderly persons", "as well as complaints raised by their families".

Parenthetically, although this act defines older people as people age 65 or older, it had an influence on preventing abuse for younger people. In the appendix of the Act, it is stipulated that the system for prevention of abuse for non-older people who need care because of their mental or physical disabilities should be discussed and implemented as soon as possible. The LTCI Act had a major amendment in 2006 when the Act on the Prevention of Elder Abuse was enacted. The Article 115 was amended to fulfill the requirement posted on the appendix. It stipulates that municipalities are responsible for providing the "community support project" of prevention of abuse for people who are eligible for LTCI. Because people age 40–64 with age-related disability (such as stroke and Alzheimer's) are eligible for LTCI, the community support project can be provided to prevent abuse for those in this age group.

The existing legislation clearly has several problems from the perspective of protecting elder rights in residential care, notably the lack of the power of enforcement. For example, there are no sanctions or punishments for acts of abuse. There are two penal provisions but they are for violation of confidentiality obligation and for being uncooperative or giving a false answer during an on-site inspection. To cite another example, the act permits a mayor of a municipality to instruct officials to do an on-site inspection only when he/she finds that "elder abuse by a caregiver may have posed a material threat to the life or health of an older person". Since care facilities tend to be closed to the community, this provision could inhibit any opportunity for detecting elder abuse in care facilities. Municipalities also have authority to do an on-site inspection with a report of elder abuse for the care facility based on the LTCI Act and the Welfare Act for Elders. However, it is "recommended" by the MHLW that the municipality should ask for the facility's cooperation and ascertain the existence of elder abuse (MHLW, 2006b). As a result, few on-site inspections have been conducted. 118 inspections (on-site inspection, audit, or review of documents) were made in 2013 out of 221 cases which were regarded as "elder abuse cases" in welfare facilities and LTCI facilities (traditional and new types). These are very small numbers considering that the total number of reports and consultation was 962 (MHLW, 2015d).

One possible reason why the provisions with strong enforcement were not included was that the main focus was on preventing abuse by informal caregivers. As cited above, this act is based only on nationwide research on elder abuse by informal caregivers. Although researches on elder abuse by facility care staff have been conducted after the enactment of the Act, no major amendments have been made on the Act based on their findings.

Key legal-regulatory framework of Japan's institutional/residential care

Because most residential care services are provided based on the LTCI, some regulations in the LTCI Act are also effective in protecting human rights of residents. They consist of the following three: surveillance on compliance to standards of designation, disclosure of information, and complaint processes. Similar regulations are stipulated in the Welfare Act for Elders for welfare facilities. Note that they would not apply to the health insurance financed facilities or to undesignated "housing". The recent media coverage of the use of restraints occurred in such undesignated "housing" owned by a medical clinic.

Regulations for the LTCI facilities
Surveillance on compliance to the standards for designation

To designate a provider as a LTCI facility, an application form is submitted show-ing that it had met the necessary staffing and physical plant requirements. On-site inspections are made for confirmation. For on-going monitoring, the attendance book of the staff is closely inspected. The number of staff per resident must be met both on a daily and a calendar month basis. Table 7.4 shows the requirements for each facility. The auditing of the LTCI facilities for compliance to standards is made in conjunction with that of compliance to LTCI reimbursement rules. The LTCI fee schedule determines the price of all services and the conditions that the provider must comply with in order to be reimbursed. Following the practice set by health insurance, when fees are revised, they are revised individually and not across-the-board at the same rate. This fine-tuning is made so as to provide incen-tives and disincentives to meet policy goals (Ikegami & Campbell, 1999; 2004). For example, in the 2009 fee schedule revision which was designed to encourage home-helper agencies to hire more experienced workers, the price per visit was set higher for an agency if one-third of their workers had either three or more years of experience, or had the qualification of a certified care worker (MHLW, 2009). By doing so, the agency's profit would increase because their temporary workers would continue to be paid at the same rate. Audits are made to verify that the agencies do meet the specifications, should the agency bill at this higher rate. Parenthetically, non-government, third party audits focused on user satisfaction surveys and self-evaluation on their management aspects are also made (Tokyo Metropolitan Government, 2011). But, except for Group Homes, they are volun-tary and providers are allowed to choose the organization conducting the survey so that they have not had much impact.

Table 7.4 Staffing regulations for institutional care

	Special Homes for Aged	HFE	Medical Long-term Care Sanatoriums
Physicians	As needed	1 per 100 residents	3 per 100 residents
Nurses	1 if less than 30 2 if 31–50 3 if >50	Nurse to care worker ratio must be >3:1	1 per 6
Care workers	1 (can be a nurse) per 3	1 (can be a nurse) per 3	1 per 6
Therapists	1 (could be nurse or certified massager)	1 PT or OT or ST per 100	PT or OT as required
Social workers	1 per 100	1 or more	No requirement
Care managers	1 per 100	1 per 100	1 per 100
Pharmacists	No requirement	As needed	1 per 150

From MHLW (2014c)

The ultimate penalty for non-compliance is revocation of its designation as a LTCI provider. During the ten-year period from the implementation of the LTCI to the end of fiscal year 2009, a total of 777 agencies have had their license revoked, of which about three-quarters were for-profit (compared with 586 for the total; MHLW, 2010b). On a yearly basis, since the average number of agencies was 964,032 during these nine years, the percentage of the total revoked averaged 0.076%, varying from 0.03% in 2001 to 0.09% in 2005 (MHLW, 2010c). The more frequently used penalty is denying the reimbursement of the services inappropriately billed. The amount returned has been about from 0.02% (2005) to 0.005% (2001) of the total billed (MHLW, 2010c). While these percentages are low, it has had a signal effect on providers because those having a record of inappropriate billing tend to have all their claims audited more closely. The number of agencies who have had their license revoked after 2009 still remains small (118 in 2010 and 166 in 2011; MHLW, 2013b).

Disclosure of information

LTCI facilities and agencies must submit an annual report to the prefectural governor. This is then posted on a website. The information is descriptive and consists of the following: name, location, contacting form, number of care workers, facility status, and charges. In addition, the results of the prefectural audit are also reported on the web, but the degree to which this is disclosed varies across prefectures.

Complaint processes

The process for dealing with complaints from residents and their families could be regarded as another system for protecting human rights. There are three complaint processes. First, complaints can be made directly to the service provider. Every provider must have a designated person to handle complaints and their records are inspected at the time of the audit. The second approach is through their care manager who must follow up on any complaints made. The third is through their LTC insurer. Should a follow-up be required, it is performed by the prefectural unions of LTCI plans which have the authority to inspect and order improvement as needed. In fiscal year 2014, there were 6,128 consultations, of which 223 were followed-up (Kokuho Chuōkai, 2014). According to a survey made in Tokyo, about a quarter of the consultations were related to a complaint (Tokyo CHI Federation, 2010).

Family members can voice their complaints through family members' associations which are established in most facilities. However, it is very rare to have representatives of the residents in the organization's board or in the management committee. This is not due to the lack of attention to human rights, but because residents generally do not have the capacity. Those who are admitted to the Special Homes for Aged are very frail.

Recently, some LTCI facilities began to utilize an ombudsperson to respond to complaints of residents and to protect human rights of residents. Civil organizations of ombudspersons have been established in all prefectures (Kitamura, 2004). However, the ombudsperson system has no legal basis and decision to utilize the ombudsperson is completely voluntary and left to the facility.

Regulations for welfare facilities

Welfare facilities are "authorized [*ninka*]" to provide services by prefectural governments based on the Welfare Act for Elders. Three regulatory actions (surveillance on compliance to standards of authorization, disclosure of information, and complaint processes) are mandated similarly to the LTCI facilities. One major difference is that in the surveillance, a visit is made directly by officials from the prefectural government. The officials inspect how residents are treated, how dignity of residents is maintained, if services are provided as planned, if the environment of the facility is safe, and compliance of staffing and facility standards. However, the period between visits could be four years if the facility receives regular audit by a third party organization and has no issues in their management. Only 34.1% (19 facilities) of the welfare facilities in Tokyo prefecture (total of 85 facilities) received an inspection in 2012 (Tokyo Metropolitan Government, 2013). Visits are made after prior notification. Therefore, this regulation might not be sufficiently effective for inspecting violation of residents' human rights.

Key issues and trends in human rights of residential care

Japanese protection systems for human rights in residential care lack the power of enforcement. A newspaper reported in 2014 that inspections by municipalities revealed the use of heavy physical restraints on elderly residents in an "apartment for seniors" (The Asahi Shimbun Digital, 2014). The "apartment" was run by a medical corporation and was not designated as Fee-Based Homes for the Elderly under the Welfare Act for Elders. However, it was advertised as an apartment with care services because it "cooperated" with the medical corporation. These care services were provided by home visiting care providers which are owned by the medical corporation. Because visiting home helpers and/or nurses provide care only for approximately 30 minutes, three to four times a day, many residents were physically restrained (e.g. tied to a bed, mittens applied) for almost 24 hours to prevent disruptive behaviors. However, following the precedence made by the Tokyo prefectural government in 2009 which decided that such housing did not fall under the Fee-Based Homes in the Welfare Act for Elders, the regulations were not applied (The Asahi Shimbun Digital, 2014). The LTCI regulations are applicable only to restricting the application of physical restraints in institutional settings, and not by designated home-visiting service providers. Despite this exposure and other past media attention, the argument for making regulations stricter has not been strongly raised in Japan. It should also be noted that even in institutional care where regulations do apply, few problems have been reported. There were 221 cases reported as "cases of abuse" in institutions in 2013 (MHLW, 2015d). Only 67 institutional care facilities have had their license revoked during the period from the implementation of the LTCI to the end of fiscal year 2011 (MHLW, 2013b). These numbers are extremely small considering that there were 30,008 LTCI designated facilities providing institutional care in 2013 (MHLW, 2014e).

The lenient regulation systems allow facilities to hide incidents, abuse, or illegal restraints. The public sympathy extended towards care workers may also contribute to make facilities closed to the community. Because the media has drawn attention to their harsh work environment, and their personal experience of providing care, many regard them as people with good personality doing a socially demanding job. For example, after the scandal of the "senior apartment" was reported, the same newspaper posted comments from readers, some justifying the application of physical restraints on the grounds of the heavy care burden. Family members of residents may also justify or ignore violations of human rights because they feel fortunate for being able to be admitted. The waiting list for Special Homes for Aged is approximately 520,000, more than the number of their beds currently available (MHLW, 2014e; MHLW, 2014f).

However, there might be some basis to why few problems have been reported. This is the relatively high quality of care workers in Japan; 96.3% of the care workers have graduated from high school or higher educational institutes and 50.6% of care workers are registered as "certified care workers [*kaigo fukushi shi*]" (literal translation "care and welfare workers"), which requires graduation from a two-year professional school or passing a national examination after experiencing three years of care work (Care Work Foundation, 2014). Care workers in the community who do not have such qualifications must have a certificate stating that they have completed 130 hours of schooling. The curriculums for these certificates include subjects not only on techniques of caregiving but also subjects on ethical matters such as "dignity of human", "life and welfare", and "understanding social welfare" (MHLW, 2008b). Thus, except for a small minority of those working in institutional settings, the greater majority have some kind of qualification that has nurtured work ethics and have had professional training on ethical issues. Some may even receive their qualifications by completing a four-year university-level course and have an undergraduate degree. There are 60 (four-year) universities which provide a professional course for certified care workers (Japan Association of Training Institutions for Certified Care Workers, 2015). Most of these courses have curriculums that would provide them with a license for certified care workers and a qualification to sit for the national examination for certified social workers on graduation. Since the latter is difficult to pass, 55.8% of the graduates pursue a career as care workers, and only 22.9% in social work related jobs (Japanese Association of Schools of Social Work, 2012). One possible reason why Japan has this unique system lies in the fact that qualifications for care work and social work were legislated at the same time by the 'Certified Social Workers and Certified Care Workers Act [*Shakai fukushishi oyobi kaigo fukushishi hō*]'.

The strict immigration policy that restricts the extensive entry of foreign workers may also have contributed to the public notion that care work is not an unskilled, demeaning job. Current policy requires immigrant care workers to pass the examination for "certified care workers" within four years. If they do not, they must return to their countries (MHLW, 2015c). As of 2014, only 241 (46.4%) of people from Philippines and Indonesia have passed the examination since the Japanese government established the program of accepting immigrant care workers in 2008 (MHLW, 2014e). However, there is some doubt on whether this policy and the quality of the workforce could be maintained in the future. Despite the qualifications required, the average annual income of care workers in LTCI facilities (2,184,000 JPY) is much lower than that of all industries (3,256,000 JPY; Ministry of Internal Affairs and Communications, 2013; MHLW, 2012a), and the current shortages would exacerbate in the future. For these reasons, the relaxation of the current strict immigration policy is being discussed (MHLW, 2015b).

One other aspect which may have contributed to assuring quality of care is the strict staffing requirements in facilities (Ikegami et al., 2014). The number of full-time equivalent care workers and nurses per resident is regulated and enforced by on-site audits. In addition, a bonus payment is made if the facility has a higher staffing ratio and/or if the proportion of the care workers with a certified care worker qualification or with three or more years of employment is above the levels set by the LTCI fee schedule. Consequently, facilities try to obtain bonuses by meeting these standards, which could be reflected in the quality. As noted, if the facility is found not be meet the bonus requirements, it must retrospectively pay back the amount they have billed inappropriately.

Conclusion

Japan has relied mostly on the training and qualification of the direct care workers to protect the human rights of older people. The greater majority have some qualifications which require training not only on the technical aspects of providing services, but also on ethical subjects. This focus may be a reflection of the positive image of care workers which has been nurtured by media and by the personal experiences of the difficulties encountered by family members in delivering care. Other countries might learn from Japan about the importance of social recognition for maintaining the quality of care workers and, thereby, protecting the human rights of those in residential homes. However, whether Japan could maintain the current quality of care workers is doubtful because of the growing shortage of care workers and the subsequent need to have more open immigration policies. Thus, stricter legislation and enforcement of human rights are likely to be needed in the future especially in the less regulated areas of special housing for older people.

References

Arai, M. (2008) Guardianship for Adults. In Coulmas, F., Conrad, H., Schad-Seifert, A., and Vogt, G. (eds), *The Demographic Challenge A Handbook about Japan* (pp. 1065–1076). Leiden: Koninklijke Brill.

The Asahi Shimbun (1995) "Poa" to yokusei ["Poa" and restraints]. June 23, 1995, p. 1.

The Asahi Shimbun (1998) "Fukuoka sengen wo zenkoku ni" Shibaru Iryō ["Make Fukuoka declaration a nation-wide movement" Restraining medicine]. November 6, 1998, p. 5.

The Asahi Shimbun Digital (2014) *Herupa- Tabō kōsoku ni nare* [The home helper was so busy and accustomed to restrain older people]. http://www.asahi.com/articles/DA3S11446617.html (Accessed February 1, 2015).

Association for Health Economics Research and Social Insurance and Welfare (2004) *Kateinai ni okeru kōreisha gyakutai ni kansuru chōsa* [Investigation on elder abuse in households]. http://www.mhlw.go.jp/shingi/2004/04/dl/s0426-6e.pdf (Accessed February 1, 2015).

Cabinet Office Government of Japan (2013) *2012 Kōrei Shakai Hakusho* [White paper on Aged Society in 2012]. http://www8.cao.go.jp/kourei/whitepaper/w-2013/gaiyou/index.html (Accessed February 1, 2015).

Cabinet Office Government of Japan (2014) *2013 Kōrei Shakai Hakusho* [White paper on Aged Society in 2013]. http://www8.cao.go.jp/kourei/whitepaper/w-2014/gaiyou/index.html (Accessed February 1, 2015).

Campbell, J.C. (1992) *How Policies Change*. New Jersey: Princeton University Press.

Campbell, J.C. (2002) 'How Policies Differ: Long-term-care Insurance in Japan and Germany', in Harald, C. and Ralph, L. (eds), *Aging and Social Policy – A German-Japanese Comparison*. Munich: Ludicium, pp. 157–187.

Campbell, J.C., Ikegami, N., Gibson, M. (2010) Lessons from Public Long-term Care Insurance in Germany and Japan. *Health Affairs*, 29(1): 87–95.

Care Work Foundation (2014) *2013 Kaigo rōdō jittai chosa kekka nit suite* [Results from survey on care work]. http://www.kaigo-center.or.jp/report/h25_chousa_01.html (Accessed February 1, 2015).

Dementia Care Research and Training Center Sendai (2009) *Kōreisha gyakutai bōshi gakushu tekisuto* [Textbook for prevention of elder abuse]. Sendai: Dementia Care Research and Training Center Sendai.

Formanek, S. (2008) Traditional Concepts and Images of Old Age in Japan. In Coulmas, F., Conrad, H., Schad-Seifert, A., and Vogt, G. (eds), *The Demographic Challenge: A Handbook about Japan* (pp. 323–343). Leiden: Koninklijke Brill.

Hieda, T. (2012) *Political Institutions and Elderly Care Policy: Comparative Politics of Long-Term Care in Advanced Democracies*. New York: Palgrave Macmillan.

Ikegami, N. (2007) Rationale, Design and Sustainability of Long-Term Care Insurance in Japan – In Retrospect. *Social Policy & Society*, 6(3): 423–434.

Ikegami, N. and Campbell, J.C. (1999) Health Care Reform in Japan: The Virtues of Muddling Through. *Health Affairs*, 18(3): 56–75.

Ikegami, N. and Campbell, J.C. (2004) Japan's Health Care System: Containing Costs and Attempting Reform. *Health Affairs*, 23(3): 26–36.

Ikegami, N., Ishibashi, T., and Amano, T. (2014) Japan's Long-term Care Regulations Focused on Structure – Rationale and Future Prospects. In Mor, V., Leone, T., and Maresso, A. (eds), *Regulating Long-Term Care Quality An International Comparison* (pp. 121–143). Cambridge: Cambridge University Press.

The Japan Association of Training Institutions for Certified Care Workers (2015) *Yōsei kō ichiran* [List of credited training schools]. http://kaiyokyo.net/search/index.php (Accessed February 1, 2015).

Japanese Association of Schools of Social Work (2012) *Shakai fukushi kei gakubu gakka sotsugyōsei no shinro tō chōsa* [Investigation on careers of graduates of social welfare related courses]. http://www.jassw.jp/data_room/course/course_201202.pdf (Accessed February 1, 2015).

Kaneko, Y. (1987) *Rōjin Gyakutai* [Elder Abuse]. Tokyo: Seiwa Shoten.

Kinzai Institution for Financial Affairs (1998) *Seinen kōken seido no kaisei ni kannsuru yōkōsian no kaisetsu: Yōkōsian, gaiyō, hosokusetsumei* [Explanation of a draft summary for the Reform of Adult Guardianship System: draft, summary, and supplemental explanation]. Tokyo: Kinzai.

Kitamura, I. (2004) Tokubetsuyōgo rōjin hōmu ni okeru seikatsu no sitsu kōjō no torikumi [Approach to Improve Quality of Life in Nursing Home]. *Bulletin of Department of Social Welfare Nihon Fukushi Daigaku*, 110, 159–169.

Kokuho Chuōkai (The All-Japan Federation of National Health Insurance Organizations) (2014) *Kujyō mōsitate oyobi sōdan uketsuke jyōkyō* [State of complaints filed and received]. Tokyo: Kokuho Chuōkai.

Kurata, S. and Ojima, T. (2014) Knowledge, perceptions, and experiences of family caregivers and home care providers of physical restraint use with home-dwelling elders: a cross-sectional study in Japan. *BMC Geriatrics*. 14:39.

MHLW (Ministry of Health, Labour and Welfare) (2001a) *1999 Shakaifukushi shisetsuto chōsa* [Survey of social welfare facilities]. Tokyo: Kōsei Tōkei Kyōkai.

MHLW (Ministry of Health, Labour and Welfare) (2001b) *2001 Kokumin seikatsu kiso chōsa no gaikyō* [Comprehensive survey of living conditions]. http://www.mhlw.go.jp/toukei/saikin/hw/k-tyosa/k-tyosa01/index.html (Accessed February 1, 2015).

MHLW (Ministry of Health, Labour and Welfare) (2006a) *Kaigo hoken seido kaikaku no gaiyō* [Summary of the reform of the LTCI system]. http://www.mhlw.go.jp/topics/kaigo/topics/0603/dl/data.pdf (Accessed February 1, 2015).

MHLW (Ministry of Health, Labour and Welfare) (2006b) *Shichōson Todōfuken ni okeru kōreisya gyakutai eno taiō to yōgosya shien ni tsuite* [Correspondence of municipalities on elder abuse and support for caregivers]. http://www.mhlw.go.jp/topics/kaigo/boushi/060424/dl/01.pdf (Accessed February 1, 2015).

MHLW (Ministry of Health, Labour and Welfare) (2006c) *Shitei shisetsu sabisu tou ni yousuru hiyou no gaku no santei ni kansuru kijun* [Standards for calculation of service fee for designated institutional care]. http://www.mhlw.go.jp/stf/shingi/2r985200000239zd-att/2r98520000023dt8.pdf (Accessed February 1, 2015).

MHLW (Ministry of Health, Labour and Welfare) (2008a) *e-Health Net*. http://www.e-healthnet.mhlw.go.jp/information/dictionary/alcohol/ya-032.html (Accessed February 1, 2015).

MHLW (Ministry of Health, Labour and Welfare) (2008b) *Kaigo fukushi shi yōsei katei ni okeru kyōiku naiyō tō no minaoshi ni tsuite* [Review of the curriculum for certificate of care work]. http://www.mhlw.go.jp/bunya/seikatsuhogo/dl/shakai-kaigo-yousei02.pdf (Accessed February 1, 2015).

MHLW (Ministry of Health, Labour and Welfare) (2009) *2007 Kaigo service shisetsu, jigyō chōsa* [Survey of LTCI institutions and facilities]. Tokyo: MHLW.

MHLW (Ministry of Health, Labour and Welfare) (2010a) *Kaigohokenhō: Shitei kaigo rōjin fukushi shisetsu · rōjin hoken shisetsu · kaigo ryōyō iryō shisetsu no jinin, setsubi oyobi unei ni kansuru kijun* [LTCI Act Standards for personnel, facilities and administration for nursing home, HFE, and hospital LTC beds] (Revision of 30 September, 2010). Tokyo: MHLW.

MHLW (Ministry of Health, Labour and Welfare) (2010b) *Kaigo hoken Shidōshitsu Kankei* [Document on the division of long-term care insurance management]. http://www.mhlw.go.jp/stf/shingi/2r985200000133sr-att/2r985200000134dd.pdf (Accessed February 1, 2015).

MHLW (Ministry of Health, Labour and Welfare) (2010c) *Kaigo sa-bisu jigyōsho ni taisuru kannsa kekka no jyōkyō* [Audit results of care service agencies]. Tokyo: MHLW.

MHLW (Ministry of Health, Labour and Welfare) (2010d) *Ryoyō byōshō no tenkan ikōto chōsa* [Survey on attitudes towards transferring LTC beds. Debriefing information presented at the October 15, 2010, meeting of the Central Social Insurance Council]. Tokyo: MHLW.

MHLW (Ministry of Health, Labour and Welfare) (2011a) *Kaigo hoken seido wo torimaku jōkyō* [Situation faced by the long-term care insurance. Debriefing information presented at the February 7, 2011, meeting of the Central Social Insurance Council]. Tokyo: MHLW.

MHLW (Ministry of Health, Labour and Welfare) (2011b) *Kaigo sa-bisu no kibankyōka no tame no kaigohokenntō no ichibu wo kaisei suru hōritsuan* [Draft act on revising the long-term care insurance and related acts for strengthening the basis of care services] April 4, 2011. Tokyo: MHLW.

MHLW (Ministry of Health, Labour and Welfare) (2012) *2012 Kaigo sa-bisu sisetsu jigyōsyo chōsa no gaikyō* [Summary of the investigation on service agencies under LTCI]. http://www.mhlw.go.jp/toukei/saikin/hw/kaigo/service12/ (Accessed February 1, 2015).

MHLW (Ministry of Health, Labour and Welfare) (2013a) *2013 Kokumin seikatsu kiso chōsa no gaikyō* [Comprehensive survey of living conditions]. http://www.mhlw.go.jp/toukei/saikin/hw/k-tyosa/k-tyosa01/index.html (Accessed February 1, 2015).

MHLW (Ministry of Health, Labour and Welfare) (2013b) *Zenkoku kaigo hoken kōreisha hoken fukushi tantō kachō kaigi shiryō ni tsuite* [Documents for the national meeting of managers of LTCI and welfare/health care of older people]. http://www.mhlw.go.jp/stf/shingi/2r9852000002xhcw.html (Accessed February 1, 2015).

MHLW (Ministry of Health, Labour and Welfare) (2014a) *2013 Iryōshisetsu (dōtai) chōsa, byōin hōkoku no gaikyō* [Summary of survey on medical institutions and report of hospitals]. http://www.mhlw.go.jp/toukei/saikin/hw/iryosd/13/ (Accessed February 1, 2015).

MHLW (Ministry of Health, Labour and Welfare) (2014b) *2013 Kaigo sa-bisu shisetsu jigyōsho chōsa no kekka* [Summary of survey on LTC services and facilities]. http://www.mhlw.go.jp/toukei/saikin/hw/kaigo/service13/index.html (Accessed February 1, 2015).

MHLW (Ministry of Health, Labour and Welfare) (2014c) *2016 Kaigo hōshu kaitei ni mukete – Kaigo rōjin hoken shisetsu, kaigo ryōyōkata iryō shisetsu nitsuite* [Issues on planned revision of LTCI payment in 2016 – HFE and Medical Long-term Care Sanatoriums] http://www.mhlw.go.jp/file/05-Shingikai-12601000-Seisakutoukatsukan-Sanjikanshitsu_Shakaihoshoutantou/0000053838.pdf (Accessed February 1, 2015).

MHLW (Ministry of Health, Labour and Welfare) (2014d) *2016 Kaigo hōshu kaitei ni mukete – Tokutei shisetsu nitsuite* [Issues on planned revision of LTCI payment in 2016 – Specified facilities] http://www.mhlw.go.jp/file/05-Shingikai-12601000-Seisakutoukatsukan-Sanjikanshitsu_Shakaihoshoutantou/0000051823.pdf (Accessed February 1, 2015).

MHLW (Ministry of Health, Labour and Welfare) (2014e) *Dai 26 kai kaigo fukushi shi kokka-shiken ni okeru EPA kaigo fukushi shi kōhosha no shiken kekka* [Results of nominee of immigrant care workers on the 26th examination for certified care worker]. http://www.mhlw.go.jp/stf/houdou/0000041984.html (Accessed February 1, 2015).

MHLW (Ministry of Health, Labour and Welfare) (2014f) *Tokubetsu yōgo rōjin hōmu no nyusho mōshikomisha no jōkyō* [Summary of people applying to admit into nursing homes]. http://www.mhlw.go.jp/file/04-Houdouhappyou-12304250-Roukenkyoku-Koureishashienka/0000041929.pdf (Accessed February 1, 2015).

MHLW (Ministry of Health, Labour and Welfare) (2015a) *2013 Shakai fukushi shisetsu tō chōsa* [Summary of survey on social welfare facilities]. http://www.mhlw.go.jp/toukei/saikin/hw/fukushi/13/ (Accessed February 1, 2015).

MHLW (Ministry of Health, Labour and Welfare) (2015b) *Gaikokujin kaigo jinzai ukeire no arikata ni kansuru kentōkai chukan matome* [Midterm summary of a meeting on acceptance of immigrant care workers]. http://www.mhlw.go.jp/file/05-Shingikai-12201000-Shakaiengokyokushougaihokenfukushibu-Kikakuka/0000072244.pdf (Accessed February 1, 2015).

MHLW (Ministry of Health, Labour and Welfare) (2015c) *Indonesia, Philippines, Vietnam kara no gaikokujin kanngoshi kaigo fukushi shi kōhosha no ukeire nit suite* [Acceptance of nominees of immigrant nurses and care workers from Indonesia, Philippines, and Vietnam]. http://www.mhlw.go.jp/stf/seisakunitsuite/bunya/koyou_roudou/koyou/gaikokujin/other22/index.html (Accessed February 1, 2015).

MHLW (Ministry of Health, Labour and Welfare) (2015d) *2012 Kōreisha gyakutai no bōshi, kōreisha no yōgosha ni taisuru sien tō ni kansuru hōritsu ni motoduku taiō jōkyō tō ni kansuru chōsa kekka* [Results from investigation based on the Act on the Prevention of Elder Abuse, Support for Caregivers of Elderly Persons and Other Related Matters]. http://www.mhlw.go.jp/stf/houdou/0000072782.html (Accessed February 1, 2015).

MHW (Ministry of Health and Welfare) (1975a) *1973 Kanja chōsa* [Patient survey 1973]. Tokyo: Kōsei Tōkei Kyōkai.

MHW (Ministry of Health and Welfare) (1975b) *1973 Shakaifukushi gyōsei gyōmu hōkoku* [Administrative report of social welfare 1973]. Tokyo: Kōsei Tōkei Kyōkai.

MHW (Ministry of Health and Welfare) (1989a) *Kōreisha Hoken Fukushi Suishin Jikkanen Senryaku Heisei 11nen made no Mokuhyō* [Goals of the Ten Year Plan to Develop Health and Welfare Services for Elders]. http://www.ipss.go.jp/publication/j/shiryou/no.13/data/shiryou/souron/17.pdf (accessed February 1, 2015).

MHW (Ministry of Health and Welfare) (1989b). *Tōmen no Rōjin Hōmu tou no arikata ni tsuite* [Opinion on the institutional care in the near future]. http://www.ipss.go.jp/publication/j/shiryou/no.13/data/shiryou/syakaifukushi/371.pdf (accessed February 1, 2015).

MHW (Ministry of Health and Welfare) (1992a) *1990 Kanja chōsa* [Patient survey 1990]. Tokyo: Kōsei Tōkei Kyōkai.

Ministry of Internal Affairs and Communications (2013) *2012 Shugyou kōzō kihon chōsa* [Employment status survey]. http://www.stat.go.jp/data/shugyou/2012/pdf/kgaiyou.pdf (Accessed February 1, 2015).

MOJ (Ministry of Justice) (2015a) *Act on Securing, Etc. of Equal Opportunity and Treatment between Men and Women in Employment.* http://www.japaneselawtranslation.go.jp/law/detail/?id=60&vm=04&re=01&new=1 (Accessed February 1, 2015).

MOJ (Ministry of Justice) (2015b) *Act on the Prevention of Elder Abuse, Support for Caregivers of Elderly Persons and Other Related Matters, Article 2.* http://www.japaneselawtranslation.go.jp/law/detail/?id=2045&vm=04&re=01&new=1 (Accessed February 1, 2015).

MOJ (Ministry of Justice) (2015c) *Civil Code Part IV and Part V, Article 858.* http://www.japaneselawtranslation.go.jp/law/detail/?id=2252&vm=04&re=01&new=1 (Accessed February 1, 2015).

MOJ (Ministry of Justice) (2015d) *The Constitution of Japan, Article 11.* http://www.japaneselawtranslation.go.jp/law/detail/?id=174&vm=04&re=01&new=1 (Accessed February 1, 2015).

MOJ (Ministry of Justice) (2015e) *The Constitution of Japan, Article 98 Section 2.* http://www.japaneselawtranslation.go.jp/law/detail/?id=174&vm=04&re=01&new=1 (Accessed February 1, 2015).

Momose, T. (1997) *Nihon Rōjin Fukushishi.* Tokyo: Chuohoki Publishing Co., Ltd.

National Association of Chronic Care Hospitals (2010) *Yōbōsho Kan Sōridaijin* (Request to Prime Minister Kan). http://jamcf.jp/chairman/100720youbou.pdf (accessed February 1, 2015).

Neary, I. (2002) *Human Rights in Japan, South Korea and Taiwan.* Oxon: Routledge.

Nomura Research Institute, Ltd (2010) *Tokubetsu yōgo rōjin hōmu ni okeru nyusyo mōshikomisha ni kannsuru tyōsa kenkyu* [Survey and research on those waiting for admission to nursing homes]. Tokyo: Nomura Research Institute, Ltd.

OECD (2011) *OECD Health Data 2011*. Paris: Organisation for Economic Cooperation and Development.

OECD (2014) *Elderly population*. http://data.oecd.org/pop/elderly-population.htm# indicator-chart (Accessed February 1, 2015).

Okuma, K. (1988) *Lupo rōjin byōtō* [Report Elder Ward]. Tokyo: Asahi Shimbunsha.

Supreme Court of Japan (2015) *Seinen kōken kankei jiken no gaikyō* [Reports on incidents related to adult guardianship]. http://www.courts.go.jp/vcms_lf/20140526koukengaikyou_h25. pdf (Accessed February 1, 2015).

Tanaka, S. (1993) *Nihon ni okeru shisetsu kea seido* [Institutional Care systems in Japan]. In Asano, H. and Tanaka, S. (eds), *Nihon no Shisetsu Kea [Institutional Care in Japan]* (pp. 245–286). Tokyo: Chuohoki Publishing Co., Ltd.

Tokyo CHI Federation (eds) (2010) *Tokyoto niokeru kaigo sa-bisu no kujyō sōdan hakusho* [Complaints White Paper on LTC service in Tokyo]. Tokyo: Tokyoto Kokumin Kenkō Hoken Dantai Rengō Kai.

Tokyo Metropolitan Government (2011) *Fukushi sa-bisu daisansha hyōka* [The welfare service third party evaluation]. http://www.fukunavi.or.jp/fukunavi/hyoka/hyokatop.htm (accessed February 1, 2015).

Tokyo Metropolitan Government (2013) *2012 Shidō kensa hōkokusho* [Report of supervisions and inspections]. http://www.fukushihoken.metro.tokyo.jp/kiban/shisaku/houkokusyo. files/24kensahoukoku.pdf (accessed February 1, 2015).

Yamada, Y. (2004) *Kazoku kaigo to kōreisha gyakutai* [Family caregiving and elder abuse]. Tokyo: Hitotsubashi Shuppan.

Yamada, Y. (2008) Kōreisha gyakutai no jittai chōsa kara yomitoreru koto [Report on results from the investigation on elder abuse]. *Japanese Journal of Geriatric Psychiatry*, 19(12), 1307–1316.

8 Residential care in the United States

A persistent struggle for quality, dignity and independence

Richard J. Mollot, JD

The United States is "an aging nation" according to the US Census Bureau, the federal agency charged with collecting data on US population dynamics.[1] This growth in the older adult population is due to the advent of the so-called "Baby Boomers" (the large numbers of children born following the end of World War II to the early 1960s), increasing average lifespan (including strong growth in the over-85 population) and decreasing birthrates from the mid-1960s on. The significant growth in the population approaching or beyond the traditional retirement age in the US (age 65), and those 85 and older, have brought on changing conceptions of aging and appropriate settings for the elderly in need of long-term care.[2] The result is an evolving and increasingly diverse residential care sector.[3]

Historically, care for older adult and disabled long-term care consumers in the US has largely been relegated to nursing homes, residential care facilities that are licensed to provide 24-hour a day skilled nursing care. In recent years, particularly since the 1990s, individuals in need of long-term care services or supports have been turning to other residential care settings, such as assisted living, that are considered less institutional. In addition, many have been seeking to remain in their homes and access care, services and accommodations there so that they can maximize their independence, including control of their schedules, care, surroundings, etc.[4] Following is an overview of residential care in the US which examines the policies and conditions that have characterized these settings and how these policies and conditions, coupled with changing ideas of aging and disability in American society, have shaped the drive toward settings that provide greater independence and quality of life.

1 US Census Bureau (2014). *Fueled by Aging Baby Boomers, Nation's Older Population to Nearly Double, Census Bureau Reports*. Retrieved from https://www.census.gov/newsroom/press-releases/2014/cb14-84. html.
2 Projected Future Growth of the Older Population. Retrieved from Administration on Aging http://www.aoa.gov/Aging_Statistics/future_growth/future_growth.aspx.
3 Ng, T., Harrington, C., Musumeci, M., & Reaves, E. (2014). *Medicaid Home and Community-Based Services Programs: 2010 Data Update*. Retrieved from http://kff.org/medicaid/report/medicaid-home-and-community-based-service-programs.
4 *Ibid*. at Figure 4.

Nursing homes

Operational overview

Despite continuing efforts toward deinstitutionalization, nursing homes continue to be the principal setting for individuals who need long-term care in the United States. This is largely due to the fact that they are the only residential setting licensed by the federal government to provide 24-hour a day monitoring and skilled nursing care. The typical US nursing home is a large, institutional setting, virtually indistinguishable from a hospital structurally. Residents live in double rooms (though this can vary) with a shared bathroom situated off a long corridor of similar rooms extending from a nurses' station. Furnishings might include two hospital beds divided by a gauzy retractable cloth screen. On each side of the divide one can usually find the same, institution-provided nightstand with drawers, wheeled bed tray and vinyl-clad chair.

As of 2011, there were 15,465 nursing homes in the US.[5] The average facility has approximately 110 beds and an 83% occupancy rate.[6] Approximately 1.4 million individuals reside in US nursing homes. This includes "2.8 % of the over-65 population and 10.2 % of the over-85 population. Fifteen percent of the nursing home population is under age 65, while 7.7 % are over 95 years."[7]

The government pays for close to 80% of nursing home care through both state and federal sources. Sixty-three percent (63%) of nursing home revenue comes from the Medicaid program, the national health insurance program for the poor, 14% comes from Medicare, the national health insurance program for the elderly and disabled, and the remaining 22% is through private pay (typically individuals' savings or insurance). Approximately two-thirds (68%) of facilities are for-profit, with one-quarter being non-profit and 6% government owned.[8] Medicaid generally covers long-term care services while Medicare generally covers short-term, post-acute residential care services, such as rehabilitation services for individuals recovering from surgery. The median cost for a semi-private room in a nursing home is $212 per day (over $77,000 per year).[9] Medicaid pays for the large portion of nursing home long-term care because the majority of people who require these services quickly spend down their financial resources when faced with these costs.

---

5   Kaiser Family Foundation. (2013). *Overview of Nursing Facility Capacity, Financing, and Ownership in the United States in 2011*. Retrieved from http://kff.org/medicaid/fact-sheet/overview-of-nursing-facility-capacity-financing-and-ownership-in-the-united-states-in-2011. Hereinafter *Overview of Nursing Facility Capacity*.

6   *Ibid.*

7   Centers for Medicare & Medicaid Services (CMS) (2013). *Nursing Home Data Compendium 2013 Edition*, pp. 165–168. Retrieved from http://www.cms.gov/Medicare/Provider-Enrollment-and-Certification/CertificationandComplianc/NHs.html.

8   *Overview of Nursing Facility Capacity* at Figure 4.

9   Genworth 2014 Cost of Care Survey (Executive Summary), March 25, 2014. Retrieved from https://www.genworth.com/corporate/about-genworth/industry-expertise/cost-of-care.html.

It is important to note that all of the figures above are average or median, as noted, and that figures wary widely across the states and, often, within states.

History

The modern history of nursing home care in the United States begins in 1987, with passage of the US Nursing Home Reform Law.[10] Five years earlier, the Administration of President Ronald Reagan, through its Healthcare Financing Administration (HCFA), had proposed federal regulations that would significantly weaken existing standards for nursing homes. The proposed changes, in response to the industry's complaints that nursing home oversight was too rigid and stringent, included easing annual inspection requirements and permitting states to outsource accreditation of nursing homes. Controversy ensued, with strong opposition voiced by senior citizen and healthcare consumer groups "and most state regulatory agencies because the proposed changes were seen as a movement in the wrong direction – that is, towards easing the stringency of nursing home regulation – and because they did not deal with the fundamental weaknesses of the regulatory system." As a result of this controversy, Congress ordered HCFA to delay implementation of the proposed changes and HCFA ordered that a study be conducted by the Institute of Medicine (IOM).

The IOM study, *Improving the Quality of Care in Nursing Homes*, looked at nursing home care across the country, including quality, state regulation, staff training and accreditation, and state Medicaid reimbursement policies.[11] Its Introduction and Summary cites over 20 studies from the 1970s and 1980s in noting the widespread "grossly inadequate care and abuse of residents" in nursing homes across the country including "neglect and abuse leading to premature death, permanent injury, increased disability, and unnecessary fear and suffering on the part of residents."[12] In addition to finding that such problems persisted in nursing homes in every state of the country, the study found that "[r]egulation of nursing homes both by state and federal governments is necessary to assure safety and acceptable quality of care for nursing home residents because of the vulnerability of the residents and the lack of institutional choices available to them. The committee is convinced that *more effective government regulation can achieve substantial improvement in quality of care in many nursing homes in all states. A stronger federal leadership role is essential . . .*"[13] Among the study's major conclusions were that "[s]pecific improvements are needed in the regulatory system. A major reorientation of the . . . system is needed to make

---

10 HR 3545 (100th): Omnibus Budget Reconciliation Act of 1987. Retrieved from https://www. govtrack.us/congress/bills/100/hr3545. Hereinafter the *Nursing Home Reform Law*.

11 National Academy of Sciences, *Improving the Quality of Nursing Home Care*, January 1, 1986. Available at http://www.iom.edu/Reports/1986/Improving-the-Quality-of-Care-in-Nursing-Homes. aspx. Hereinafter "IOM study." The last quote in the previous paragraph is from the IOM study's introduction.

12 *Ibid*. at 3.

13 *Ibid*. at 21. Emphasis added.

it focus on the care being provided to residents and the effects of the care on their well-being. This will require revision of . . . nursing home performance criteria and standards (the 'conditions of participation' and 'standards' [necessary to receive federal payment for services]), the surveillance (survey) process, compliance (enforcement) policies and procedures, and the systems for collecting and analyzing the data and other information needed for effective regulation."[14]

Rather than pave the way for implementation of the Reagan Administration's proposal to loosen care standards and oversight, the findings of the IOM study laid the foundation for strengthening nursing home standards. The result was the Nursing Home Reform Law, which to this day is the principal law for nursing home requirements and standards, and oversight thereof, across the United States.

The Nursing Home Reform Law

As one author aptly stated, the Reform Law "changed forever society's legal expectations of nursing homes and their care."[15] It established national standards for care and residents' rights for people in nursing homes. At its heart is the requirement that each resident must be provided with care and services sufficient to attain and maintain his or her highest practicable physical, mental, and psychosocial well-being. To realize this mandate, many new federal requirements were established, including: a resident assessment process leading to development of an individualized service plan, the right to organize and participate in family or resident councils, the right to be free of unnecessary restraints (physical or chemical), and specific requirements for those most responsible for resident dignity and care: nursing home inspectors (surveyors), long-term care ombudsmen and direct care workers.

Though the law pertains only to nursing homes that receive federal funding through Medicaid and/or Medicare, because the vast majority of facilities are certified to receive such funding, the law has served as a *de facto*, industry-wide standard. The Reform Law provides for a number of important staffing standards, including a requirement that nursing homes have an RN (registered nurse) director of nursing, an RN on duty for at least eight hours a day, seven days a week, and a licensed nurse (either an RN, LPN (licensed practical nurse) or both) on duty around the clock. The law established minimum standards for certified nurse aides (CNAs), who provide approximately 90% of the direct care to residents: they must undergo a state-approved training curriculum of a minimum of 75 hours, pass a certification exam and undergo continuing education for the duration of their careers. Given that CNAs provide the critical services necessary to sustain residents, including feeding, dressing, and bathing, many states have recognized the need for additional training by instituting higher training requirements. For instance, New York State mandates a minimum of 100 hours of training. While this is a substantial improvement, it is still a fraction of the training required by

14 *Ibid.* at 22.
15 Turnham, Hollis, *JD.*, *OBRA'87 Summary*. Available from http://theconsumervoice.org/home.

the government for many paraprofessionals who do not provide important care services to a vulnerable population, such as massage therapists (1,000 hours) or manicurists (250 hours).

The law also requires that there be "sufficient" nursing staff. It is important to note that the law does not specify a numerical standard for numbers of staff or for minimum hours of care per resident; rather, this standard focuses on the expected outcomes for nursing home residents. This distinction has been a divisive issue in the country and in individual states ever since, for while it mandates a level of staffing that will seemingly ensure resident well-being and dignified treatment, the lack of an easily measurable, quantitative requirement has proven disastrous for nursing home residents because, in effect, it has meant that there is no staffing level requirement whatsoever.

As a result, though numerous studies have indicated that staffing levels are probably the most important determinant of a facility's quality of care, about 97% of US nursing homes have insufficient care staff according to the last national study on the issue, *Appropriateness of Minimum Nurse Staffing Ratios in Nursing Homes*, published in 2001.[16] That study found that, based upon the needs of individual residents, "there was a pattern of incremental benefits of increased nurse staffing until a threshold was reached . . . [ranging] between 2.4–2.8, 1.15–1.30, and 0.55–0.75" hours of care time per resident per day for nurse aides, licensed staff (RNs and LPNs combined), and Registered Nurses, respectively.

The Reform Law established a set of basic rights for residents:

- the right to freedom from abuse, mistreatment, and neglect;
- the right to freedom from physical restraints;
- the right to privacy;
- the right to accommodation of medical, physical, psychological, and social needs;
- the right to participate in resident and family groups [for family members of residents];
- the right to be treated with dignity;
- the right to exercise self-determination;
- the right to communicate freely;
- the right to participate in the review of one's care plan, and to be fully informed in advance about any changes in care, treatment, or change of status in the facility; and
- the right to voice grievances without discrimination or reprisal.[17]

16 Abt Associates 2001, *Appropriateness of Minimum Nurse Staffing Ratios in Nursing Homes, Report to Congress: Phase II Final, Volume I*. It is important to note that this threshold relates to health outcome "benefits" only and does not relate to quality of life or dignity, though these are important components of the Reform Law's standards.

17 Klauber, M. and Wright, B., The 1987 Nursing Home Reform Act, AARP, from: Public Policy Institute, February 2001. Retrieved from http://www.aarp.org/home-garden/livable-communities/info-2001/the_1987_nursing_home_reform_act.html#BACKGROUND.

It is important to note that all of these rights, as well as the aforementioned mandate that each resident is to receive the care and services he or she needs to attain, and maintain, his or her highest practicable physical, emotional, and social well-being, relate to the individual resident. In other words, the law specifies these as individual rights, and nursing homes are required to meet them on an individual basis. Providing sufficient staffing or care to meet the needs of the "average" nursing home resident is not, in itself, sufficient to be in compliance with the law.

This is a critical point for a number of reasons. Fundamentally, it signifies that the focus of the law, and thus the system operating under the law, is on the consumer (the nursing home resident). Providers are not simply licensed and paid to provide a certain amount of goods and services, as in a typical contractual arrangement, but rather (as the aforementioned mandate states) to provide care and services appropriate and sufficient to ensure that each and every resident is able to attain, and maintain, his or her highest practicable physical, emotional and social well-being. It recognizes not only the vulnerability of this population (most nursing home residents, for instance, cannot simply walk out of their facility when the services they receive are poor or inadequate), but also the uniqueness and value of residents' lives; care and services must be tailored to meet their needs.

To that end, another noteworthy facet of the Reform Law and its implementing regulations is their recognition of the importance of quality of life and dignity. Nursing homes are responsible for providing a home-like environment; meeting the needs and desires of residents in terms of waking up and going to sleep, dining, dressing, bathing, etc.; and promoting care for residents in a manner and in an environment that maintains or enhances each resident's dignity and respect in full recognition of his or her individuality.[18] Thus, for example, federal guidelines state that a facility must encourage and assist residents to dress in their own clothing (rather than hospital-style gowns); promote resident independence and dignity in dining (by avoiding the use of bibs, paper plates and plastic cutlery); and respect residents' private spaces (by knocking on bedroom doors and requesting permission to enter, closing doors as requested by residents, etc.).[19]

Enforcement of the Reform Law: the nursing home survey system

As a result of the Reform Law, the nursing home survey system (the inspection system that is the backbone of government quality assurance and oversight efforts) was markedly improved, with an increased focus on outcomes for residents and tougher enforcement mechanisms, including monetary penalties. The protections

18 CMS. (2009). Pub. 100–07 State Operations Provider Certification, Transmittal 48.
19 *Ibid.* at p. 6.

and requirements in the Reform Law are codified in federal regulations, which provide specific requirements for nursing homes such as for resident services, physical structure and fire safety.[20]

In turn, these regulatory standards are enforced by nursing home inspectors, known as surveyors, through a system comprised of what are known as "F-Tags" (data tags associated with the specific federal nursing home regulations) and written guidance to help surveyors understand the regulatory requirements and how to evaluate for compliance with them. The F-Tag system covers the full range of care and services provided by nursing homes, including nursing, dietary, dental and physician services; residents' rights; quality of life and quality of care (from resident self-determination to comfortable sound levels to no development of mental problems); and facility administration.[21]

Because, as noted earlier, the law and standards are grounded in the federal insurance programs that pay for the great majority of nursing home care, Medicare and Medicaid, principal responsibility for ensuring that nursing homes meet the Reform Law's standards falls to the federal government. The federal agency responsible for both paying for and overseeing care is the Centers for Medicare and Medicaid Services (CMS).[22] CMS is a sub agency within the US Department of Health and Human Services, which is a Cabinet-level agency (meaning that its operations fall under the President of the United States and the Secretary (head) of the Department is a presidential appointee).[23]

As federal law notes, "It is the duty and responsibility of the Secretary to assure that requirements which govern the provision of care in nursing facilities . . . and the enforcement of such requirements, are adequate to protect the health, safety, welfare, and rights of residents and to promote the effective and efficient use of public moneys."[24] To ensure that the nation's 15,000+ nursing homes meet these standards, CMS delegates responsibility to state governments, which oversee quality assurance in the nursing homes within their states. This delegation is carried out through a written contract with each state, usually a state's department of health, to conduct surveys (inspections) of individual nursing homes[25] as well as to provide other quality assurance functions, such as responding to complaints about a facility's care. Under these contracts, state survey agencies are required

---

20 Title 42 of Federal Regulations, Part 483, Requirements for States and Long Term Care Facilities (42CFR483). Available at http://www.access.gpo.gov/nara/cfr/waisidx_01/42cfr483_01.html.

21 For a chart of all F-Tags and their descriptions see LTCCC 2014, *Antipsychotic Drug Use in NY State Nursing Homes* at 48. Available at http://www.nursinghome411.org/articles/?category=antipsycho ticlaws.

22 The aforementioned Healthcare Financing Administration's name was changed to CMS in 2001.

23 The US President's cabinet is comprised of the heads of agencies operating within the executive branch. Though appointed by and working under the President, Cabinet heads are subject to approval by the US Senate.

24 US Social Security Act, §1919 (f)(1).

25 State personnel usually simultaneously assess compliance with federal certification and state licensure requirements for the participating facilities in the state.

to conduct surveys of facilities at least once every 15 months, with the statewide average interval for these surveys not to exceed 12 months, and conduct complaint investigations. Because these contractual activities are the principle means by which nursing home providers are held accountable for meeting federal standards, they are critical to ensuring both quality of care for nursing home residents across the country as well as appropriate use of the government funding that pays for a substantial portion of nursing home care.

While this system is comprehensive, as a result of serious shortcomings in its implementation widespread problems continue in many US nursing homes and the majority fail to achieve the minimum standards mandated in the Nursing Home Reform Law. In 2003, 15 years after passage of the Reform Law, the US Government Accountability Office (GAO) issued a report entitled *Prevalence of Serious Quality Problems Remains Unacceptably High, Despite Some Decline*.[26] The GAO found that "[t]he magnitude of documented serious deficiencies that harmed nursing home residents remains unacceptably high, despite some decline . . .[O]ne in five nursing homes nationwide . . . had serious deficiencies that caused residents actual harm or placed them in immediate jeopardy. Moreover, GAO found significant understatement of care problems that should have been classified as actual harm or higher – serious avoidable pressure sores, severe weight loss, and multiple falls resulting in broken bones and other injuries . . ."[27] Other studies over the years, as well as publicly reported data on nursing home quality, staffing and inspections, indicate that these problems are widespread and persistent. Most recently, a 2014 study by the US Inspector General found that one-third of the individuals who went to a US nursing home for short-term Medicare rehab are harmed in the nursing home and that 59% of the time harm is "clearly or likely preventable." All of the harm described in the report was "attributable to the care provided . . . [in the facility due to] substandard treatment, inadequate resident monitoring, and failure or delay of necessary care."[28]

Underlying the persistence of serious problems in US nursing homes is the persistent failure of the states and CMS to utilize meaningful enforcement mechanisms. When facilities are found to be out of compliance with minimum standards, there are a range of enforcement remedies available to the states and CMS. These include: monetary fines (known as Civil Money Penalties or CMPs), denial of government payment for new admissions to the facility (DOPNA), directed plan of correction of the problem (DPOC), imposition of an independent monitor of facility operations and removal from the Medicaid/Medicare reimbursement systems. The last remedy typically results in a facility's sale or closure. While

26 GAO (2003). *Prevalence of Serious Quality Problems Remains Unacceptably High, Despite Some Decline – Highlights.* Retrieved from http://www.gao.gov/products/GAO-03–1016T.
27 *Ibid.*
28 Office of Inspector General (2014). *Adverse Events in Skilled Nursing Facilities: National Incidence Among Medicare Beneficiaries – Executive Summary.* Retrieved from oig.hhs.gov/oei/reports/oei-06-11-00370. pdf.

these are strong remedies, because they are underutilized they have limited effect on nursing home performance.[29]

For instance, in 2012, CMS launched a national campaign to reduce antipsychotic drugging and improve dementia care in US nursing homes. At the time, close to 24% of nursing home residents were receiving antipsychotics, though only about 1% of the population will ever be diagnosed with a psychotic condition. These drugs are typically used as a form of chemical restraint, despite the "blackbox" warning from the US Food and Drug Administration against use of these drugs on elderly people with dementia.[30]

In 2011, a review by the US Office of Inspector General (OIG) determined "that 83 percent of Medicare claims for atypical antipsychotic drugs for elderly nursing home residents were associated with off-label conditions and that 88 percent were associated with the condition specified in the FDA boxed warning . . . [It] further determined through medical record review that 22 percent of the atypical antipsychotic drugs associated with the claims were not administered in compliance with CMS standards . . ."[31] In response, CMS launched its campaign in March 2012 and established a national goal of 15% reduction in antipsychotic drugging by the end of the year (nine months later) and undertook various activities to (1) improve enforcement of the Reform Law's longstanding prohibitions against, *inter alia*, inappropriate drugging and the use of chemical restraints and (2) educate and engage nursing homes.[32]

Despite the campaign, nursing homes failed to achieve this goal at the end of 2012 and, in fact, did not achieve this goal until 2013 (21 months after the nine-month goal was set). At the same time, a review of all antipsychotic drug enforcement citations in seven states "found that 95% of the deficiencies were described as 'no harm,' meaning . . . that the facilities were unlikely to be sanctioned, regardless of actual effects on residents."[33] As a result of the lack of enforcement and

29 The US Government Accountability Office (GAO) has published numerous assessments over the years identifying significant and persistent weaknesses in the enforcement of federal minimum standards for nursing homes. In addition to the study discussed in the text, see, for examples, *Nursing Home Quality: CMS Should Improve Efforts to Monitor Implementation of the Quality Indicator Survey.* 2012. Retrieved from http://www.gao.gov/products/GAO-12-214 and *Nursing Homes: Addressing the Factors Underlying Understatement of Serious Care Problems Requires Sustained CMS and State Commitment.* 2009. Retrieved from http://www.gao.gov/products/GAO-10-70.

30 US Food and Drug Administration. (April 2005). *Public Health Advisory: Deaths with Antipsychotics in Elderly Patients with Behavioral Disturbances.* Retrieved from http://www.fda.gov/Drugs/DrugSafety/PostmarketDrugSafetyInformationforPatientsandProviders/ucm053171.htm.

31 Office of Inspector General, US Department of Health and Human Services. (May 4, 2011). *Medicare Atypical Antipsychotic Drug Claims for Elderly Nursing Home Residents*, report number OEI-07-08-001. Retrieved from https://oig.hhs.gov/oei/reports/oei-07-08-00150.pdf.

32 For links to both surveyor and nursing home trainings, as well as related CMS guidance and other resources, see http://www.nursinghome411.org/articles/?category=antipsychotic.

33 Edelman, T. and Lerner, D. Center for Medicare Advocacy. (June 27, 2013). Examining Inappropriate Use of Antipsychotic Drugs, Part One: How Seven States Cite Antipsychotic Drug Deficiencies. Retrieved from http://www.medicareadvocacy.org/examining-inappropriate-use-of-antipsychotic-drugs-part-one-how-seven-states-cite-antipsychotic-drug-deficiencies.

failure of the campaign, as of late 2014, an estimated 80,000 more nursing home residents were being given dangerous antipsychotic drugs every day because CMS failed to reach and sustain its initial goal.[34]

As noted earlier, in addition to conducting annual surveys (inspections) the states are responsible for responding to complaints about resident care. Unfortunately, this aspect of oversight and quality assurance is also weak, overall. In 2011, the US Government Accountability Office conducted an assessment to address these issues, noting that "many state survey agencies had difficulty meeting some of CMS's nursing home complaint standards."[35] This finding collaborates with perceptions of consumer representatives across the country, who have for years complained that complaints are not thoroughly investigated, even when resident harm is alleged. For instance, family members of residents will often complain that their state only interviewed the provider, and not family members or residents, when investigating an allegation of abuse.

To a significant extent, the persistence of nursing home problems and lack of accountability are due to the varying political will and priorities of both state and federal policymakers and the power of provider industry groups to weaken enforcement and regulatory interpretation. State and federal regulators often refer to the nursing homes (which they are supposed to be overseeing) as their "partners." In terms of the antipsychotic drugging campaign discussed above, for instance, despite the utter failure to meet the goals that CMS set in collaboration with the industry, in November 2014 the director of the CMS nursing home division referred to the industry's progress to date in reducing inappropriate antipsychotic drugging as "fantastic."[36]

Nursing home care is a multi-billion dollar a year industry in the United States. The Medicaid program spends over $50 billion per year on nursing home care[37] while the Medicare program spends close to $29 billion per year for nursing home care.[38] In addition, as noted earlier, approximately 20% of nursing home revenues are from private resources. As a result, the nursing home industry is quite

34 Mollot, R. The Long Term Care Community Coalition. (December 2014). *Left Behind: The Impact Of The Failure To Meet & Sustain The Initial Goal Of The National Campaign To Reduce Antipsychotic Drugging Of U.S. Nursing Home Residents.* Retrieved from http://www.nursinghome411.org/articles/?category=antipsychotic.

35 GAO. (April 2011). *More Reliable Data and Consistent Guidance Would Improve CMS Oversight of State Complaint Investigations.* Retrieved from http://www.gao.gov.

36 Tritz, K. (2014, November 4). National Partnership to Improve Dementia Care – November Quarterly Stakeholder Call. For an assessment of antipsychotic drugging reduction in US nursing homes over the course of the federal campaign see Mollot, R. (2014). *Left Behind: The Impact Of The Failure To Fulfill The Promise of The National Campaign To Improve Dementia Care.* Retrieved from http://www.nursinghome411.org/?articleid=10091.

37 Kaiser Family Foundation, State Health Facts, Distribution of Medicaid Spending on Long Term Care (Source: Urban Institute estimates based on data from CMS (Form 64) (as of 9/16/13)). Retrieved from http://kff.org/medicaid/state-indicator/spending-on-long-term-care.

38 Medicare Payment Advisory Committee (MedPAC), *MedPac Report to the Congress: Medicare Payment Policy,* March 2015, Chapter 8 – *Skilled Nursing Facility Services Payment System.* Retrieved from http://medpac.gov/documents/reports/march-2015-report-to-the-congress-medicare-payment-policy.pdf?sfvrsn=0.

powerful on both the state and federal levels. There are numerous lobbying associations, most prominently LeadingAge (representing the not-for-profit sector of the industry) and the American Health Care Association (AHCA, representing the for-profit sector of the industry) and their state affiliates. Along with numerous law firms, general lobby firms and regional lobbying associations, these groups endeavor to represent the industry's interests in the development of laws and policies relating to payment, oversight, and accountability and in the implementation of those laws by both the state and federal governments.

Nursing home consumer and public advocacy, on the other hand, is miniscule in comparison. A minority of the states have independent not-for-profit organizations, known informally as Consumer Advocacy Groups (CAGs).[39] CAGs monitor nursing home care and represent the interests of residents individually (helping to resolve individual complaints) and/or systemically (representing the interests of residents with state and federal policymakers and the news media). In addition, there are only a few consumer-focused national organizations in the US, including the National Consumer Voice for Quality Long Term Care,[40] the Center for Medicare Advocacy[41] and the Coalition for Quality Care.[42] Larger state groups, such as those in New York[43] and California,[44] often try to bridge this gap, working with national policymakers and other stakeholders. However, for residents in most states, there are no consumer-based resources to help them individually or to counter the industry's significant influence systemically.

US law also provides for an important, quasi-governmental consumer advocate: the Long Term Care Ombudsman Program (LTCOP). The LTCOP is charged with protecting nursing home residents by monitoring nursing homes, advocating for residents and helping to resolve problems in resident care, quality of life and dignity. While the LTCOP does not have regulatory authority (and thus cannot penalize nursing homes), LTCOPs operate in every state under statutorily mandated functions and responsibilities delineated in the Older Americans Act.[45]

39 There are approximately 17 state groups though this number is somewhat fluid. It is worth noting that some of these groups have professional (paid) staff while others are all volunteer based.
40 Formerly known as the National Citizens' Coalition for Nursing Home Reform (http://www. theconsumervoice.org), the Consumer Voice was one of the consumer organizations responsible for the Nursing Home Reform Law.
41 The Center (http://www.medicareadvocacy.org) conducts legal and policy advocacy on behalf of nursing home residents and other consumers.
42 The Coalition (http://coalitionqualitycare.org) is comprised of state and regional CAGs working together to share information and coordinate advocacy.
43 The Long Term Care Community Coalition (http://ltccc.org/ and http://www.nursinghome411. org) is a New York based consumer group that conducts research and advocacy on both state and national long-term care policy issues.
44 California Advocates for Nursing Home Reform (http://www.canhr.org) is likely the largest state consumer organization in the country. It has had a significant, leading role in numerous consumer advocacy efforts, most recently in the national campaign to reduce the widespread use of antipsychotic drugs as chemical restraints on nursing home residents.
45 The State Long Term Care Ombudsman Program was established by Title III of the Older Americans Act (OAA) in 1978 as a demonstration program and was transferred to a new Title VII of the OAA (which also includes other programs) in 1992. See HR 782–106th Congress: Older Americans Act Amendments of 2000 (http://www.govtrack.us/congress/bills/106/hr782).

These include: (1) identifying and resolving complaints made by or on behalf of residents, (2) representing the needs of residents to policymakers and the public, (3) advocating for systemic change by advocating or seeking to change laws and systems on behalf of residents, (4) providing information and educational materials about long-term care, and (5) advocating for the health, safety, welfare, and rights of people residing in residential care settings. More than any other entity, LTCOPs have the advantage of being "on the scene" in nursing homes, since LTCOP staff or trained volunteers are assigned to individual nursing homes and, typically, visit their facility on a weekly basis. However, because states have significant leeway in how they operate the program within their state, the state programs vary widely in terms of their ability to monitor care and help residents.[46,47]

Additional oversight and accountability mechanisms

As noted earlier, there are two principal federal entities that have the ability to monitor and assess program integrity related to nursing financing and services: the Government Accountability Office (GAO) and the Office of the Inspector General (OIG).[48] In addition, federal law provides for state Medicaid Fraud Control Units (MFCUs), "federal and state-funded law enforcement entities that investigate and prosecute provider fraud and violations of state law pertaining to fraud in the administration of the Medicaid program. In addition, the MFCUs are required to review complaints of resident abuse or neglect in nursing homes and other health care facilities."[49] Because nursing home providers agree to meet or exceed the care standards provided for in the Nursing Home Reform Law when they are paid by the Medicaid program, a failure to meet these standards constitutes fraud. MFCUs in several states have used hidden camera and other types of investigations to capture incidents of abuse and neglect, such as failing to give a resident prescribed medication, failing to provide appropriate monitoring to prevent pressure sores or resident abuse.[50] While many MFCUs have been highly successful in identifying and punishing incidents of resident abuse and neglect, the size and scope of work of the MFCUs is significantly limited. In other words, they

46 Colello, K. (2009). Older Americans Act: Long-Term Care Ombudsman Program. Congressional Research Service, 7–5700.

47 Mollot, R. (2014). The New York State Long Term Care Ombudsman Program: An Assessment of Current Performance, Issues & Obstacles. Retrieved from http://www.nursinghome411.org/?articleid=10080.

48 Both the OIG's website (http://oig.hhs.gov) and the GAO's website (http://www.gao.gov) provide a wealth of resources in terms of analyses and studies of nursing home care. However, it is important to note that assessing nursing home care and related program integrity issues represent a very small part of both agencies' scope of work.

49 National Association of Medicaid Fraud Control Units. Available at http://www.namfcu.net. [July 7, 2014.] MFCUs operate in every US state except for North Dakota.

50 For examples of MFCU investigations in New York go to http://ltccc.org (search "MFCU"). For further details on the genesis of the federal MFCU program go to http://www.ltccc.org/documents/10709-LongTermCareCommunityRemarks.doc.

lack the capacity to provide the system-wide oversight and quality assurance for which the state survey agencies are responsible (but too often fail to accomplish).

Nursing home residents and their families (if the resident lacks capacity or has died) may also bring a legal claim when the resident has been harmed as the result of poor or inadequate care, neglect or abuse. In some ways such lawsuits provide a strong mechanism for improving care, since (when the plaintiff is successful) they can be costly to the nursing home, often much more so than state or federal fines.[51] In the past, there were very few of these lawsuits, due to the fact that US civil court system places less monetary value on the lives of individuals who have little or no income. However, over the years courts have been more inclined to provide compensation for a resident's pain or suffering as the result of poor care and negligence, and this has made abuse and neglect cases more viable.

It is critical to note that this viability varies greatly from state to state, as some states place significant limitations on the amount of a punitive award while others provide for specific monetary claims. Some states allow nursing homes to place clauses in their residency contracts requiring that any future civil dispute (including one relating to poor care that resulted in death) be resolved through arbitration, rather than a court of law. From a consumer viewpoint, this severely limits the public's ability to hold nursing homes accountable for inadequate care, neglect or abuse.

On the other hand, some states have taken steps to recognize a monetary value for nursing home residents' lives, irrespective of those individuals' future earnings expectations. For example, in New York, the public health law provides that a nursing home that deprives a resident of any right or benefit shall be liable to the resident for any injuries suffered as a result of that mistreatment.[52] This has resulted in a number of cases, such as that of Gertrude Kash. Ms Kash had been admitted to Jewish Home of Rochester for short-term rehabilitation. Three weeks into her stay, a nurse failed to perform the required daily catheterization of her bladder, which was part of her care plan. As a result, Ms Kash had to get up in the middle of the night to empty her overfull bladder. She was unable to make it and was found on the floor by the nursing staff after slipping in her own urine. She complained immediately of back pain.

The gravity of this injury was not diagnosed by staff, including her doctor, and was treated only with pain medicine. A week later she was found again on the floor of her room. At that point she was sent for a CT scan which revealed a fractured vertebrae. She returned to the Jewish Home after the CT scan but no treatment of her fracture and declining neurological condition was offered other than increased pain medication for her steadily increasing pain. She was never evaluated again by her doctor or any other physician or nurse practitioner after the CT scan.

---

51 As discussed earlier, nursing home abuse and neglect tend to be under-identified by surveyors. Thus government fines are relatively rare.

52 New York State Public Health Law § 2801-d. Private actions by patients of residential healthcare facilities.

Ms Kash continued to decline precipitously in health and pleas from her family for more medical intervention went unheeded. Finally a relative from out of town who is also a doctor came to see her and determined that she was paralyzed from the chest down. As her daughter reported in an article in *The LTCCC Monitor*, "It had now been two weeks since the first fall. She was rushed to the hospital where it was determined that the damage to her spinal cord caused by the fracture, swelling and bleeding was now irreversible. She lived for an additional three years confined to a wheelchair paralyzed from the chest down."[53,54]

Nursing Home Compare and other resources for the public

There has been a growing movement in the US to provide the public, including long-term care consumers, with more information on healthcare providers and their quality. From a consumer perspective this has both positive and negative implications. On the one hand, such information can help individuals make good decisions. On the other hand, it is sometimes used as a substitute for quality assurance and enforcement. Additionally (and importantly), public information is only valuable to the extent that it is accurate. In recent years the federal government has developed several databases to help the public find information on a variety of healthcare service providers. "Nursing Home Compare,"[55] part of the US government's medicare.gov website, contains information about every Medicaid and Medicare-certified nursing home in the United States. The public can view information about individual facilities such as the facility's staffing levels (self-reported, as of July 2015), measures that indicate a facility's qualities in certain categories (also self-reported), the dates and results of recent inspections, and the level and frequency of penalties. The public can also compare these statistics against other facilities and statewide and national averages. In addition, Nursing Home Compare contains a comprehensive database with information for every facility that is searchable and which can be used to identify, for instance, state and national trends relating to quality measure performance, citations, and fines. The major problem with Nursing Home Compare, however, is that the data presented have limited reliability. As noted above, staffing and quality measure data are self-reported by nursing homes and unaudited by the government. Both, to varying degrees, are widely understood to be inflated. In addition (as also discussed earlier), survey inspections are of limited value due to the fact that nursing home problems tend to be under-identified by the survey system. As one report stated, Nursing Home Compare and the other nursing home quality reporting systems

53 *Settlement Approved in Brighton, New York Fall Case*. New York Nursing Home Abuse Lawyer Blog. (2010). Retrieved from http://www.newyorknursinghomeabuselawyerblog.com/2010/12/settlement-approved-in-brighto.html.

54 Kash, L. (2013). *My Mother's Nursing Home Nightmare*. The LTCCC Monitor. Retrieved from http://www.ltccc.org/newsletter/documents/ltccc_spring2013_web.pdf.

55 Nursing Home Compare website available at http://www.medicare.gov/nursinghomecompare/search.html.

currently in use are much better at identifying poor facilities than they are at identifying potentially "good" ones.[56]

In addition to Nursing Home Compare and the individual state websites (providing similar information in varying formats) there are a number of public and private entities across the country which provide assistance with accessing nursing home and other long-term care services and supports. The public (government) entities tend to provide basic information on the range of services available in different communities, payment options and other resources[57] while private entities generally hold themselves out as a free public service but, in fact, receive payment by nursing homes and other providers for listing and/or referrals.[58]

The *Olmstead* decision and the movement away from institutional care

In the 1999 US Supreme Court case *Olmstead v. L.C. and E.W.*,[59] the Court held that states are required to place individuals in the least restrictive setting possible as appropriate for each individual. The case involved two women who were relegated to institutional care despite their professional caregivers' opinion that they could live safely in the community. Their state, Georgia, had been approved by the federal government for 2,100 Medicaid community-based waiver "slots" to enable 2,100 individuals to access care outside of a nursing home. However, Georgia had only funded 700 of these slots. The Court found that this situation amounted to bias in the administration of a state program, and set forth parameters for states to reduce the institutional bias of long-term care in states throughout the country. In accomplishing this, the Court mandated that states make reasonable modifications (though not fundamental alterations) to their Medicaid-funded programs to foster such placement.

Olmstead is a landmark decision in respect to expectations for dignity and quality of life for long-term care consumers. However, because the states were given significant leeway and flexibility, implementation has been slow, with most states making little progress in the years since the Court's decision. This means that many people who could live safely in their own homes, with appropriate services, continue to be relegated to nursing homes and other institutional settings. To a large extent this is a result of the failure by most states to develop and implement

56 Phillips, C., Hawes, C., Lieberman, T., and Koren, M.J. (2007) "Where should Momma go? Current nursing home performance measurement strategies and a less ambitious approach," BMC Health Serv Res. 7: 93. Retrieved from http://www.ncbi.nlm.nih.gov/pmc/articles/PMC1920506.

57 See, for example, the US Center for Disability and Aging Policy (CDAP) Aging & Disability Resource Centers Program/No Wrong Door System at http://www.acl.gov/Programs/CDAP/OIP/ADRC/index.aspx.

58 See, for example, A Place for Mom at http://www.aplaceformom.com.

59 527 US 581 (1999).

concrete policies to facilitate de-institutionalization.[60] However, it is also important to note that there are often significant practical hurdles. In urban areas, high real estate costs often making finding an affordable home a significant challenge while, in rural areas, access to home caregivers can be a challenge. Increasingly, however, individuals, grassroots advocates and policymakers are succeeding in making the promise of *Olmstead* a reality for the elderly and disabled individuals who need long-term care. Systemically, this has been due to increasing availability of (and funding for) what are known as Home and Community Based Services (HCBS). HCBS include a range of services, from personal assistance (such as help with meal preparation) to healthcare services (such as intravenous (IV) therapy). Payment for HCBS can be private (including through privately held insurance) or, increasingly, public (through the Medicaid program).

Assisted living

As part of the movement away from nursing home care, more and more individuals have been turning to other settings when they need or desire residential long-term care. Assisted living residences (ALRs)[61] generally provide a combination of housing and supportive services for individuals who do not need to be in a nursing home (which are meant to provide around-the-clock skilled nursing care) but do require (or desire) personal care, health services and/or monitoring in a residential setting. It is important to be aware that the federal government does not define assisted living and states have developed their own definitions, standards, and regulatory structures.[62] Because these definitions vary greatly, it is difficult to identify how many assisted living facilities exist. According to the National Center for Health Statistics' 2013 Overview, there are 22,200 licensed (non-nursing home) residential care communities in the US, serving just over 700,000 residents.[63]

Even within some states, different types of ALR facilities may exist in which one would find different resident populations, with different services offered, different regulatory requirements and, quite often, different payment mechanisms. Some facilities market themselves to individuals with certain physical or mental conditions (such as individuals who utilize a wheelchair or have Alzheimer's Disease), while others may not accept them – and might ask people who develop such conditions to leave. Accommodations and services also can vary. Some ALRs

---

60 There have been several lawsuits by consumers to force states to take more substantive actions to implement *Olmstead*. Courts have generally sided with states, though there are signs that this is changing.

61 "Assisted living" is probably the most commonly used name for these facilities, which go by different names across the country, including "senior living," "board and care," residential care facility," and "adult home."

62 See, for example, New York State's assisted living law and regulations. Assisted Living in New York State. (2013). Assisted Living 411. Retrieved from http://assisted-living411.org/nyassistedliving. php.

63 Harris-Kojetin, L., Sengupta, M., Park-Lee, E., and Valverde, R. (2013). *Long-Term Care Services in the United States: 2013 Overview*. Retrieved from http://www.cdc.gov/nchs/nsltcp.htm.

provide apartments with kitchenettes, while others offer private or shared rooms. In some places, services may be limited to housekeeping and personal care, such as help with bathing and dressing, while others offer more significant levels of service, such as dementia care, physical therapy or medication management. Typical services include meals that are served in a common dining room, personal care, housekeeping, and activities.

These wide variations have both positive and negative repercussions for consumers. The variety of ALRs and, in some areas, the competition between them, can provide a variety of options for consumers. An individual seeking assisted living may be able to choose a facility that can help him or her maintain important activities and community connections, for instance having regular shuttle service to that individual's religious or social institution, providing a weekly card game or hosting a book club. Where there are a range of providers, individuals can also often choose facilities that are tailored to meet their particular needs, such as for dementia care.

On the other hand, these variations can have serious pitfalls for consumers. The rights and protections mandated in the Nursing Home Reform Law do not extend to ALRs. Thus, the lack of federal standards (and, hence, standardization of services and relevant criteria), and the general weakness of state assisted living requirements and oversight, has left the provider industry with significant leeway in not only the kind of care it provides, but who provides it, how and at what cost. For example, while assisted living facilities often hold themselves out as a place where people with Alzheimer's Disease and other dementia can live safely, there are, in fact, generally very limited standards for providing this care in terms of training or licensure requirements for care staff, safety of the facility's environment, the appropriateness of services provided, etc. The result can be disastrous for a vulnerable resident and his/her family who, because of lax oversight, generally have limited meaningful ability to file a complaint with the government oversight agency or even make a legal claim.

This is of particular concern given the continued growth of this sector of the residential care marketplace. While the majority of (though not all) ALR residents pay privately, there are numerous efforts in the states and by the federal government to use public funds for this purpose. There are two ostensible benefits to this trend: (1) assisted living facilities tend to be less institutional settings than the traditional nursing home, thus fulfilling the public's interest in avoiding institutionalization (and the mandate of the Supreme Court's *Olmstead* decision, discussed earlier) and (2) assisted living care is, generally speaking, far less expensive than nursing home care (thus having the potential to reduce state and federal expenses).[64]

---

64 The principal public program involved in so-called "affordable assisted living" is the Medicaid program which, as noted earlier, pays for the majority of nursing home long-term care. Some states, with federal approval, have instituted small Medicaid assisted living program in which providers are paid a percentage of the Medicaid nursing home reimbursement rate for residents who meet financial and functional criteria.

In addition to wide variations in quality and the system-wide absence of meaningful standards and oversight, it is also important to note that there is great variation in ALRs' ability to fulfill the so-called promise of assisted living: to provide care and safety in a less restrictive environment than that which is available in a typical nursing home. Due to the lack of cognizable standards, many ALRs have been found to operate with the same rigidity as the traditional nursing home in terms of resident choice and autonomy.

Conclusion

Institutional care in nursing homes has been the traditional setting for older and disabled individuals who need long-term care in the United States. Despite numerous efforts over the years to improve nursing home care and quality of life, beginning with the 1987 national Nursing Home Reform Law and continuing to this day with various government, consumer, and industry efforts to improve quality and change the culture of nursing homes, the majority of facilities continue to be highly institutional settings. Though there are numerous criteria relating to quality of care, quality of life and dignity, persistent weaknesses in oversight and enforcement have limited their usefulness. As a result, the large majority of US nursing homes are widely believed to be failing to meet minimum standards and lack, on a regular basis, sufficient care staff to meet the basic needs of their residents.

As a result of these problems, changing perceptions of quality of life for older and disabled long-term care consumers and a US Supreme Court case favoring de-institutionalization, the US has been moving towards more Home and Community Based Services (HCBS) for long-term care. This includes both residential care in assisted living and the delivery of care and other services to individuals' homes. However, in the absence of strong standards and meaningful oversight, the safety and appropriateness of care in these settings is, now and in the future, uncertain.

9 Dignity as a theoretical and legal construct in the context of care for older persons and the developing human rights agenda for older persons

Haris Kountouros* and Nicola Rees

Spurred by social and demographic developments, the subject of residential care is gaining increasing importance in public debate with a consequent heightened sensitivity to the need to ensure that older persons in care live in conditions which respect their dignity. The matter concerns us all. As more and more of us are expected to live longer, we face the prospect of spending the last years of our life in residential care. Respect for the dignity of older persons is ultimately respect of our dignity. At the same time, current trends, especially at the international and supranational levels, indicate attempts to develop a human rights approach specifically geared towards older persons (Megret 2011; Doron and Apter 2010; Tang and Lee 2006). As the Explanatory Memorandum to the 2014 Council of Europe *Recommendation on the promotion of human rights of older persons* states, 'The increasing number of older persons in European societies augments the need to address the issue of their position in societies, including the need to promote their autonomy and to ensure their protection from a human rights perspective' (Council of Europe 2014a, p. 1). In a similar vein, AGE Platform Europe argues that long-term care should be developed 'using a rights-based approach' (AGE Platform Europe 2014, p. 3). Beyond the area of older persons, the UN Convention on the Rights of Persons with Disabilities illustrates clearly this trend.

Concurrently with the foregoing, however, in the legal context and especially in judicial adjudication, the concept of 'dignity' is fraught with difficulties and legal uncertainty. Older persons are entitled to live with dignity, numerous declarations state, yet what does this mean in concrete legal terms? This dichotomy raises significant questions, in particular whether dignity can be operationalised in the legal context. Doubts about the value of the concept of dignity in judicial adjudication are certainly not limited to the context of care of older persons (see Macklin 2003; Hyman 2003; McCrudden 2008). Scholars and others remark that judicial practice does not indicate either a uniform treatment of the concept, or a universal understanding of what it means (McCrudden 2008; Glensy 2011). Some even go so far as to argue that dignity is a useless concept (Macklin 2003), or that it has become a burden for certain human rights claimants (see *R v. Krapp* (SCC 41, par. 23), *per* McLachlin CJ and Abella J).

* The author writes in his personal capacity. Views and opinions expressed herein do not necessarily represent the position of the Institution for which he works.

Against this background, this chapter examines the concept of dignity as a theoretical and legal construct in the context of care for older persons. The discussion seeks to provide a better understanding of the potential, but also limitations of dignity in the examined field, and to highlight a number of important developments in the area of human rights for older persons.

Dignity in philosophical discourse

Law does not operate in a vacuum, but interacts with, *inter alia*, politics, philosophy, economics, social norms and customs. For a better understanding of the role of dignity in the legal context, it is useful to first outline some theoretical aspects relevant to the issue. Like many other notions met in philosophical texts, dignity has followed a conceptual trajectory – it still does. It is also the case that the concept is met in both the vernacular and philosophical discourse and thus further nuances exist as concerns its meanings.

For instance, we can immediately comment on two common usage meanings of dignity which have derived from the times of antiquity. The first relates to *status* and thus to the position, rank or decorum someone has in society (Rosen 2012, p. 11; Waldron 2009, p. 225). The rulers, the clergy and the military have for centuries been typical examples of groups of people enjoying dignity by virtue of their status. The law has often been used as a means to protect this type of dignity (Waldron 2009, p. 225). The other has to do with 'carrying oneself with dignity', which implies behaving in a certain manner appropriate to certain norms (Schroeder 2010, p. 2). An element of self-control is implicit in this understanding of dignity, while there may be a link between this and the first meaning of dignity. Thus, just as a diplomat enjoys dignity by virtue of her office, she is at the same time expected to conduct herself in a manner fit to that status.

Yet, the second meaning of the term is broader than the first one – one does not have to be of a certain social class to act with dignity. Indeed, the philosophical school of the Stoics that flourished in the third century BC maintained that even in the face of the worst adversity, one can still choose to remain dignified. In one of his discourses, Epictetus says:

> I must die. Must I then die lamenting? I must be put in chains. Must I then also lament? I must go into exile. Does any man then hinder me from going with smiles and cheerfulness and contentment? . . . Me in chains? You may fetter my leg, but my will not even Zeus himself can overpower.
>
> (Epictetus 1998, Bk 1, Ch. 1)

During the Middle Ages and onwards philosophical thinking in Europe evolved against a background marked by heavy religious influence and tensions between various social classes – royalty, church, bourgeoisie and peasantry. This has had an impact on the treatment of the concept during that period. For thinkers such as Aquinas and Pico della Mirandola, dignity is bestowed upon all human beings by God, has an intrinsic value and is discovered by reason (*cf.* Rosen 2012, pp. 14–18; McCrudden 2008, pp. 658–659). Christian doctrine also proceeds on the belief that dignity is a gift from God and that we all possess it by virtue of being God's creatures born in His image. Yet as Rosen remarks, for a very long time, Christian, in particular Catholic, doctrine also promoted an explicitly status-specific understanding of dignity, which resulted in a very illiberal application of the concept (*cf.* Rosen 2012, pp. 13–14, 50–53).

Modern theoretical discussions on dignity emphasise the influence of Immanuel Kant, the German philosopher whose more important body of work was written in the late eighteenth century. Kant provides a theory on dignity which is merged into a larger web of concepts and ideas. Like Aristotle and Plato before him, Kant was concerned not merely with the individual but also with the individual's place within the organised society and, further, with the State (*cf.* Russell 2004, p. 240).

Dignity for Kant is the only universal value. It has its kernel in our humanity; it is discovered by reason and is realised by consequent actions/duties. Central to this understanding of dignity are reason, morality and autonomy. Following established philosophical tradition, Kant gives reason a central place in his philosophy. It is reason that gives humans their uniqueness and allows us to discover, and act in accordance with, our inherent morality. In like terms the ethical element is intrinsic to Kant's work. In an oft-quoted passage Kant says that 'morality, and humanity insofar as it is capable of morality, is that which alone has dignity' (AK 4:435). Morality for Kant is something that is transcendal and inherent in us and forms 'the ground of the dignity of human nature' (AK 4:436).

In turn, autonomy is also key because it determines our capacity to act. State oppression removes that capacity – this is a central element to Kant's work. His distinction from the Stoics should be evident. However, autonomy in Kant should never be seen merely as freedom to acquiesce, to choose, to say yes or no, or even as the capacity to defend oneself, and the like. Rather, autonomy primarily embodies the notion of having the capacity to act morally (Allison 2011, pp. 216–218). A range of ethical duties follow, principal amongst which is the Kantian 'categorical imperative', whose second formulation states that we should always treat people as ends-in-themselves and never merely as means to an end (AK 6:395). What is more, we owe a duty of *respect* to our own dignity and to that of every other human being; for ultimately, it is only through respect that human dignity can be realised (*cf.* AK 6:434–435, and see Rosen 2012 p. 157; Wood 2008; Dillon 2011). 'Capacity' and 'reason' are thus not sufficient in themselves: for Kant 'morality' remains the bridge one must cross to reach the *telos* – the 'moral act'.[1]

---

1 As a footnote we may note that here lies a big distinction between the Kantian and Aristotelian *telos*. For the former, the moral act signifies the *telos*; for Aristotle though, the moral act is a step towards a longer journey whose *telos* is 'eudaimonia'. Eudaimonia (also found in English as eudemonia) is often translated as 'happiness' or 'human flourishing' and denotes a state of being which is achievable through a life based on virtue, reason, but also the necessary material goods which can enable one to satisfy their basic needs and flourish intellectually, emotionally, physically etc. In Aristotelian philosophy 'chance' (or fortune) in one's life also plays a significant role to this end. Aristotle distinguishes 'eudaimonia' from 'euzoeia', which means 'good life', and essentially maintains that only philosophers can ultimately attain the former, the rest can aspire to a good life, though not necessarily a eudemonic one). *Cf.* Mastoraki.

Modern theoretical perspectives on dignity

Impressive as the theories of the old greats may be, they are also problematic in their application, especially in the modern world. The severely mentally disabled, the foetus, animals and plants do not fit well with the old works on dignity, commonly (though not exhaustively) because the capacity for rational thought is lacking. Yet, with the advent of social and scientific developments we are, today, more aware and more sensitive to these issues. We therefore wish to see a more ethical treatment of a widening range of sentient and non-sentient beings. Modern theoretical discourse draws upon earlier works but seeks to modify them to fit our era (see, *inter alia*, Korsgaard 1996; Christiano 2008; Nussbaum 2008; Shell 2008; Waldron 2009; Rosen 2012; Evans and Kleinig 2013).

It is characteristic of this discourse not to pay much attention to the moral obligations of the dignity bearer him/herself, unless they relate to law, but rather to concentrate on the rights that human – and other – beings have by virtue of their innate dignity. It is not the purpose of this chapter to provide a review of contemporary theoretical literature on dignity. Suffice here to note that this phenomenon has resulted in an even larger number of nuances to the concept and a debate about the 'correct reading' of some of the older texts which still continues.

It is within this broader framework that one also reads the sprawling literature on dignity in the context of care for older persons. Literature in this field attempts to clarify what dignity means and also seeks to operationalize it in the context of care of older persons. A distinctive characteristic of many of the writings in this area is the explicit elaboration of dignity by means of distinctions and taxonomies. An important distinction in this regard is between 'subjective' and 'objective' meanings of dignity. Another is between a person's internal feelings and external world, or dimensions.

Anderberg *et al.* (2007) provide a literature review of the issue and conclude that 'dignity consists of inherent and external dimensions, which are common for all humans and at the same time are unique for each person, relating to social and cultural aspects. The attributes of preserving dignity are individualized care, control restored, respect, advocacy and sensitive listening' (*ibid.*, p. 635). The authors also stress the role of support structures and processes, including professional knowledge, responsibility, reflection and non-hierarchical organisations. The consequences are strengthening life spirit, an inner sense of freedom, self-respect and successful coping. In their paper Shotton and Seedhouse (1998) explain dignity with reference to the relation between capabilities and circumstances, arguing that dignity is considered to be lacking when faced with undignifying circumstances. Restoring dignity requires changing these circumstances and the capability to do so.

A significant contribution to the debate is made by Nordenfelt (2003). He borrows from the Kantian tradition in acknowledging an intrinsic dignity (*menschenwürde*) but also identifies three other concepts of dignity which may be referred to as extrinsic or contingent values. These are (a) dignity of merit; (b) dignity of moral stature; and (c) dignity of personal identity. Common to all is that dignity entails a set of rights, in the case of basic dignity the set of rights which we call human rights. He argues that there is some dignity peculiar to older people that is over and above the basic *menschenwürde*. One of the implications of this analysis relates to the obligations of carers and nurses. Carers are expected to pay attention to all four varieties of dignity and also exhibit dignity in their own character (*cf.* Gallagher *et al.* 2008, p. 4). In turn, Mann (1998) elaborates on a taxonomy of dignity violations, following discussions with students, anthropologists, sociologists and bioethicists. These violations include (a) not being seen; (b) being seen but only as a member of a group; (c) injuries to dignity resulting from violations of personal space; and (d) humiliation. Restoring dignity requires addressing these violations and building an environment which prevents their recurrence.

A further contribution to the debate on dignity in the context of the care of older people is provided by Tadd *et al.* (2010). The authors undertook a multidisciplinary study involving nurses, philosophers, sociologists, psychologists, clinicians, health service researchers and NGOs from six EU countries: the UK, Spain, Slovakia, Ireland, Sweden and France. After looking at some of the contemporary theoretical approaches to the concept, including some of the ones outlined above, the authors proceed to an empirical evaluation of the meaning of human dignity with the help of the focus groups that served as the basis for the research in each country. As the authors state, dignity 'was seen as a highly relevant and important concept that, when experienced, enhanced self-esteem, self-worth and well-being' (*ibid.*, p. 261).

The authors remark that 'in general, participants found it easier to identify situations when dignity was lacking than when it was present or what it meant' (*ibid.*, p. 261) and, similarly, that they 'found no difficulty in describing what they considered to be undignified care or in citing examples in relation to older people' (*ibid.*, p. 269). This is quite significant, for if we cannot provide a precise definition of what dignity means, it is at least possible to agree on what 'undignified' care is, and therefore take appropriate action towards redressing it. In this sense, there is a clear similarity to Mann's own study in relation to the matter. Tadd *et al.* argue that by identifying what constitutes undignified care and vulnerability, it is possible to understand what '"dignity-enhancing-care" *de-facto* means' (*ibid.*, p. 275). In this respect, the authors emphasise the importance of empirical research, both qualitative and quantitative.

Three overarching themes were identified: respect and recognition; participation and involvement; and dignity in care. As far as respect is concerned, participants in the study identified as dignity both what relates to 'dignity of merit' and to 'dignity of moral stature' (*ibid.*, pp. 261–262). As the study makes clear, a big problem in the relevant context is that many older people feel excluded from family and community life. Accordingly, opportunities for service in the community, especially in a voluntary capacity, would be much welcome as these 'would enhance self-esteem and a sense of identity and dignity of merit' (*ibid.*, p. 263). Participants to the study also emphasised the importance of *autonomy*. In this context, the procedures followed in care centres and assistance with older persons are much relevant, particularly the extent to which they include – or exclude – older persons from relevant decision making (*ibid*. pp. 263–265). Additionally, participants criticised 'prevailing ideologies of managerialism and [of] and "economic approach" as incompatible with dignified care for older people' (*ibid*. p. 270). At the end of their report, the authors remark that 'the concept of dignity elaborated in this study demonstrates that dignity is the result of caring interactions between the caregivers and the elderly persons' (*ibid*. p. 274).

What one concludes from the above is the evolution of dignity in a context that emphasises the subjective experience of the (older) person and also looks at the objective characteristics of the care that is provided. The result is a much broader understanding of what dignity means, which is informed by social and scientific developments, and increasingly involves multidisciplinary research to provide appropriate taxonomies of desiderata. There is certainly a link to old theories on dignity, which provide a normative basis and a moral justification. Yet, new theories are not concerned so much with the spiritual or the moral in itself, but more with actions that need to be taken to safeguard and promote an older person's presumed dignity.

Dignity in the legal context

Kantian philosophical thought has had a powerful impact on the development of legal thought, norms and practice. Following the Second World War, the concept of dignity has been used as a catalyst for the development of important legal instruments, ranging from state constitutions to human rights declarations (see McCrudden 2008, pp. 668–675 for an overview of international and domestic texts in which dignity forms a key concept). Notable amongst these are the German Basic Law (*Grundgesetz*) and the Universal Declaration of Human Rights. The former regards dignity as the foundational stone for all rights which are protected under the constitution; while the latter builds its moral force on the premise of an inherent dignity of human beings (see Ebert and Oduor 2012, p. 44; Rosen 2012, p. 80; van Aggelen 2000, p. 143).

In like terms, the Charter of Fundamental Rights of the European Union (hereafter 'EU Charter'), which following the Treaty of Lisbon has legal effect, places 'dignity' at its core. The entire first chapter is dedicated to it, while Article 1 states, in now familiar fashion, that: 'Human dignity is inviolable. It must be respected and protected'. The Charter applies to the EU institutions and also its Member States when applying EU law (see Article 51). The formulation of Article 1 makes it clear that both negative and positive obligations flow from its wording (Jones 2012, p. 287). Article 25 of the EU Charter deals specifically with 'the rights of the elderly', stating that: 'The Union recognises and respects the rights of the elderly to lead a life of dignity and independence and to participate in social and cultural life'.

Yet, in their interaction, the law's constant need for clarity is confronted with dignity's fluidity as a concept. Neither its philosophical, nor our vernacular, understanding of dignity are easily transposed into legal practice. While therefore its value as a powerful normative-foundational concept which lends moral status and even practical impetus to human rights instruments is almost universally accepted, many doubt its value in judicial adjudication and many more doubt we can draw any coherent logic or theory from its use (see, *inter alia*, Macklin 2003; Hyman 2003). In his analysis of a series of judicial decisions from different jurisdictions McCrudden (2008, p. 655) concludes that 'beyond a basic minimum core, [dignity] does not provide a universalistic, principled basis for judicial decision-making in the human rights context'. 'Dignity is therefore context-specific, varying significantly from jurisdiction to jurisdiction and (often) over time within particular jurisdictions' (*idem.*). What is more, significant variations exist in the understanding of what is moral across cultures and therefore of what dignity actually means (*ibid.*, p. 712).

It is indeed not an easy task for a judge to make up her mind as to whether dignity is a value to be considered along with other values or *the* value, and even if the latter whether any other specific values should be protected rather than being trumped at all times. Nor is it easy to decide whether 'dignity' is an amalgam of values, or rights, which must be shown respect – for what are these rights and how do they measure between them? (*cf.* Hughes 2014). More complex still is the precise determination of dignity within legal architecture, in particular its position or function as a human right in itself, or a foundation of human rights. For instance, in Germany, dignity is regarded as the foundation of the Basic Law, yet courts have also approached it as a substantive right, which, nevertheless, in practice is pleaded alongside more specific rights protected under the constitution (Ebert and Oduor 2012; Rosen 2012; Enders 2010).

More differences are observed as regards the weight of dignity as a value, or right, when this conflicts with other values. While in Germany, for example, dignity will trump all other rights (see Ebert and Oduor 2012, p. 48; *cf.* Glensy 2011, p. 98), in other countries, such as Canada, courts have weighted dignity against other values and at times decided that these other values took precedence (see, for instance, *Rodriguez v. British Columbia (Attorney General)* [1993] 3 SCR 519). Another difficulty with the judicial application of dignity lies in the fact that, while a violation of dignity is often posed as a subjective issue (*cf.* Shultziner and Rabinovici 2011), this is not necessarily the case. Ultimately, it is the courts' view of what constitutes a violation of dignity that counts, rather than that of an individual. This does not only apply in those cases where an individual claims that his/her dignity has been violated. It also applies to cases where public measures prescribe certain activities with the justification that these violate human dignity even though the persons affected may not themselves regard the activities in question as violating their dignity (Rosen 2012 pp. 63–69, discussing the prohibition of dwarf-tossing in France).

Moreover, while some scholars in the US seem to believe that a substantive right to dignity would not interfere with freedom of speech (see Glensy 2011, p. 125, but *cf.* Carmi 2007, pp. 959–960), practice in several jurisdictions indicates the opposite (see the *Grudens* case in Germany (BVerfGE 30/173); *Shinui Party v. Chairwoman of the Central Election Committee* in Israel (HCJ 06/2194 (2006); and *R v. Keegstra* in Canada [1990] 3 SCR 697). Even within the same legal system, lack of coherence in the judicial treatment of dignity has been noted by McCrudden and other authors (for instance, Rosen 2012, p. 114 in relation to the interpretation of the German Basic Law, Glensy 2011 in relation to the US).

An illustration from the English courts

An interesting case, not least with respect to the deep scepticism with which dignity is treated by the judiciary, is the English legal system. In the area of care, in particular, dignity has had a very poor record in judicial adjudication. *McDonald* – a case that will be looked at in some detail further below – demonstrates the limitations of dignity as a legal construct. Two other major cases in the field of health care, *R v. Gloucestershire* and *R (KM) v. Cambridgeshire* were decided without any reference to dignity in the rulings.

If one were to offer an explanation for this phenomenon it would begin with the fact that this concept, at least in its normative sense, does not form part of the legal or philosophical tradition of the United Kingdom. A caveat should be made here inasmuch as dignity in the meanings ascribed to it at the beginning of this chapter – i.e. as status and as code of behaviour – does appear in old legal texts and cases (see Waldron 2009). Yet the deontological and metaphysical theories of Kant never found much appeal in the United Kingdom. British philosophy in the eighteenth century was dominated by empiricism and thinkers such as Locke, Berkeley and Hume (Russell 2004, p. 637). In a similar vein, legal theory was much influenced by utilitarianism and its proponents, like Bentham, who expressly rejected and mocked normative, morality-infused approaches to human rights.

This is a point which, in our view, helps to understand the difficulties in elaborating a body of case law using this concept within the English legal system. It is arguably a point which is also relevant to other countries where, for historical reasons, the English legal tradition had much influence, such as Australia, Canada and the United States. At a less theoretical level, it can also be suggested that as the United Kingdom did not succumb to the Nazi invasion and as the constitutional order in this country has remained relatively stable for centuries, dignity has not generated the appeal it has in post-war Germany and elsewhere: countries following dictatorship (like Greece and Spain); ex-communist states like Hungary; post-colonial constitutions like India and South Africa following the end of apartheid; Kenya in its new constitution of 2010 after the civil war etc. It is of course true that English law has previously incorporated concepts which had not previously formed part of its corpus, including notably the principle of state liability for breaches of EU law (see Joined Cases C-6/90 and C-9/90, *Francovich v. Italy* and *Bonifaci v. Italy* [1991] ECR I-5403; Joined Cases C-46/93 and C-48/93, *Brasserie du Pêcheur SA v. Federal Republic of Germany* and *The Queen v. Secretary of State for Transport, ex parte Factortame Ltd and Others* [1996] ECR I-1029). Interaction with EU law and the Strasbourg court's jurisprudence on human rights has been instrumental to this process. Yet, the prospect of a more dynamic engagement with dignity by English judges seems neither easy nor problem-free.

Searching for coherence and common trends

The above notwithstanding, several authors have sought to identify at least some common trends or develop a more coherent use of dignity within judicial adjudication. For example, Carozza (2003) believes that it is possible to detect an interpretative use of dignity which is being exemplified through the use of comparative law and theory and which can eventually lead to a universal normative understanding of the concept. McCrudden himself, though not sharing Carozza's view, concludes that dignity has an undiminished judicial popularity and has served to 'enable a much looser coordination of human rights adjudication to take place, with significant room for disagreement and divergence over specific practical applications' (McCrudden 2008, p. 724). Thus, 'rather than providing substantive meaning, a significant use is institutional' and provides judges with a language to justify their decisions (*idem.*).

Jones takes an active reading of the Charter of the Fundamental Rights of the EU, Article 1 in particular, and holds that this 'potentially offers one of the best ways of positively expanding the rights of people in the EU in *all* areas of EU activity' (Jones 2012, p. 286; see also Jones 2004). She explores three areas which 'demonstrate the possible breadth of human dignity in creating an EU that truly is closer to its citizens' (Jones 2012, p. 294): asylum, victims of crime (including minors, victims of trafficking and protection orders in relation to possible victims of crime), and sexual orientation discrimination. In his contribution, Glensy examines the judicial treatment of dignity in the US system. In search of a more coherent treatment of the concept he offers four approaches, ranging from regarding dignity as a substantive right linked to a 'positive rights approach', to the concept serving as a 'hortatory tool' in what he calls 'the expressive approach' (Glensy 2011). Glensy himself opts for regarding dignity as a 'heuristic-cognitive device' that acts to guide judges in their decisions (*ibid.*, pp. 126 ff). In this approach dignity operates 'by proxy' and is attached to other, more specific rights.

Another attempt towards a more coherent legal conceptualisation of dignity is made by Shultziner and Rabinovici who argue for a decisively subjectivist approach that anchors dignity in the psychology of the self, that is, 'in the universal human need for positive self-worth (self-esteem)' (Shultziner and Rabinovici 2011, p. 45). The authors claim that dignity within the legal context should be delimited in this 'thin' meaning. Violations to it are those which pertain to 'threats and injuries to self-worth such as humiliation, denials of social recognition like exclusion, and diminution of one's social status in comparison to one's citizen peers' (*ibid.*, p. 46). To support their approach, the authors examine a series of cases from the US, ECtHR and Israeli jurisdictions and conclude that, implicitly or explicitly, this approach to human dignity is already applied. The fields of application encompass the treatment of detainees and prisoners, equality, the protection granted to one's privacy, reputation, and freedom of speech. They emphasise that they 'do not argue that dignity as self-worth must trump all other considerations in every case' (*ibid.*, p. 47) – a view which, in Germany at least, would pose problems. In their view, their approach to dignity has the additional merit that it can be 'evaluated and studied more objectively along considerations of mental health and well-being' and is one that can evolve with time and with the help of social, scientific and other developments (*idem.*).

Praiseworthy as the above attempts to provide a more coherent legal discourse on dignity may be, it is arguably rather difficult to see how they can provide a practical impetus to the judicial adjudication on dignity in the context of care for older persons. Interpretative approaches to dignity in the abstract, as Carozza and Glensy suggest, do not seem to add much to the current situation, while Jones' argumentation does not apply to the field of care for older persons. What is more, even Shultziner and Rabinovici's subjectivist approach, though in theory pertinent to the field of care for older persons, does not include this field in its scope. In fact, an examination of the case law in the context of the European Convention of Human Rights portrays the inadequacy of the current legal framework.

Dignity in the European Convention and the European Court of human rights

The European Convention of Human Rights (ECHR) makes no mention of dignity. Despite this, the ECtHR has held that the 'very essence of the Convention is the respect for human dignity and human freedom' (*Pretty v. UK*, par. 65). It is also clear that the Charter can give rise to positive obligations for States. In practice, dignity is cited along other, specific rights in the Convention, in respect of which the threshold is set high. Typically, 'human dignity' is cited alongside Article 2 (right to life), Article 3 (prohibition of torture and inhumane or degrading treatment) and Article 8 (protection of personal and family life). The Court's jurisprudence to date indicates that experience of significant physical or psychological suffering should occur for a claim to succeed. As Shultziner and Rabinovici (2011, p. 30) note:

> A review of the 600 odd judgments in which the word 'dignity' was employed reveals that its use as a tool for the interpretation of the ECHR was almost exclusively limited to circumstances in which physical or mental harm was inflicted on the applicant, mostly in the context of Article 3 of the ECHR.

It is therefore the case that, in the absence of a grave case of abuse or humiliation, the ECHR does not provide a sufficient basis for the protection of the dignity of older persons in the terms that scholarly discourse envisages (Spanier, Doron, and Milman-Sivan 2013). Positive obligations, moreover, are limited to a minimal level (for instance, basic medical care, or a minimum level of subsistence) which are not sufficient to raise standards in the field of care. Indeed, time and again, the Strasbourg Court has confirmed 'the wide margin of appreciation enjoyed by states' in striking a balance between the interests of an individual applicant and what the Court sees as the 'interests of the community as a whole'. This margin of appreciation is even wider when 'the issues involve an assessment of the priorities in the context of the allocation of limited state resources' (see *James and others v. the United Kingdom (Appl. 8793/79, 21/2/1986); Shelley v. the United Kingdom (Appl. 23800/06, 4/1/2008)*).

Three cases exemplify these difficulties. *Sentges v. The Netherlands* (*Appl. 27677/02*, 8/7/2003) concerned a sufferer from muscular dystrophy complaining of a refusal by the State to supply him with a robotic arm; a decision which severely harmed his ability to establish any meaningful relationships or have any sense of autonomy. In *Pentiacova v. Moldova* (*Appl. 14462/03*, 4/1/2005) the applicants suffered from renal failure and complained of insufficient funding for their haemodialysis treatment. In *Molka v. Poland* (*Appl. 56550/00*, 11/04/2006) the applicant was confined to a wheelchair and without positive assistance was unable to vote in local elections. The complaints in all three cases, all of which made a plea to Article 8 ECHR, were unanimously held to be manifestly ill-founded and thus inadmissible. In all cases, financial considerations provided the necessary justification for the States' decisions.

Similarly, in *Watts v. UK* (*Appl. 53586/09*, 4/5/2010), an application by a 106-year-old woman, following the closure of her care home for budgetary reasons by the City Council that owned and managed it, was held to be ill-founded and thus inadmissible. Though the Court accepted that a badly managed transfer of elderly residents of a care home could well have a negative impact on an older person's life expectancy (citing expert evidence submitted during the hearing), it nonetheless held that, having regard to the operational choices which must be made by local authorities and the steps which had been undertaken to minimise any risk to the applicant's life, the authorities had met their positive obligations under Article 2 of the Convention. Moreover, while the Court was prepared to accept that there was interference with Article 8(1) of the Convention, this was neither unlawful nor disproportionate. The Court referred to Article 8(2) to highlight 'the wide margin of appreciation afforded to States in issues of general policy, including social, economic and health-care policies' (par. 100).

In *McDonald v. UK* (*Appl. 4241/12*, 20/5/2014) the ECtHR examined a complaint by a 71-year-old lady against the decision of the Royal Borough of Kensington and Chelsea to reduce night staff at her care home, which was managed by the Borough. The decision meant that she had to wear incontinence pads in the evenings although she was not incontinent but suffering from a bladder condition which caused her to urinate several times during the night. In Ms McDonald's view this constituted 'an intolerable affront to her dignity'. The case had previously been heard by the UK Supreme Court which rejected her application (*R (on the application of McDonald) v. Royal Borough of Kensington and Chelsea* [2011] UKSC 33). In delivering his judgment, Lord Brown referred to *Sentges*, *Pentiacova* and *Molka*, noting that 'one only has to consider the basic facts of those three cases to recognise the hopelessness of the Article 8 argument in the present case' (par. 16). His Lordship concluded that while he had 'the greatest sympathy for the appellant's misfortunes and a real understanding of her deep antipathy towards the notion of using incontinence pads', no interference could be established with her Article 8 rights (par. 19). And this is not all, for he added that 'even if such an interference were established, it would be clearly justified under Article 8(2) . . . on the grounds that it is necessary for the economic well-being of the respondents and the interests of their other service-users and is a proportionate response to the appellant's needs because it affords her the maximum protection from injury, greater privacy and independence, and results in a substantial costs saving' (par. 19).

The ECtHR agreed partly with this analysis. Though the Court was prepared to accept that there had been interference with Article 8 ECHR, it held that this 'pursued a legitimate aim, namely the economic well-being of the State and the interests of the other care-users'. Moreover, the interference 'was both proportionate and justified in terms of the requirement of "necessity in a democratic society" under Article 8(2)' (par. 58).

Dignity in the jurisprudence of the Court of Justice of the European Union

The jurisprudence of the Court of Justice of the European Union has so far largely followed on a path not dissimilar to that of the Strasbourg Court in the sense that neither Article 1 nor Article 25 have been relied upon by the Court directly as substantive rights (Doron 2013). Prior to the Treaty of Lisbon which gave legal effect to the Charter the Court had stated that dignity forms a fundamental principle of Community law which the Court has an obligation to protect (EU Network of Independent Experts on Fundamental Rights 2006). Thus, in *P v. S and Cornwall City Council* (Case C-13/94, ECR [1996] I-2159), the Court held that to dismiss an employee undergoing gender reassignment constituted sex discrimination and further that:

> To tolerate such discrimination would be tantamount, as regards such a person, to a failure to respect the dignity and freedom to which he or she is entitled, and which the Court has a duty to safeguard.
>
> (Case C-13/94, par. 22)

An important case that was decided in 2004 concerned the banning in Germany of a game using laser toy-guns which involved simulated killings on the grounds that it constituted an affront to human dignity. In *Omega*, the Court had to decide whether the banning constituted a violation of the freedom to provide services (Case C-36/02 [2004] ECR I-9641). In her Opinion, Advocate General Stix-Hackl remarked that the concept of human dignity enjoys protection across Members States in various forms, 'primarily as a general article of faith or – often in the case-law – as a fundamental, evaluation or constitutional principle, rather than as an independent justiciable rule of law' (par. 84). She noted that the German position, which regards dignity 'not just a "fundamental constitutional principle" but also a separate fundamental right, must . . . be considered the exception' (*idem.*). As the Advocate General stated:

> 85. One principal reason for this must be that it is not until human dignity is shaped and formulated in each individual fundamental right that it acquires

more concrete substantive form and functions as a criterion of evaluation and interpretation in relation thereto. The concept of human dignity itself – like the concept of mankind to which it directly relates – is in fact a generic concept for which there is not, as such, any traditional legal definition or interpretation in the true sense; it is rather the case that its substance has to be set out in more concrete form in each individual case, especially by way of judicial findings.

86. Instead of direct recourse to human dignity, therefore, the codification and application of individual concrete guarantees of fundamental rights would therefore seem appropriate from the point of view of justiciability and judicial methods in general.

The fact that the Court had already acknowledged that 'respect for human dignity constitutes an integral part of the general legal tenets of Community law and a criterion and requirement of the legality of acts under Community law' was not sufficient to determine the question whether dignity forms a substantive right or a principle of interpretation (par. 90). Ultimately, the Advocate General did not provide an answer to this, but contended with considering dignity a principle which could justify derogations from the free movement principle. The usual tests of necessity and proportionality apply, yet Member States retain discretion in assessing the level of protection that is necessary to safeguard dignity in their territory. As the Advocate General noted, 'There is no question here of any general opinion in the Member States' (par. 105).

In its ruling, the Court avoided the question of whether, within the Community legal order, dignity constitutes merely a principle of interpretation or, rather, a substantive right. Rather, it approached the matter from the more traditional perspective of acknowledging public policy concerns that Member States may legitimately safeguard and general principles which the Court has a duty to protect. In a cleverly drafted passage the Court states that:

> the Community legal order undeniably strives to ensure respect for human dignity as a general principle of law. There can therefore be no doubt that the objective of protecting human dignity is compatible with Community law, it being immaterial that, in Germany, the principle of respect for human dignity has a particular status as an independent fundamental right.
>
> (Case C-36/02, par. 34)

Protection of human dignity was reaffirmed as a public policy objective which could impose restrictions on fundamental freedoms, such as the freedom to provide services subject to the tests of necessity and proportionality. Moreover, even more explicitly than its Advocate General, the Court recognised that States may have different levels of desired protection of human dignity (pars 38–39).

To sum up, the Court's rulings in cases concerning dignity are important in acknowledging the concept as a general principle of law and as a public policy issue which can be validly pursued. On the other hand, it is also true that the concept is primarily confined to the area of equality and a few other areas, such as biotechnology, or where it is pleaded as a justification for restriction of the fundamental freedoms which are protected under the Treaty (see the Opinion of AG Stix-Hackl in *Omega*, pars 87–89). Even following the Treaty of Lisbon the Court does not show that it is prepared to rely upon the Charter to develop a case law which draws directly upon the concept of dignity (de Búrca 2013).

In *M'Bodj v. Belgium* (Case C-542/13, decided 18/12/2014), the Court examined the case of a Mauritanian national who was granted a residence permit in Belgium for medical reasons (a major eye disability), on the basis that his removal to Mauritania would subject him to a real risk of inhuman or degrading treatment due to the lack of adequate medical treatment. The Belgian authorities had not granted Mr M'Bodj either refugee status or subsidiary protection, and subsequently denied him income allowance and income support. The question for the Court was whether this refusal breached Directive 2004/83 *on minimum standards for the qualification and status of third country nationals or stateless persons as refugees* ('the Qualification Directive'), which expressly states that it 'respects the fundamental rights and observes the principles recognised in particular by the Charter of Fundamental Rights of the European Union . . . and seeks to ensure full respect for human dignity' (Preamble, 10th recital). The Court ruled that the Qualification Directive does not require Member States to grant social welfare and health care benefits to an applicant who suffers from a serious illness, and who has been granted leave to reside in that State, and where the national's country of origin cannot provide appropriate treatment, provided that the national has not been *intentionally* deprived of health care in that country (see further Da Lomba 2014).

In *Dano v. Jobcenter Leipzig* (Case C-333/13), also decided in 2014, the Court held that economically inactive EU citizens who go to another Member State solely in order to obtain social assistance may be excluded from certain social benefits. The ruling made headlines for restricting so-called 'benefits tourism'. What went mostly unreported was the last part of the ruling which dealt with a plea in respect of Article 1 of the Charter of Fundamental Rights of the EU. What is interesting about that part of the ruling is the very restrictive view taken by the Court on the application of the Charter. The Court was at pains to emphasise the limitations to the application of the Charter under Article 51, as well as the restricted scope of the preliminary ruling procedure under Article 267 TEFU (pars 86–88). It then held that when Member States lay down the conditions for the grant of special non-contributory cash benefits, as defined in Article 70 of Regulation 883/2004, and the extent of such benefits, they are *not* implementing EU law, because these conditions result neither from Regulation 883/2004 nor from Directive 2004/83 or other secondary EU legislation (par. 90). In a similar vein Member States were free to determine the extent of the social cover provided by such benefits. As a consequence the Court decided that it did not have jurisdiction to answer the question on the application of the Charter.

The ease with which the Court arrived at the conclusion that the Charter was not applicable is quite remarkable. Of course, from a political point of view, it would have been very dangerous for the Court to hold otherwise. Indeed the possibility cannot be excluded that if considerations of dignity came into the picture, the Court would have ruled in favour of Ms Dano. This self-imposed limitation signals strongly that the Court is very careful not to extend the scope of the Charter in politically sensitive areas. In light of this, arguably, an elaboration of the concept of dignity along the lines proposed by the Advocate General in *Omega*, that is, by 'codification and application of individual concrete guarantees of fundamental rights' offers better prospects from the point of view of justiciability and adequacy of standards. A number of current developments at the international and supranational levels show some tentative trends towards this direction though, as we shall see, the picture is not uniform across the board.

Developments at the United Nations

A first development which should be highlighted concerns attempts at the UN level to develop a legal instrument specific to older persons. Initiatives in the area of older persons at the UN level continue along a long trajectory of cautious steps, beginning with the 1982 International Plan of Action on Ageing. This was the first major international instrument on ageing and was endorsed by the General Assembly following the World Assembly on Ageing that was held in Vienna the same year. Almost a decade later, in 1991, the United Nations adopted a set of Principles for Older Persons (Resolution 46/91). Eighteen principles tackle five rubrics: independence, participation, care, self-fulfilment and dignity. 'Dignity' appears both as a separate rubric which includes two principles,[2] and in the context of 'care', where the relevant principle states that 'older persons should be able to enjoy human rights and fundamental freedoms when residing in any shelter, care or treatment facility, including full respect for their dignity, beliefs, needs and privacy and for the right to make decisions about their care and the quality of their lives'.[3]

It took another decade until the issue was taken up again at the United Nations. In 2002 the Second World Assembly on Ageing, held in Madrid, updated the International Action Plan. The revised Plan states that 'effective care for older persons needs to integrate physical, mental, social, spiritual and environmental factors' (par. 70). It sets as objectives, *inter alia*, the improvement of 'the coordination of primary health care, long-term care and social services and other community services', the inclusion of 'older persons in the planning, implementation

---

2 Principle 17: 'Older persons should be able to live in dignity and security and be free of exploitation and physical or mental abuse'. Principle 18: 'Older persons should be treated fairly regardless of age, gender, racial or ethnic background, disability or other status, and be valued independently of their economic contribution'.

3 Principle 14. See also principle 11: 'older persons should have access to health care to help them to maintain or regain the optimum level of physical, mental and emotional well-being and to prevent or delay the onset of illness'.

and evaluation of social and health care and rehabilitation programmes', and the 'integration of 'the needs and perceptions of older persons in the shaping of health policy' (pars 76–77).

The recognition of the need for an international level protective instrument particularly drafted for older people from a foundation of human rights garnered academic commentary (Doron and Apter 2010). Another ten years later, in 2012, the Social, Humanitarian and Cultural Committee of the General Assembly of the United Nations adopted Resolution 67/139, titled 'Towards a comprehensive and integral international legal instrument to promote and protect the rights and dignity of older persons' (A/RES/67/139). The Resolution was sponsored by El Salvador and was supported by 53 states. Another 102 states abstained, including all the Member States of the European Union, Israel, Australia, China and Japan. Three states voted against the Resolution: the United States, Canada and Somalia. The Preamble to the Resolution remarks that, while there are numerous implicit obligations *vis-à-vis* older persons in many human rights treaties, explicit references to age in core international human rights treaties are scarce, and that no such instrument exists at the international level. In light of this, the Resolution mandated the Open-ended Working Group on Ageing to:

> present to the General Assembly, at the earliest possible date, a proposal containing, inter alia, the main elements that should be included in an international legal instrument to promote and protect the rights and dignity of older persons, which are not currently addressed sufficiently by existing mechanisms and therefore require further international protection.

In August 2014 the Working Group on Ageing adopted its Fifth Working Session Report where the launch of work on two parallel tracks is announced: first, on deepening the level of protection of the human rights of older persons within the current framework; and, second, work on the elements of a new international instrument (UN General Assembly 2014). It is difficult not to feel frustrated by the slow pace towards an international instrument on older persons. Demographic transformation is continuing at an accelerating pace and whilst even a quarter of a century ago this was mainly the concern of developed countries, today half of the world's older population lives in the Asia-Pacific region. The most rapid increase in older persons is currently happening in developing countries. By 2050 the region of Asia-Pacific is expected to triple its older population. Worldwide, by the same year, more than 20 percent of the global population will be over 60 years of age (see UN ESCAP 2012). Yet, as long and arduous the process is, it must also be welcomed for it offers a unique prospect for the adoption of legally justiciable standards that tackle specifically older persons.

Developments in the Council of Europe

A second important development in the field of rights for older persons is the adoption in February 2014 by the Committee of Ministers of the Council of

Europe of a Recommendation on the promotion of human rights of older persons (CM/Rec(2014)2). The Recommendation is addressed to the Member States, which are invited to ensure compliance with its principles in national legislation and practice relating to older persons. The Recommendation emphasises that older persons must be ensured respect of their inherent human dignity and acknowledges the need for specific protection of older people due to their vulnerability and gaps in existing legal instruments. The central message of the Recommendation is that older persons 'should be able to fully and effectively participate and be included in society and that all older persons should be able to live their lives in dignity and security, free from discrimination, isolation, violence, neglect and abuse, and as autonomously as possible' (Preamble, 14th recital).

The Recommendation includes titles on non-discrimination, autonomy and participation, protection from violence and abuse, social protection and employment, care and administration of justice. For each title the document lays out a number of best practices with the express intention to disseminate these across Member States and relevant stakeholders. Annex 1, at the end of the chapter, synopsises the 54 specific recommendations ('OP' refers to 'older persons'). With particular respect to residential care for older people the Recommendation emphasises the following points:

- Member States should provide for sufficient and adequate residential services for those older persons who are no longer able or do not wish to reside in their own homes (rec. 40);
- older persons who are placed in institutional care have the right to freedom of movement. Any restrictions must be lawful, necessary and proportionate and in accordance with international law (rec. 41);
- Member States should ensure that there is a competent and independent authority or body responsible for the inspection of both public and private residential institutions (rec. 42);
- Member States should provide for easily accessible and effective complaint mechanisms and redress for any deficiencies in the quality of care (rec. 42);
- older persons in principle should only be placed in residential, institutional or psychiatric care with their free and informed consent. Any exception to this principle must fulfil the requirements of the European Convention on Human Rights, in particular the right to liberty and security as guaranteed in Article 5 (rec. 43).

The Recommendation is not legally binding. However, as Andorno remarks, 'soft law is law, not just ethical statements'. As such, it may herald a process towards 'harder' legal instruments, such as treaties, or lead to the creation of customary law (Andorno 2009, pp. 225–226). The immediate significance of this Recommendation lies in the wide-encompassing elaboration of several factors which ultimately affect the dignity of older people and of a number of best practices across Member States which should be included in a shared information system accessible to the public. Five years following its adoption (i.e. in 2019), the Committee of Ministers is meant to assess its implementation (see Council of Europe 2014b, II par. 6). The explicit recognition in the Explanatory Memorandum to the Recommendation of the inadequacy of existing instruments offers a prospect of an eventual adoption of standards which are able to 'eliminate barriers preventing older persons from fully enjoying their human rights and to respect their autonomy and legal capacity' (*ibid.*, I, par. 2). Having said that, the lukewarm approach taken by the very Member States that belong to the Council of Europe to the adoption of a legally binding instrument at the UN level, by definition limits the expectations for substantive action in this area.

Developments in the European Union

At the European Union level the institutional approach to older persons is limited by the fact that, within the area of health, the Union has only a coordinating competence. What is more, older persons are not included in the any of the main titles of the Treaty. The *2010–2020 European Innovation Partnership on Active and Healthy Ageing*, one of the flagship initiatives of the Union on ageing, concentrates merely on (a) supporting the aims of healthier, more active and independent EU citizens until old age, and (b) creating more sustainable and efficient social and health care systems, through the collaboration of public and private stakeholders (European Commission 2013).

While initiatives bringing together a range of stakeholders are welcome, the character of this initiative shows the same predilection for market-driven measures that is observed more widely in regard to the policies of the Union. Efficiency and sustainability are not bad objectives, but they become so if they become the sole or dominant objectives. As the European Parliament's resolution on the relevant initiative emphasises, 'restrictions and limitations in regard to healthcare, care services, social protection and social security adopted and implemented by the Commission and/or the Member States in an effort to make financial and budgetary savings and cuts in public (health and social) expenditure in the wake of the current economic and financial crisis should in no way interfere with, or negatively affect, basic human needs and dignity' (A7–0029/2013, point 25).

A more encouraging picture emerges through the actions taken by social partners with the support of the Union. In 2010 a consortium of 11 partners from nine countries, under the coordination of AGE Platform Europe, adopted a *European Charter of rights and responsibilities of older people in need of long-term care and assistance* (June 2010; hereinafter LTCC to avoid confusion with the EU Charter). The LTCC explicitly seeks to provide a springboard for action in the field, which includes fostering best practices in Member States and raising awareness amongst the wider public. The LTCC is particularly important because it is the result of social dialogue between older persons, their families, caregivers associations and other relevant stakeholders in the field.

The LTCC is addressed directly to older people. Article 1 states that 'You have the right to respect for your human dignity and welfare, regardless of your age, race, colour, national or social origin, financial means, beliefs, sex, sexual orientation or identity and the degree of care and assistance you require'. Further provisions in Article 1 deal specifically with the physical, psychological and emotional well-being of older persons, protection against medical and pharmaceutical abuse and neglect. In addition, the LTCC includes the right to self-determination, which concerns, *inter alia*, the right to participate at decisions affecting older people (Article 2), the right to privacy (Article 3), the right to high quality and tailored care (Article 4) and the right to personalised information, advice and informed consent (Article 5). The LTCC also includes the right to continued communication, participation in society and cultural activity (Article 6), the right to freedom of expression and thought/conscience (Article 7), the right to palliative care and support, and respect and dignity in dying and in death (Article 8), and the right to redress (Article 9). Finally, the LTCC lays down a number of responsibilities, including respecting the rights of carers and staff to be treated with civility and work in an environment free from harassment and abuse (Article 10).

As noted above, the LTCC is the result of a project involving several actors across different Member States. It enjoys the advantage of being well informed by research in the area and of being a collectively agreed instrument – including, significantly, care providers' associations. The provisions of the LTCC also formed a basis for reflection during the process of adoption of the Council of Europe Recommendation, while the Explanatory Memorandum to that Recommendation makes explicit references to the LTCC, indicating a process of cross-fertilisation of standards. In the aftermath of the adoption of the LTCC, the consortium of the original 11 partners was enlarged to 18, within the framework of a new project also financed by the EU (see WeDo 2013).

The new project sought to 'set up a lasting and open European, national and regional/local stakeholders committed to improving the quality of services for older people in care and assistance and to fight elder abuse' (*ibid.*, p. 3). The project ended in December 2012 with the launch of a European Quality Framework on long-term care services. This targets all stakeholders in the area and aims to move further the effort for improvements in the area of care with elaborated quality tools, methodologies and further dissemination of best practices. Following the end of the formal project, the partnership has now been opened to all interested parties from all EU Member States.

Conclusion

This chapter examined the concept of dignity as a theoretical and legal construct in the context of care for older persons, within a wider framework of emerging trends which seek to develop a human rights approach specifically geared towards older persons. A number of issues may be highlighted by way of conclusion. First of all, we see that dignity does not have a single meaning, but is rather a concept whose meaning is contextually variable. As McCrudden rightly notes, everyone may agree on a common basic core understanding on dignity, but beyond that the concept does not provide a universal basis for judicial adjudication (McCrudden 2008, p. 655). This fact has obvious implications on what we can expect from dignity in the context of residential care, but at the same time it is perhaps possible to develop an appropriate jurisprudence which is context-specific. In other words, it may be the case that dignity is best functionalised if understood within the specific context in which it operates.

Within the context of older persons, the examination of the theoretical literature on the issue shows dignity to be an explicitly multidimensional concept, pertaining to the physical, mental and emotional state of older persons. As such, it is affected by a wide range of factors which, in turn, are the subject of a growing body of research – often multidisciplinary and conducted across several countries. Theoretical and/or ethical discourse and empirical research increasingly evolve within a synergistic framework, seeking to inform policy and law in the area (see Tadd *et al.* 2010, p. 279). At the same time, it remains the case that, within the legal context, dignity remains an elusive concept. The legal understanding of dignity is neither as sophisticated, nor as wide encompassing as the theoretical discourse shows it to be.

Within judicial adjudication dignity remains tied to a rather small number of specific rights enshrined in constitutional or human rights instruments, like the ECHR. As such it is contingent upon successfully establishing a violation of a human right protected under the Convention (or other instruments). As a consequence, successful claims are rare and are typically limited to the most serious cases of abuse, neglect, inhumane or humiliating treatment, or discrimination. The overwhelming majority of everyday violations to the dignity of older persons goes either unreported or fails in court. We agree with the opinion of Advocate General Stix-Hackl in *Omega* about the value of 'codification and application of individual concrete guarantees of fundamental rights' as an appropriate method of ensuring justiciability for the concept of dignity.

Beyond all the rhetoric on dignity, it is still the case that all too often basic standards of care for older persons remain desperately inadequate. This is exacerbated by the fragmented nature of policies on long-term care protection at national level (AGE Europe 2014, p. 2). In a similar vein, existing terminologies are not suitable to the field of older persons. For instance, it is wrong to group together disabled persons with older persons, since old age is not the same as disability. The elaboration of appropriate terms is necessary, like 'frailty', which describes the need for care and support while advancing in age (AGE Europe 2014, p. 7). In short, existing structures – be they physical, legal or social – are not sufficiently geared towards the needs of older persons. Against this background, dignity is ultimately a metaphor for standards and structures which can properly address these needs.

Moreover, the continuing economic crisis, which has been accompanied by a wave of public expenditure and job cuts across the board, has had a disproportional effect on older persons. *McDonald* illustrates the impact of job cuts on the provision of decent care. As the Dutch report on the ten-year review of the implementation of the Madrid International Plan of Action remarks, 'even the most obvious individual rights, such as the right to a daily shower and to spend some time each day in the open air sometimes are no longer respected in the context of elder care' (AGE Platform Europe 2014, p. 3). What is more, in far too many cases, training of carers remains utterly insufficient.

In light of this, the adoption of legally binding standards which specifically deal with older persons emerges as an urgent need. It is not simply a matter of providing greater legal clarity in the area. It is also a matter of ring-fencing existing rights and preventing further deterioration of conditions in care and more widely in the area. What is more, in these times of record unemployment the creation of specific standards in the relevant field could provide an impetus to job creation, greater investment in research and development, and improvements in infrastructure. Standards should be precise, set high and be forward looking. The prospect of a UN Treaty on older persons is particularly important, though – as we have seen – most developed countries have not so far given the project the support it deserves. It is also significant that within the – non-legally binding – instruments that have been developed by both the Council of Europe and the partnership of stakeholders under the aegis of AGE Europe at the EU level, the rights which are set out are not compromised by references to economic considerations. Nor should they be. Dignity in care cannot be compromised by cost considerations. To be sure, the language in these instruments could be made more precise. Yet, even with the existing wording, progress should be possible. For example, a term found on several occasions in the Council of Europe Recommendation is 'appropriate'. While this term may be difficult to define precisely, functionally, it may be understood as 'fit for purpose'. Obviously, when structures or adopted measures do not adequately meet their objectives they cannot be judged as 'appropriate'.

A final caveat is needed. It is clear that within the human rights approach on older persons the notion of 'autonomy' holds a prominent position. The term, as we have seen, is intimately related to dignity. As such it complements dignity and signals an approach which seeks to expand the capabilities of older persons. But we should be cautious of autonomy being used as a byword for the transfer of responsibilities from the State and related public authorities to individual older persons. Autonomy cannot justify the absence of State involvement from the field of elderly care, closures of care homes, or cuts in the provision of support for older persons in care and more broadly. With this in mind, the overall conclusion is that dignity has an important role to play in the field of care for older persons, particularly as a contextualised concept which is best functionalised through the elaboration of specific rights and obligations in the area. In this respect dignity can form a point of consensus amongst those agreeing to relevant instruments, as well as lend moral credibility to the instruments and provide the *telos* of the rights enumerated therein.

I Scope and general principles

1 Purpose of the Recommendation to promote, protect and ensure the full and equal enjoyment of all human rights and fundamental freedoms of OP and to promote respect for their inherent dignity

2 Recommendation applies to persons whose older age constitutes, alone or in interaction with other factors, including perceptions and attitudes, a barrier to the full enjoyment of their human rights, and their full participation in society on an equal basis

3 OP shall fully enjoy rights under the ECHR and ESC (to the extent that Member States are bound by them)

4 OP should have access to sufficient information about their rights

5 OP should be appropriately consulted, through representative organisations, prior to adoption of measures which impact upon their human rights

II Non-discrimination

6 OP shall enjoy their rights and freedoms without discrimination on any grounds including age

7 Member States should consider referring to 'age' in anti-discrimination legislation

8 Member States should take effective measures to prevent multiple discrimination

III Autonomy and participation

9 OP have the right to respect for their inherent dignity. They are entitled to lead their lives independently, in a self-determined and autonomous manner. This includes decisions regarding their property, income, finances, place of residence, health, medical treatment or care, as well as funeral arrangements. Any limitations should be proportionate to the specific situation and provided with appropriate and effective safeguards to prevent abuse and discrimination

10 OP should have the possibility to interact with others and participate in social and public life

11 OP have the right to dignity and respect for their private and family life

12 OP enjoy legal capacity on an equal basis with others

13 OP have the right to third party support for exercising their legal decisions

14 Member States should provide legislation allowing OP to regulate their affairs in the event that they are unable to express their instructions at a later stage

15 Member States should ensure all relevant measure provide appropriate safeguards to prevent abuse

IV Protection from violence and abuse

16 Member States should protect OP from violence, abuse and neglect

17 Member States should provide for awareness-raising to protect OP from financial abuse

18 Member States should raise awareness among medical staff, care workers and other persons providing services to OP to detect violence or abuse in all settings

19 Member States shall carry out effective investigation into claims of violence or abuse

20 OP who have suffered abuse should receive appropriate help and support. Where Member States fail to meet their positive obligation to protect them, OP are entitled to an effective remedy and, where appropriate, adequate redress.

(Continued)

V Social protection and employment

21 OP should receive appropriate resources enabling them to have an adequate standard of living and participate in public, economic, social and cultural life

22 Member States should facilitate mobility of OP and proper access to infrastructure

23 Member States should provide measures to enable OP to have housing adapted to their needs

24 Member States should promote sufficient supplementary services, such as nursing care

25 Member States are invited to consider ratifying the Protocol to the ESC providing for a system of collective complaints and to be bound by Article 23 (right to social protection of OP)

26 Member States should ensure that OP do not face discrimination in employment

27 Member States should promote participation of OP in labour markets in employment policies

28 Member States should pay attention to safety and health problems of older workers

VI Care

A *General principles*

29 Member States should take appropriate measures to promote, maintain and improve the health and well-being of OP. They should also ensure that appropriate health care and long-term quality is available and accessible

30 Services should be available in the community to enable OP to stay as long as possible in their own homes

31 Member States should promote a multidimensional approach to health and social care

32 Care providers should treat personal date with confidentiality and respect for privacy

33 Care should be affordable and cost assistance programmes should be in place

34 Care givers should receive sufficient training and support

35 Member States should operate a system of regulation and assessment of care

B *Consent to medical care*

36 OP should receive medical care only upon their free and informed consent

37 Where consent is not possible, the wishes of the OP, should – in accordance with national law – be taken into account

38 Where an OP does not have capacity to consent, any intervention may only be carried out with the authorisation of a representative, an authority or a body provided by law

39 In emergency situations, medical interventions may be carried out immediately for the benefit of the health of the OP concerned

C *Residential and institutional care*

40 Member States should provide for sufficient and adequate residential services

41 OP in institutional care have the right to freedom of movement. Any restrictions must be lawful, necessary and proportionate and in accordance with international law. There should be adequate safeguards for review of such decisions

42 Member States should ensure the existence of a competent and independent authority responsible for the inspection of public and private residential institutions, and of accessible and effective complaint mechanisms and redress for deficiencies

43 OP should only be placed in residential, institutional or psychiatric care with their free and informed consent. Exceptions must be compatible with ECHR, esp. Art 5

(*Continued*)

Annex 1 (Continued)

D **Palliative care**

44   Member States should offer palliative care for OP suffering from life-threatening or life-limiting illness ensuring their well-being and to live and die with dignity

45   OP in need of palliative care should be entitled to access it without undue delay

46   Family members and friends should be encouraged to accompany OP who are terminally ill or dying and should receive professional support

47   Health care providers should fully respect patients' rights and comply with standards

48   Education and research in the field should be led by trained specialists and programmes on palliative care should be incorporated in all health and social-care trainings

49   Member States should ensure availability and accessibility of palliative care medicines

50   Member States should take into account of CoE Recommendation 2003/24 on the organisation of palliative care

VII   Administration of justice

51   OP entitled to fair trial within the meaning of Art. 6 ECHR. Member States should accommodate the needs of OP in the judicial proceedings, including by free legal assistance

52   Competent judicial authorities should pay particular diligence in handling cases in which OP are involved, especially their age and health

53   Member States shall ensure that detention of OP does not amount to inhuman or degrading treatment

54   Member States shall safeguard the well-being and dignity of OP in detention

References

Allison H.E. (2011) *Kant's Groundwork for the Metaphysics of Morals: A Commentary* (Oxford University Press, Oxford).

Anderberg, P., Lepp, M., Berglund, A.L. and Segesten, K. (2007) 'Preserving Dignity in Caring for Older Adults: A Concept Analysis' 59 *Journal of Advanced Nursing* 635.

Andorno, R. (2009) 'Human Dignity and Human Rights as a Common Ground for a Global Bioethics' 34 *Journal of Medicine and Philosophy* 223.

AGE Platform Europe (2014) 'Human Rights of Older Persons in Need of Care', Special Policy Briefing, 25 July 2014, http://www.age-platform.eu/images/FINAL__policy_briefing_human_rights_of_older_persons_in_need_of_care_AGE_Platform_Europe.pdf, accessed 22 December 2014.

Carmi, G.E. (2007) 'Dignity – The Enemy from Within: A Theoretical and Comparative Analysis of Human Dignity as a Free Speech Justification' 9 U Pa J Const L 957.

Carozza, P. (2003) 'My Friend Is a Stranger: The Death Penalty and the Global Ius Commune of Human Rights' 81 *Texas Law Review* 1031.

Christiano, T. (2008) 'Two Conceptions of the Dignity of Persons' 16 *Jahrbuch für Recht und Ethik* 101.

Council of Europe (2014a) Explanatory Memorandum of Recommendation CM/Rec(2014)2 of the Committee of Ministers to Member States on the promotion of rights for older persons (CM(2013)173 final).

Council of Europe (2014b) European Commission and AGE Platform Europe, 'Report on the proceedings of *Human Rights for Older Persons: Who Cares?*', 23 June 2014, http://

www.age-platform.eu/images/FINAL_Report_event_23_June_morning_AGE_CoE_
DGEMPL.pdf, accessed 30 December 2014.

Da Lomba, S. (2014) 'The ECHR, Health Care and Irregular Migrants', in Freeman,
M., Hawkes, S. and Bennett, B. (eds), *Law and Global Health: Current Legal Issues*, Vol. 16,
(Oxford University Press, Oxford) pp. 149–164.

de Búrca, G. (2013) 'After the EU Charter of Fundamental Rights: The Court of Justice
as a Human Rights Adjudicator?' *New York University Public Law and Legal Theory Working
Papers.* Paper 420.

Dillon, R.S. (2011) 'Respect' in *Stanford Encyclopaedia of Philosophy*, http:plato.stanford.edu/
entries/rights, accessed 30 December 2014.

Doron, I. (2013) 'Older Europeans and the ECJ' 42 *Age and Ageing* 604–608.

Doron, I. and Apter, I. (2010) 'The Debate Around the Need for an International Convention on the Rights of Older Persons' 50(5) *The Gerontologist* 586–593.

Ebert, R. and Oduor, R.M.J. (2012) 'The Concept of Human Dignity in German and
Kenyan Constitutional Law' 4 *Thought and Practice: A Journal of the Philosophical Association
of Kenya (PAK)* 43.

Enders, C. (2010) 'The Right to Have Rights: The Concept of Human Dignity in German
Basic Law' *Revista de Estudos Consitucionais, Hermenêutica e Teoria do Direito*, Vol. 2, pp. 1–8.

Epictetus (1998) *Discourses and Selected Writings*, trans. R. Dobbin (Penguin, London).

EU Network of Independent Experts on Fundamental Rights (2006) *Commentary of the Charter of Fundamental Rights of the European Union*, http://ec.europa.eu/justice/fundamental-
rights/files/networkcommentaryfinal_en.pdf, accessed 15 December 2014.

European Charter of the Rights and Responsibilities of Older People In Need of Long-
Term Care and Assistance (June 2010) http://www.age-platform.eu/images/stories/
22204_AGE_charte_europeenne_EN_v4.pdf, accessed 10 December 2014.

European Commission (2013) 'Long-term Care in Ageing Societies – Challenges and Policy Options', SWP(2013) 41 final.

European Parliament (2012), 'Resolution of 6 February 2013 on the European Innovation
Partnership on Active and Healthy Ageing' (2012/2258(INI), A7-0029/2013).

Evans, N. and Kleinig, J. (2013) 'Human Flourishing, Human Dignity and Human Rights'
32 *Law and Philosophy* 539.

Gallagher, A., Li, S., Wainwright, P., Rees Jones, I. and Lee, D. (2008) 'Dignity in the Care of
Older People – A Review of the Theoretical and Empirical Literature' 7 *BMC Nursing* 11.

Glensy, R.D. (2011) 'The Right to Dignity' 43 *Columbian Human Rights Law Review* 65.

Hughes, A. (2014) *Human Dignity and Fundamental Rights in South Africa and Ireland* (Pretoria
University Law Press, Pretoria).

Hyman, D. (2003) 'Does Technology Spell Trouble with a Capital T?: Human Dignity and
Public Policy' 27 *Harvard Journal of Law & Public Policy* 3.

Jones, J. (2004) '"Common Constitutional Traditions": Can the Meaning of Human Dignity under German Law Guide the ECJ?' 1 *Public Law* 167.

Jones, J. (2012) 'Human Dignity in the EU Charter of Fundamental Rights and its Interpretation Before the European Court of Justice' 33 *Liverpool Law Review* 281.

Kant, I. (1996) *Metaphysics of Morals*. transl. M.J. Gregor (Cambridge University Press,
Cambridge) (AK 6) .

Kant I. (2007) *Critique of Pure Reason*, transl. Norman Kemp Smith (2nd edition, Palgrave
Macmillan, 2007) (AK 4).

Korsgaard, C.M. (1996) *Creating the Kingdom of Ends* (Cambridge University Press, Cambridge).

Macklin, R. (2003) 'Dignity is a Useless Concept' *British Medical Journal* 1419.

Mann, J. (1998) 'Dignity and Health: The UDHR's Revolutionary First Article' 3 *Health
and Human Rights* 31.

Mastoraki, A. 'Η Έννοια της Αρετής στον Αριστοτέλη', http://www.pneuma.gr/downloads/areth.doc, accessed 18 December 2014.

McCrudden, C. (2008) 'Human Dignity and Judicial Interpretation of Human Rights' 4 *European Journal of International Law* 655.

Megret, F. (2011) 'The Human Rights of Older Persons: A Growing Challenge' 11(1) *Human Rights Law Review* 37.

Nordenfelt, L. (2003) 'Dignity and the Care of the Elderly' 6 *Medicine, Health Care and Philosophy* 103.

Nussbaum, M. (2008) 'Human Dignity and Political Entitlements', in The President's Council for Bioethics: *Human Dignity and Bioethics: Essays Commissioned by the President's Council on Bioethics*, https://bioethicsarchive.georgetown.edu/pcbe/reports/human_dignity/chapter14.html, accessed 20 December 2014.

Rosen, M. (2012) *Dignity. Its History and Meaning* (Harvard University Press, Cambridge, Massachusetts).

Russell, B. (2004) *History of Western Philosophy* (Routledge Classics, London).

Schroeder, D. (2010) 'Dignity: One, Two, Three, Four, Five, Still Counting' 19 *Cambridge Quarterly of Healthcare Ethics* 1.

Schultziner, D. and Rabinovici, I. (2011) 'Human Dignity, Self- Worth and Humiliation: A Comparative Legal-Psychological Approach', http://ssrn.com/abstract=1964371, accessed 20 December 2014.

Shell, S.M. (2008) 'Kant's Concept of Human Dignity as a Resource for Bioethics', in The President's Council for Bioethics: *Human Dignity and Bioethics: Essays Commissioned by the President's Council on Bioethics*, https://bioethicsarchive.georgetown.edu/pcbe/reports/human_dignity/chapter13.html, accessed 20 December 2014.

Shotton, L. and Seedhouse, D. (1998) 'Practical Dignity in Caring' 5 *Nursing Ethics* 246.

Spanier, B., and Doron, I. and Millman-Sivan, F. (2013) 'Older Persons use of the ECoHR' 28 *Journal of Cross Cultural Gerontology* 407–420.

Tadd, W., Vanlaere, L. and Gastmans, C. (2010) 'Clarifying the Concept of Human Dignity in the Care of the Elderly: A Dialogue between Empirical and Philosophical Approaches' *Ethical Perspectives* 253.

Tang, K.L. and Lee, J.J. (2006) 'Global Social Justice for Older People: The Case for an International Convention on the Rights of Older People' 36(7) *British Journal of Social Work* 1135.

UN ESCAP (2012) Report of the Asia-Pacific Intergovernmental Meeting on the Second Review and Appraisal of the Madrid International Plan of Action on Ageing, 10–12 September 2012, Bangkok.

UN General Assembly (2014) Report of the Open-ended Working Group on Ageing, 15 August 2014 (A/AC.278/2014/2).

Waldron, J. (2009) 'Dignity, Rank, and Rights' *The Tanner Lectures on Human Values*, http://tannerlectures.utah.edu/_documents/a-to-z/w/Waldron_09.pdf, accessed 10 December 2014.

WeDo (2013), *European Quality Framework for Long-Term Care Services. Principles and Guidelines for the Wellbeing and Dignity of Older People in Need of Care and Assistance*, http://wedo.tttp.eu/system/files/24171_WeDo_brochure_A4_48p_EN_WEB.pdf, accessed 10 December 2014.

Wood, A.W. (2008) *Kantian Ethics* (Cambridge University Press, Cambridge).

van Aggelen, J. (2000) 'The Preamble to the United Nations Declaration of Human Rights' 28 *Denver Journal of International Law and Policy* 129.

Conclusion: from 'residential care' to 'ageing with dignity'

Israel Doron, Nicola Rees, Helen Meenan

More than half a century has passed since Goffman's depiction of nursing homes and homes for the aged in dark colours of total institutions (Goffman, 1961). Not only has the number of older persons living in residential care increased dramatically (as a result of the ageing of the world population), but the landscape of residential care for an older population has changed significantly. As has been described in the different chapters of this book, in many countries around the world new models of residential care settings have been established, new ideologies regarding the means and ways of care have been presented, and new legal frameworks to regulate and supervise these care facilities have been enacted.

However, what has been undoubtedly demonstrated by this book is that the world is still struggling to resolve the need for more and better care for older people within residential care settings. In an ageing world, current thinking, planning and resources are scaling up from previous estimates but within this framework for tackling the issue, the people at the centre of it find themselves without voice or choice, echoing the shadows of the total institutions. Phrases are used which give hope of a subjective-centred approach – human rights, dignity and autonomy, among others, but as the chapters here evidence, worldwide there is little evidence to support the theory in practice. Older people are not a commodity to be priced up per unit, given care that costs a minimum price to ensure profit, nor should they be silent players in their own lives. Older people should have a status that ensures they are seen to possess and are given a dignified position in the society of which they are part.

A diverse world of regulatory frameworks: different histories and different legal stories

The first – and not surprising – theme that can be extracted from the different chapters of this book, is that every country has its own history and legal 'story' regarding its regulation of residential long-term care of older persons. The book discusses regulation of the care home sector as it is relevant to each contributor. This shows some distinct differences between the different countries with regard to the regulatory framework of residential care of older persons.

The merits of the English system are a long-standing system of regulation, a supervisory body, the CQC, which now has a separate head of social care to oversee the latest more rigorous inspection system, the incorporation of experts by experience in the inspections, publication of inspection results and many NGOs and campaigning organisations to provide information and guidance to the public on, for example, how to choose a care home. We also have a vigilant media which has given this subject a platform.

The drawbacks of the English system as discussed by Helen Meenan in this volume are that the system remains risk-based. There are financial benefits for the state in concentrating resources where they are needed most but this has failed to detect some of the worst care homes with shocking and inhumane treatment of older people. She suggests that each new home have a 'new home' inspection in the first six months of opening. This should not be resource intensive as only a certain number of new homes open each year. . She also highlights the apparent tenderness with which home owners and managers are treated and would like to see a proper test of their knowledge of the applicable law and regulations before they can be registered. It is imperative that they are aware of their duties to their residents *before* they are registered. It is clear that there is still not much of a deterrent effect for the minority of disengaged or disinterested owners and managers and the minority of care workers. Meenan would also like to see a nationally accredited qualification for this sector. England is too large a country with too many variations in service throughout a national standard for training would be beneficial in helping to even out these bumps.

Dignity has become a pervasive concept in the English regulatory 'spirit' and the CQC has adopted the principle of promoting equality and diversity and human rights. It asserts that it has developed a human rights approach to regulation and that this approach is embedded in its new inspections. Apart from applying the FREDA principles and rights of staff to its five key questions in inspections, it also aims to encourage improvement of service providers. England has uniquely highlighted the divide between public and private care home residents and the continuing inability of private residents to invoke human rights and human rights remedies even in a shared care home. However, we also see a realisation in England that human rights can be used to tremendous persuasive effect for the cause of those older people to whom they apply. England appears to be much further along in certain key bodies embedding a human rights approach in what they do, for example the CQC and in NGOs exploring human rights as a persuasive tool. Where human rights are missing it is as a core and compulsory element of any training curricula and in the adoption of a voluntary human rights approach by residential care homes.

In Kenya, we have seen that there is a basic principle that care homes are to be rejected and, instead, there should be investment and legislation designed to help families care for their older people at their homes as would be the Kenyan tradition. In the 2014 National Policy on Older Persons and Ageing, however, there is the proposal that care homes for those 'neglected, homeless and/or with special needs' should be provided by the state. The same basic principle applies in Egypt and the wider Arab world where it is the cultural and spiritual norm for families to care for their older people within the family home but again, there is a growing demand for residential care homes and therefore a specific regulatory structure to govern them.

Australia has a strong regulatory framework which includes the 'National Ageing and Aged Care Strategy for People from Culturally and Linguistically Diverse (CALD) Backgrounds'. This accounts for a very recognisable and defined Aboriginal population but such 'selective diversity' would not work for more integrated nations. This explains the differences with other common law tradition countries where separate groups are not singled out for specific protections.

Japan's regulatory structure could be more robust. The authors state that there is little sanction for failing to adhere to regulatory requirements and the regulations are themselves very 'young' and presumably therefore, still to be thoroughly tested. What does stand out about adherence and enforceability in Japan is that residential care homes are enclosed communities, not open to those in the 'outside' community which helps to explain the emphasis on legislation that offers protection against abuse for the older people who live in them. Despite the recent provision of an ombudsman system for complaints about residential care, few cases are taken and even fewer are followed up. Without an open and transparent system of regulation, Japan may legislate to avoid harm to their older people, but the legislation will be a toothless tiger.

The People's Republic of China has been undergoing a rapid economic and cultural transformation in respect of its population. Older people are being left behind in the rural parts of China when their families move to the growing cities and urban areas. As a culture that would have expected that care for older people was carried out by family, this has led to a fast developing regulatory structure for the care of older people, which does not have human rights at its foundations, but rather builds on the existing health and social care systems. The sheer scale of the issue in China is daunting. The authors state that there will be a requirement for 6,000,000 old-age care workers in the country by 2020. Regulating such a massive sector will be challenging but ensuring compliance with those regulations will be a bigger challenge. The law as it stands is drafted broadly with detail being added at a local level thereby leading to uncertainty in the system. Enforcement for care homes that are found to have breached a regulation is the instruction to rectify the situation although there is the possibility of withdrawal of the licence for the home.

In the United States of America (US) there is a strong regulatory structure that helps to represent the industry's voice, but there is little such regulatory support for residents especially around advocacy and complaints (examples such as the National Consumer Voice for Quality Long Term Care and Coalition for Quality Care). In fact, the authors state 'that there are no consumer-based resources to help them individually or to counter the industry's significant influence systemically' in most states. There is the Long Term Care Ombudsman Program (LTCOP), but this is regulated at a local level and monitoring and the capacity to offer help are therefore irregular. While there is some movement towards placing people in the least restrictive setting (as shown in *Olmstead*) in the US there is a long history of institutionalisation of older people, a more 'out of sight, out of mind' culture that will be severely tested as the ageing population spill out of the hospitals and require care in their homes.

In Israel, the initial regulatory framework was created from the health and social care sector (as in China) where residential care homes were smaller than seen in many other western societies (England and US as examples). There is now a new act, the Assisted Living Act 2012 which provides a more robust structure for assisted living facilities (a development in the provision of care for older persons) and where residents have more of a voice, however, as noted by the author, regulation in Israel is paternalistic in nature, leading to assumption that the older person cannot regulate their own affairs and needs protection provided by professionals. In essence, the regulations treat the older person as a child. This leads to the conclusion that human rights are not the basis for regulation in this sector, rather like the Japanese system.

Common themes, common stories: dynamic times of change

While each and every country described in this book has experienced a unique history and social development of its regulatory framework of residential long-term care for older persons, some common themes emerge from all these different histories. We will hereby describe these key similarities and common themes.

Demographic changes in residential care: ageing, diversity and complexity

All countries in this book experience the phenomenon of the ageing of their societies. While these ageing processes occur at a different pace and with different characteristics, nevertheless, their outcome is similar: a significant growth both in the numbers of older persons (especially, in the 'older old'), and the percentage rate that they represent within the general population. This 'ageing transition' creates a common policy challenge to re-design the long-term care services for this ageing and growing older population, both in the community and in residential and institutional settings. For example, in Kenya, the number of people aged 60 years and above is projected to rise sharply from 2.1 million today to 9.2 million by 2050. More specifically, in the realm of residential care, in Australia, statistical data reveals that the number of persons residing in aged care facilities was only 132,420 in 1999, increasing to 165,032 in 2011, while most recent figures indicate that in the 2012–2013 period, 226,042 persons received permanent care in RACFs.

The common outcome of these demographic changes is a reality of change and instability in the existence and character of residential care. In some countries (e.g. Kenya or Egypt) or in some segments of the societies within them (e.g. the Arab minority in Israel), where historically and traditionally, no residential care facilities existed, suddenly new settings have been established, and new populations have started to use them. In other countries (e.g. China), where institutional care was previously associated with negative social stigma, new trends have 'normalised' such care and made it more socially acceptable.

Finally, in countries where residential care facilities and institutional care for older persons have been around for more than a century (e.g. the UK or USA), these settings are experiencing significant changes. These changes can be in the characteristics of their residents (older, more dependent, with more complex health needs, with more cognitive impairments, and more diverse in their ethnic, cultural, religious, and sexual orientations). These changes can be in the organisational characteristics of the facilities (more for-profit and privately owned). And finally, these changes can be in the more modern and novel care settings (not 'institutions' or 'care' but 'assisted living', retirement villages, or continuing care settings).

It is clear then, that all over the world, residential care for older persons is characterised by movement and change: in countries where no tradition or history of residential care settings have existed in the past, a new trend of the development of a whole new world is being experienced. And in countries with a long history of residential care for older persons, the care setting experience is a whole new world of change in both their populations and their characteristics. It clear then that law and regulation cannot ignore these changes and must adapt themselves in order to be relevant and effective.

The changing landscape of residential care: individualisation, privatisation and globalisation

As described above, all countries share stories of change in the 'demographics' of residential care settings for older persons. But it is not only the changes in the mere existence of such services, or the nature of the characteristics of the populations that resides in these facilities. There are some key similarities in broad-general trends that cross countries, in the field of residential care for older persons:

Individualisation and the decline in informal care solutions for the long-term care of older persons: in almost all countries described in this book, the mix between family care and residential care is in constant change. In most countries, especially the more developing countries, one can witness the reduction in the ability of the state to rely on traditional filial responsibility care, and the increase in need for formal community-based or residential care to supplement and sometimes even replace informal family care or non-existent informal community based long-term care.

These developments were seen in the experience of Japan, China or Egypt, where historically, older persons were provided care within the community by their family members. This was done as part of the tradition, culture and religion. Yet, modernisation, urbanisation and changing landscapes of families (e.g. decline in fertility rates and shrinkage of family size) and traditions, have all contributed to a decline of the existence of informal social networks that can provide the necessary community-based, long-term care for their ageing societies. While this does not necessarily lead to an increase of residential care solutions, it does give rise – in the absence of community-based alternatives – to a growing pressure for residential care solutions and for legal regulation.

Japan is a good example of such developments. Traditionally, Japan was regarded as an elder-friendly society because of its Confucian tradition. There is a national holiday called the 'Respect for the aged day *(keirō no hi)*' which celebrates and honours older people. Traditionally, Japanese households were composed of three generations: parents, the eldest son and his wife, and their children. In these households, it was the responsibility of the daughter-in-law to take care of the parents. However, as described in the chapter on Japan, in reality, socio-demographic changes have reduced the percentage of older persons receiving care in a 'three generation households' from 32.5% in 2001 to only 18.4% in 2013.

Egypt provides another unique and interesting perspective: despite a strong Islamic tradition and culture of filial responsibility for older family members, recent trends of ageing and deteriorating economic conditions (especially after the Arab Spring uprising) have increased the phenomenon of homelessness, mainly among older persons. This new social phenomenon was addressed in part less by the government but more by Islamic charity organisations or other private NGOs.

This kind of development has direct implications regarding the regulation of residential care and understanding of the future challenges. The potential outcome of the moral commitment of the social ability of family members or religious institutions to provide long-term care in the community, and the rising significance of residential long-term care, means that the role of the legal regulation becomes more important to preserve the human rights of the older residents. These residents are not only older and more disabled, but they also lack close family/cultural support or care to supervise or protect their rights.

Privatisation and globalisation: another common theme that is found in most of the countries described in this book is that of privatisation. In times of financial constraints and erosion of many welfare states on the one hand, and the realisation that there is a 'market' for residential care solutions for middle and upper classes on the other hand, it is not surprising to find that in many countries the private sector has started to 'fill in' the demand for new and private residential care solutions for older persons. Privatisation is experienced in many countries as a double-edged sword: while it provides new residential care solutions in the absence of public solutions and it can improve quality of care through competition and choice (as was described by the Israeli experience). On the other hand, privatisation can create new problems of abuse, exploitation and discrimination, which sometimes follow mere greed and search for quick financial profit.

The Israeli experience can serve as a good example for these trends in privatisation. As described in the chapter on Israel, until the early 1980s, the vast majority of residential care settings were operated or owned by the government or by not-for-profit organisations. However, in the last three decades, private for-profit enterprises established many new facilities, taking a large market share by housing the majority of older residents. The privatisation and the market competition that followed has increased not only the choices available for older persons but also the quality and standard of care. However, in recent years, new cases of abuse and exploitation have been exposed, which in part were the outcome of attempts to cut the costs and increase profits.

These privatisation trends are accompanied by globalisation. Within the residential care context, globalisation appears in different ways and forms. One example, as described in some of the countries in this book, concerns foreign/migrant workers, who are called from distant lands to supply the shortage in the much needed work force for residential (and community) care for older persons. This is more explicit in more developed countries (e.g. US, England or Israel), where the shortage in working hands in residential care settings is being solved by legal and non-legal migrant workers, who are usually low-paid and non-professional. It is also evident that even Japan, with its higher value and training of the work force, need to recruit from outside their borders. The other, which is still in its 'starting' point, can be seen in some advertisements, where residential settings in countries like Turkey or India offer low-cost solutions for older persons from developed countries.

Overall then, it seems that the landscape of residential care all over the globe is becoming much more complex in its reality. Older residents themselves are much more diverse in their characteristics and are much more heterogeneous in their medical needs. In addition, the financial context is more challenging with public financial constraints and private interests for profits. Finally, a globalised world with low-paid non-professional work force crossing continents, alongside new and novel international care industries that can 'ship' older persons across borders, have caused residential care to become 'international' and not only local or national.

An age of policy and law reform

Another important common theme that was clearly seen in all countries covered in this book is the fact that all were involved or are being involved in the process of policy and legal reform in the field of ageing in general and in the field of the regulation of residential long-term care for older persons specifically. Some countries started these legal reforms three or four decades ago as part of the human rights and de-institutionalization movements; some have started it only in recent years as part of new demographic trends of ageing and changes in family traditions; and finally, some are in the midst of ongoing regulatory reforms as this book is being written and being published. Yet, all countries described in this book are currently involved or very recently have made significant new legal reform in the field.

When discussing the rights of older persons in general, these new policy and legal reforms have been shaped in many different ways. For example, in Kenya, in 2009 a new National Policy on Older Persons and Ageing was presented in line with broad parameters set by UN Madrid International Plan of Action on Ageing and the African Union Framework and Plan of Action on Ageing. This was further developed in 2013, when Kenya established for the first time a new and specific Division on Older Persons and Social Welfare within the Department of Social Development in the Ministry of Labour, Social Security and Services. This department has started to address questions of long-term care, as well as residential care for older persons.

Australia can also serve as an excellent example for these times of reform. In April 2012 the Commonwealth Government introduced a number of reform packages to aged care, marking the start of a ten-year programme aimed 'to create a flexible and seamless system that provides older Australians with more choice, more control and easier access to a full range of services, where they want it and when they need it'. To date the Australian Government has: changed Community Care to Home Care Packages, and provided supplements to both home care and residential care; developed a national website entitled 'My Aged Care'; established a national contact centre; established the Australian Aged Care Quality Agency to oversee the quality of aged care; established the Aged Care Pricing Commission, the role of which is to examine fees associated with extra services, and accommodation fees that are higher than those determined by the Minister. Finally, over the next two years, the Australian Government aims to further increase access and choice for consumers of aged care and establish a framework to undertake a five-year review. Over a five-year period it is the Government's intention to work with the aged care sector to identify and develop further reforms.

This book has provided many other examples: in Japan, significant policy reform regarding older persons started in the first 'Gold Plan' in 1989, only to be revised by the 'New Gold Plan' of 1994; in Israel, a novel legislation addressing the new industry of 'assisted living facilities' for older persons was very recently enacted; and in China, only recently the central government adopted a new framework for a three-tier care model for older people, to be implemented across all of China by the year 2020: the first, bottom, tier involves the 'foundation' of home-based care; the second, middle, tier involves the 'backing' of community-based care; and the third, top, tier involves the 'support' of institutional care.

It is within this new and dynamic 'elder law' world that the future regulation of residential care for older persons needs to be located and situated. Residential care is only a small part of a much larger policy puzzle that countries all over the world are struggling to resolve, in order to accommodate the new needs and rights of the ageing population. Yet, from a human rights perspective, this is one of the most important pieces of the puzzle, as it concerns the weakest portion of the older population: that which is the most dependent and vulnerable.

It is all about money: the funding issue

Finally, from the different analyses presented in the different chapters of this book, the question of financial costs and funding was quite evident. Residential care is expensive – and the costs of high quality care for older persons within residential settings, especially those providing high levels of care, are expensive. As described in the USA chapter, nursing home care is a multi-billion dollar a year industry, as Medicaid spends over $50 billion per year and while Medicare spends over $31 billion per year for nursing home care. It is quite clear then that resolving the funding question is not easy: should residential care be part of the national social security programme, and be recognised as a social and universal entitlement? Or is it up to the individual and his or her family members to fully fund the costs of residential care, either directly from personal savings or from privately purchased insurance?

The different countries presented in this book each had its own unique 'cocktail' of financial arrangements, which included distinctive (and quite complex) mixtures of both public and private funding. In Australia, for example, residential aged care is not free, although there are provisions in the Aged Care Act to assist persons who have little if any income. Prior to entering a RACF the prospective resident or their legal representative (such as their attorney pursuant to a power of attorney, or their financial manager pursuant to a financial management order) can request to have an income and asset assessment test. This test is undertaken by the Government. Even if the prospective resident does not request the assessment prior to entering a facility, the Government will assess their income and assets on admission. The test is designed to determine the amount of fees and accommodation charges that the resident will be charged whilst residing in the facility.

In the USA, the Government pays for close to 80% of nursing home care through both state and federal sources. Sixty-three per cent (63%) of nursing home revenue comes from the Medicaid programme, the national health insurance programme for the poor, 14% comes from Medicare, the national health insurance programme for the elderly and disabled, and the remaining 22% is through private pay (typically individuals' savings or insurance). Approximately two-thirds (68%) of facilities are for-profit, with one-quarter being non-profit and 6% government owned. Medicaid generally covers long-term care services while Medicare generally covers short-term, post-acute residential care services, such as rehabilitation services for individuals recovering from surgery. The median cost for a semi-private room in a nursing home is $212 per day (over $77,000 per year). Medicaid pays for the large portion of nursing home long-term care because the majority of people who require these services quickly spend down their financial resources when faced with these costs.

These two examples are only the tip of the iceberg of the critical question of 'who pays' for the residential care of older persons. One cannot realise a 'right' to residential care if he or she cannot afford to pay for it or if the government does not establish a social insurance programme to ensure adequate funding and financial support. The diversity in the financial solutions presented in this book only stresses this key dimension: defining the right to residential care for older persons as a human right is of utmost importance. It will mandate governments and countries to allocate appropriate financial resources to ensure that every older person will be able to enjoy residential care, regardless of his or her personal financial ability.

The common new challenge: can 'dignity' transform the legal regulation of residential care?

From the analysis of the different regulatory frameworks described in this book, some common elements regarding the ways to promote the human rights of older residents in residential care settings were clearly seen. We will describe what we believe the key elements are.

The significance of regulating the elder care workforce

The relationship between the quality of workforce in residential and institutional care setting of older persons and the quality of care provided in them is well studied in the gerontological literature. If one cares for the health and well-being of older persons in a residential care setting, one needs to ensure the quality of the workers who actually provide the care. This 'interconnectedness' between those who provide the actual care and the older persons themselves is a key element for all regulatory frameworks of residential care. A real example of such positive connectedness was provided in the Japanese example, where the high training and qualification required from direct care workers have contributed to the preserving of the human rights of older residents.

Nevertheless, in many countries described in this book, significant regulatory gaps were found regarding the quality of the workforce in residential care. For example, in China, there are no mandatory requirements that only qualified old-age care workers are responsible for taking care of older persons. While there were 322,703 old-age care worker positions in the public residential care sector by the end of 2012 (Ministry of Civil Affairs, 2013a) and the state projected a need of 6,000,000 old-age care workers for the whole country by 2020 (State Council, 2010), only 10,967 people received the old-age care workers' training and 9,491 received the qualification within 2010–2013 under the government promotion (Vocational Skill Assessment and Guidance Centre of Ministry of Civil Affairs, 2014). Such significant discrepancy between demand and supply of old-age care workers in the market implies older persons in residential care homes are not taken care of by a state-recognised worker.

In the USA, the law does not specify a numerical standard for numbers of staff or for minimum hours of care per resident; rather, the legal standard focuses on the expected outcomes for nursing home residents. As a result, though numerous studies have indicated that staffing levels are probably the most important determinant of a facility's quality of care, about 97% of US nursing homes have insufficient care staff. Moreover, the minimum standards for certified nurse aids (who provide most of the direct care for residents) is very limited compared to the amount of training required by government to other paraprofessionals (e.g. massage therapists or manicurists).

It was quite evident, from all the different countries represented in this book, that appropriate professional training and appropriate professional staffing is crucial to safeguard the dignity, human rights and quality of care for older persons in residential care settings. Future training reform must aim to improve and incorporate human rights discourse and preserve and promote dignity, and is urgently required if the current 'under-professionalisation' of the care of older persons is to be overcome.

On the importance of bridging the gap between law and reality

The analysis described in the various chapters in this book suggest that many times there is a significant gap between the law and regulation 'on paper' as opposed to the reality many older persons experience in real life in residential care settings. This has been shown quite eminently in the British experience regarding the well-publicised scandals around the quality of care in nursing homes – scandals that occurred despite a well-regulated industry and a well-developed regulatory environment.

In some countries, this gap is the outcome of the legal regulatory structure which includes non-enforceable 'recommendations'. In other countries, the regulations are vague, too general, or lack appropriate enforceability mechanism. For example, in China, an older person's right to residential care is now endorsed in 15 provisions of LPRIE, specifically in the chapter on social services. Yet these provisions are nothing more than simple directives to command various government departments, to competently equip the state with sufficient professional, technological and regulatory standards to provide residential care. Under LPRIE, the registration requirements for establishing a residential care home are only specified in the briefest of terms while the scope and the methods of supervision by the Civil Affairs Department of the People's Government are unclear and abstruse. Without any detailed specifications, it simply invests the 'relevant departments' of the State Council with the power, and their own discretion, to formulate rules to regulate the construction of care service facilities for older persons, to form category regulations for residential care homes, and to assess and maintain the provision and quality of service (Article 42).

Similar gaps were found in other countries as well. For example, in Japan, it was described how the Japanese protection systems for human rights in residential care lack the power of enforcement, and how the lenient regulation systems allow facilities to hide incidents, abuse or illegal restraints. In the USA, despite a comprehensive monitoring system, as a result of serious shortcomings in the implementation, widespread problems continue in many US nursing homes and the majority fail to achieve the minimum standards mandated in the Nursing Home Reform Law. Hence, while the gap between 'the law on paper' and 'the law on the streets' is well known, it seems that it receives significant relevance and importance in the context of regulation residential care of older persons.

Transparency, publicity and active participation as human rights instruments

One very interesting theme that arose from the analysis of the different national regulatory analysis was the issue around transparency, publicity and active participation of older persons in the inspection process. Each concept is rich and complex within itself, but there were some broad and clear mutual themes around these concepts.

For example, in China, it was described how new regulation mandates publishing the inspection report to the public (Article 28) and recommend involvement of older persons in supervision of the management and services rendered by residential care homes (Article 26). In Japan, long-term care facilities must submit an annual report to the prefectural governor, and these reports are publicly posted on the internet. And in Israel, since the beginning of 2015, the public inspection reports of nursing homes are publicly available on the internet.

Another good example of these elements was presented in the American example, where there has been a growing movement to provide the public, including long-term care consumers, with more information on healthcare providers and their quality. In recent years the American federal government has developed several databases to help the public find information on a variety of healthcare service providers. 'Nursing Home Compare', part of the US Government's medicare.gov website, contains information about every Medicaid and Medicare-certified nursing home in the United States. The public can view information about individual facilities such as the facility's staffing levels (self-reported, as of July 2014), measures that indicate a facility's qualities in certain categories (also self-reported), the dates and results of recent inspections, and the level and frequency of penalties. The public can also compare these statistics against other facilities and statewide and national averages. In addition, Nursing Home Compare contains a comprehensive database with information for every facility that is searchable and which can be used to identify, for instance, state and national trends relating to quality measure performance, citations and fines.

While such trends have their known limitations (information is sometimes limited and based on self-report), they provide an important tool for consumer empowerment and greater choice to older persons and their family members. They promote positive competition, and they provide older persons with power: the power of knowledge, which is essential for advancing their rights.

The significance of specific international human rights norms

Unlike other minority or weakened populations such as children or persons with disabilities, there is no international human rights convention for the rights of older persons. This is true not only at the UN/global level, but also at the international-regional levels: the European Union (EU), the African Union (AU) and the American region (the OAS – Organization of American States) do not have a specific protocol for the rights of older persons (Doron & Spanier, 2012).

However, yet again, this field is a dynamic state (Doron & Apter, 2010): on the global level there are discussions regarding the need for a new convention; and both at the African and American regional levels, there are already preliminary drafts of new human rights protocols specifically aimed at the rights of older persons. For example: Africa Union Protocol on the Rights of Older People in Africa which was passed by African Ministers of Social Development and is due to be adopted in the near future. In its Articles 11 and 12, the Protocol commits Member States to both (1) 'identify, promote and strengthen traditional support systems . . . to enhance the ability of families and communities to care for older family members' but also to (2) 'enact or review legislation that ensures that residential care is optional for older persons' and 'Ensure older persons in residential care facilities are provided with care that meets national minimum standards' (AU 2014).

It is important to realise that these international human rights developments have an important potential to influence the future regulations and human rights of older persons in general, and those living in residential care settings in specific. For example, as described in the chapter on Japan, the international human rights movements and the ratification of key human rights conventions (e.g. the ICCPR and the ICESCR), have significantly contributed to the promotion and respect of human rights in Japan, and to the development of national human rights legislation and regulation. In Egypt, it was also shown how regional inter-state cooperation (e.g. the Islamic States) can produce policy documents (e.g. the Cairo Declaration of Human Rights in Israel of 1993, or the Universal Islamic Declaration of Human Rights of 1981), which can serve as a platform to promote human rights of older persons specifically.

It is clear that any future developments in the regulation of residential care for older persons will be influenced by the future developments on the international – global and regional – human rights level. If indeed a future international convention for the rights of older persons is established, or if any of the draft specific protocols for the rights of older persons is accepted by the regional bodies of the African Union or the Organization of the American States, this will potentially provide an important drive to reform existing regulations to conform with the new human rights standards that will be set.

'Dignity': the future conceptual platform for regulating residential care for older persons

Finally, it should be recognised that perhaps *the key* for resolving the challenges described above is the need for a much deeper and material change in the regulatory framework of residential care. It seems that the 'core' ideology that serves as the foundation of residential care settings in many countries is still ageist and paternalistic. It assumes that older persons who eventually find themselves in residential care are people who need supervision and protection as they cannot truly care for themselves or decide how to best preserve their interests. It mandates minimum universal standards that assume and pretend that 'command and control' are the best regulatory regime to ensure that older persons are not abused or exploited. Eventually, they treat older persons in the same social and legal ideology as children, and other disadvantaged social groups.

Even in some countries (e.g. the UK or USA), where rhetoric of honouring autonomy or promoting patient-centred care have become more significant within the regulatory reforms, or even in countries where dignity was used in the rhetoric of long-term care reforms (e.g. Japan and Australia), the impression is that they have still failed to transform the actual reality of the living experience of older residents in residential care settings. Both from the 'bottom' experiences (e.g. the scandals or inhumane care exposed in the UK), or from the 'top' experiences (e.g. the heavy federal and extensive legal command-and-control of American and Australian regulation), reality suggests that a more encompassing concept is needed as a foundation for future reforms in this field.

The chapter on dignity presents in our view a basis for an alternative foundation for the future legal regulation of residential care of older persons around the world. To begin with, its ideology and rationale are rooted not only in 'objective' human rights philosophy, but also on a 'subjective' understanding of what 'dignity' means for older persons themselves. Moreover, dignity is a multi-dimensional concept, pertaining not only to the physical, mental and emotional state of the older person, but also to nature of the interaction between the older residents, the staff and owners of the facility, and the legal authorities which regulate the care.

Dignity is not a synonym for autonomy. As deeply analysed in the chapter on dignity, an 'automatic' adoption of 'autonomy-based' human rights discourse will not resolve the regulatory challenges that are faced by residential care settings for older persons. When it comes to these unique social environments, dignity forces us to contextualise our understanding of human rights, and reframe 'autonomy' in a more relational term: it is not only about the older residents, but it is also about the family members, care-takers, staff, and the organisational structure of the regulations and the state. Dignity is also about multi-culturalism and respecting ethnic, religious and cultural diversity. Or, applying Charles Foster's model of dignity, maximising the amount of dignity and making older residents thrive must include the dignity of those who surround them (Foster 2011).

There is no naivety in arguing for adopting 'dignity' as a conceptual foundation for future legal regulatory reform of residential care for older persons. As described in the chapter on dignity, rhetoric of dignity – in and by itself – cannot prevent the infringement of the most basic human rights of older persons. However, reframing the regulatory environment of older persons in residential care under the legal foundation of commitment to dignity, in our view, can ultimately provide better outcomes not only in preserving but in actually promoting the human rights of older residents.

If we can agree that the future of legal regulation of residential care for older persons lies in adopting a dignity-based framework that results in human rights standards for the policies and regulations that would then emerge, then the real challenge is clear: how to operationalise dignity in the context of residential care for older persons. Whether this is through training programmes that are designed with dignity as the foundation, or through state policy which has dignity as the basis for building a human rights framework for care homes, this is not an easy task and neither can it be the same in all countries. This also was not the aim of this book. What has been clearly evidenced in these chapters is that most countries find themselves at different stages in the development of a residential care sector for older people but whether these countries have a well-established regulatory structure, or whether they are at the beginning of building one, incorporating a human rights approach into regulatory structures can only enhance the living conditions for those older residents. While it is true that a human rights approach could be adopted anytime by individual care-home owners or managers, if regulation and inspection systems and processes incorporate these human rights principles, the standards would then be generally expected rather than available at the whim of individuals. However, if in light of the insights from this book, different countries around the world will accept that the conceptual starting point for any future regulatory reform of residential care for older persons lies in the contextual operationalisation of securing and promoting the 'dignity' of the older residents – this will be, in our view, a most significant step forward to promote the human rights of older persons in these places.

Bibliography

Doron, I. & Apter, I. (2010). The Debate around the Need for an International Convention on the Rights of Older Persons. *The Gerontologist, 50(5)*, 586–593.

Doron, I., & Spanier, B. (2012). International Elder Law: The Future of Elder Law. In I. Doron and A. Soden (eds). *Beyond Elder Law: New Directions in Law and Ageing* (pp. 125–148). Berlin: Springer Publications.

Foster, C. (2011). *Human Dignity in Bioethics and Law*. Oxford: Hart.

Goffman, E. (1961). *Asylums: Essays on the Social Situation of Mental Patients and Other Inmates.* NY: Anchor Books.

Index